Shells in Aegean Prehistory

Lilian Karali

BAR International Series 761
1999

Published in 2016 by
BAR Publishing, Oxford

BAR International Series 761

Shells in Aegean Prehistory

ISBN 978 0 86054 966 6

BAR Publishing is the trading name of British Archaeological Reports (Oxford) Ltd.
British Archaeological Reports was first incorporated in 1974 to publish the BAR
Series, International and British. In 1992 Hadrian Books Ltd became part of the BAR
group. This volume was originally published by Archaeopress in conjunction with
British Archaeological Reports (Oxford) Ltd / Hadrian Books Ltd, the Series principal
publisher, in 1999. This present volume is published by BAR Publishing, 2016.

Printed in England

BAR
PUBLISHING

BAR titles are available from:

BAR Publishing
122 Banbury Rd, Oxford, OX2 7BP, UK
EMAIL   info@barpublishing.com
PHONE   +44 (0)1865 310431
FAX   +44 (0)1865 316916
www.barpublishing.com

To my precious ones

John, Theodora and Virginia

CONTENTS

ABBREVIATIONS

AAA	Athens Annals of Archaeology
ΑΔ	Αρχαιολογικόυ Δελτίον
AE	Αρχαιολογική Εφημερίς
AJA	American Journal of Archaeology
AM	Mitteilungen des Deutschen Archäologischen Instituts. Athenische Abteilung
BASRP	Bulletin of the American School of Prehistoric Research
BCH	Bulletin de Correspondance Hellenique
BSPF	Bulletin de la Societe Prehistorique Francaise
CMS	Corpus der minoischen und mykenischen Siegel
DACIA	Dacie, Recherches et Decouvertes Archeologiques en Roumanie
EtCrete	Etudes Cretoises
Hesperia	Hesperia. Journal of the American School of Classical Studies at Athens
Jconch	Journal of Conchology
JAS	Journal of Archaeological Science
JFA	Journal of Field Archaeology
JHS	Journal of Hellenic Studies
ManMem	Memories of the Manchester Philological Society
MonAnt	Monumenti Antichi dell'Accademia dei Lincei
ΠΑΕ	Πρακτιά της εν Αθήναις Αρχαιολογικής Εταιρείας
PPS	Proceedings of the Prehistoric Society
ProcMalSoc	Proceedings of the Malacological Society
PZ	Prähistorische Zeitschrift
RA	Revue Archéologique
MP	Furumark A., *Mycenaean Pottery*, Stockholm 1941.
PM	Evans A.J., *Palace of Minos*, London 1921.
TAW	Hardy D.A. et al., *Thera and the Aegean World III*, London 1990.
BM	British Museum
NAM	National Archaeological Museum, Athens
HM	Herakleion Museum

ACKNOWLEDGEMENTS

Twenty years have passed since I first began my research concerning sea-shells. Through the scientific presentation of old and new finds and archaeological evidence from the Neolithic world, my work aims to show the paleoenvironment, the diet, the wealth, originality and aesthetic inquiries of man in the Neolithic and Bronze Age.

A project of this kind would never have been possible without the positive response of the Ephorates of Antiquities undertaken by the directors of the excavations who kindly allowed me to study malacological material from a number of sites. I am particularly grateful to Dr Ch. Koukouli for the Kastri Theologo, Skala Sotiros; Dr D. Grammenos for Dimitra, Pentapoli, Vassilika; Professor Chr. Doumas for Akrotiri of Thera; the late Professor J. Deshayes for Dikili Tash; Dr A. Sampson for Tharrounia, Kaloyerovrysi and Cyclop's Cave; Professor J.-Cl. Poursat for Malia-Quartier Mu; Professor L. Marangou for Markiani of Amorgos; Dr D. Reese for exchanging views and information about shell material and many other specialists for their contribution.

Sincere thanks are due to my students who helped and supported me in this effort.

The difficult task of translating my work in English was completed thanks to my friend Mrs Alex Doumas who tried to put my text in a proper scientific English language.

To all those mentioned by name, and to all those who have contributed in various unseen ways, to bringing my efforts to fruition, I express my heartfelt thanks.

P.S. This work has been completed in 1995, therefore bibliography does not include more recent publications.

Chapter I

Introduction

Archaeology and the Environment

The discipline of archaeology seeks to investigate and to illuminate aspects of human activity in the past. It seeks to locate and to elucidate man's achievements, to reconstruct the natural environment in which man acted and to determine the relations of interdependence between man and his environment. To complete the reconstruction of the distant past the study of the material remains and the technology, that is the stage of development and evolution of culture, is essential. Consequently, in addition to the works of art, the movable finds and the architectural remains, the archaeological value of which is well-known, every piece of evidence that emerges during the course of excavating a site can shed light on the parameters of existence, habitation and growth of the settlement, and therefore merits attention.

Modern archaeological research deals with all the evidence brought to light in excavation, that is the artifacts and the biological remains. All are essential for studying the past, which is confronted as a total of elements and events (Shackley 1981, 1985).

In the framework of environmental archaeology evidence is provided by materials that at first glance go unnoticed, such as macro- and micro-floral remains, faunal and human remains, fossils etc.

Of considerable significance among these remains are molluscs[1], particularly in Greece. Molluscs constitute critical environmental indicators because the existence of each species depends closely on factors such as climate, the ecology and the morphology of the sea bed, as well as the more general character of the marine environment (tides, currents, composition of the water - whether it is fresh, salty, brackish etc.). In the eastern Mediterranean, from Crete to Lycia and from Thessaly to Egypt, during the Cenozoic era the same species of molluscs are encountered under more or less same conditions (Karali 1979, 3-20).

Information on shells is obtained from direct and indirect sources, that is from the study of the molluscs found in excavations, from references in texts, from representations, from evidence of trade and wider relations between sites and populations, and lastly from laboratory examination of remains such as pottery or purple dye (*porphyra*).

Historical Background

The first scientific information on living organisms is found in the work of Aristotle. In his three major treatises of biological content, *Historia Animalium, Parts of Animals, Generation of Animals*, he describes in detail the constituent elements (e.g. blood, bones, hair) and the organs of the body, the ways in which animals reproduce, their dietary habits, ecosystems and behaviour. His field of enquiry ranges from man to bee, from the European bison to the shells of the Mediterranean, and includes examination of marine organisms such as fish, crustaceans, cephalopods and so on. Aristotle's work was not forgotten and from the first to the sixth century AD it constituted the subject of study and source of inspiration for many scholars. In the twelfth century it passed into medieval Europe where it was translated into Latin and influenced the development of science in the West.

In Roman times Pliny the Elder (1st century AD), drawing on the works of some five hundred Greek and Roman authors, compiled a 37-volume *Natural History*. This provides *inter alia* important information on the world of the sea and molluscs (*Zoology*, books 8-11). Pliny's work was also one of the bases of modern biological knowledge.

Molluscs, like other animal species, concerned later scholars, not only from the standpoint of biology and anatomy, but also from that of systematic taxonomy and scientific onomatology. Not only was there confusion due to local names but also due to the use of the same term for different species on account of some superficial similarity. From the fifteenth century, as consequence of voyages of exploration, there was a marked proliferation in the number of plant and animal species known (Fig. 1 a-b). John Ray (1627-1705) was the first to distinguish the genus and the species of organisms, and proceeded to a natural and biological classification. However, C. Linnaeus (1707-1778) is generally acclaimed as the founding father of

---

[1] This study is a guide for archaeologists. It does not replace biological examination but investigates the archaeological importance of remains of the particular order of the animal kingdom. The short list of mollusc species refers only to those found in excavations in Greece and therefore of importance for the study of archaeological sites in the Aegean.

classification. His *magnum opus, Binomial nomenclature*, published in 1758, established a system of rules for the scientific naming of animals and plants.

In the international bibliography a series of Latin terms indicates exactly where the organism in question belongs. Every animal is identified by denoting the *genus*, the species, and the name of the first scholar to publish and date it (Οντρια 1987, 16-20). The first full scientific study of molluscs living in the Aegean sea was published by Forbes in the mid-nineteenth century (Forbes 1843, 130-193).

Archaeology and molluscs

In the framework of the possibility of extracting information from the study of molluscs observations on the evolution and the changes the molluscs themselves have undergone in space and time as well as changes in the form and level of the coastline are included (Evans 1978).

The study of the environment is the subject of several disciplines, among them of modern archaeology. As a discipline with theoretical ramifications, archaeology faces methodological problems, not least with regard to clarifying its subject and to the manner of reconstructing the past. Its theoretical inquiries are concerned at a primary level with the way in which information can be drawn from material remains. Whereas the classical approach separates and discriminates between these remains, modern archaeology is concerned with the total of remains brought to light in excavation.

The conclusions drawn from the remains that were possible to collect and study differ according to environmental conditions and the circumstances of their preservation. What must be established first is to what extent an environment is archaeological. Man's presence and activity in a particular place is that which makes it a subject of study for the environmental archaeologist. The archaeological significance of each find in the excavation is indubitable, because all are directly connected with man's presence. Molluscs appear as both ecofacts (remains of natural organisms) and artifacts, for which reason the presence of a specialist scholar who can attribute to each find its true value is imperative. At some coastal sites, for example, it is difficult to recognize among the abundance of shells those that were used by man from those that are there because this was their habitat. Land snails present an analogous problem; a relatively modern species penetrates via plant roots to a considerable depth in the ground and so may appear in earlier horizons.

Study and classification of malacological material produces meaningful results, even if these appear self-evident to the specialist. In essence nothing should be considered self-evident, while things that today seem simple, required centuries of theoretical and experimental work before they were fully accepted. Although in some cases the interpretation of mollusc remains may be relatively easy, in others it is difficult and complicated, demanding comprehensive knowledge and correlations with other fields, such as typology, ethnology, religion and so on. Moreover, the study of this material is not integrated if the mollusc remains are treated as a separate entity, for they constitute part of the total of finds from a specific context. Only in this way it is possible to extract findings of a quantitative nature, which lead to further explanations (e.g. in the Late Bronze Age the number of molluscs consumed as food decreases markedly as a consequence of the rise in the standard of living and the appearance of a more complex diet).

The presence of shells at an archaeological site provides specific and reliable information on its environment, since molluscs are organisms that live in strictly defined micro-environments, whereas larger animals are more mobile and can participate in diverse habitats concurrently. So it is obvious that the information molluscs yield on the immediate locus of human activity is relatively exact.

In addition to the analytical treatment of the malacological material (identification of species, calculation of minimum and maximum number of specimens of each species, percentage of occurrence, provenance, habitats etc.) a synthetic view is required. This is the most difficult part of its study, mainly because it demands a knowledge of typology in order to classify the finds according to their use (e.g. spoon-shaped or triangular objects made from mussel shells). This entails recognition of objects which have been worked by man and had some utilitarian function. Sometimes the interpretation of such material is hasty and superficial, resulting in conclusions that may be impressive but are not necessarily reliable.

The main aim of studying malacological material is not to discover and describe the very few - and sometimes non-existent - exotic species that may have been imported, but to elucidate clearly archaeological problems concerning man's way of life, his adaptation to the environment, the transmission and diffusion of traditions, techniques and methods of working shells, as well as the ascertainment of common spheres of influence in the aesthetic and religious-symbolic spheres. Generalizations are dangerous because they can lead to theories of dubious scientific value.

The presentation of catalogues of malacological material found in excavation is no more than the introduction to the study of sea shells. The value and significance of this study lies in the potential for synthetic confrontation of the subject and the drawing of conclusions regarding human activities. Lists of species that are not accompanied by further synthetic treatment and archaeological interpretation can be compared with any archaeological find that is treated as a work of art, detached from its cultural milieu and regardless of the material from which it is fashioned.

With regard to the way of life of human groups, the study of sea shells can yield important, often unexpected information. This concerns the quantities of molluscs collected, the prevailing species consumed as food (edible) and/or used as bait, the shells preferred for ornament on account of their beauty, those that had an exchange value on account of their rarity, the species used for making objects such as tools (spoons, needles, buttons, scrapers etc.) and vessels for everyday use.

To a degree shells can shed light on contacts and transactions between population groups in periods for which there are no other testimonies. The discovery, for example, of bracelets of spondylus shell from the Aegean in the heartland of the Balkans, a long distance from the sea, points to some kind of relations between the inhabitants of these regions, perhaps implicating a further exchange of ideas. The same is true of the decorated pottery incised with cardium shell. The discovery of notable quantities of murex shells and the location of installations for extracting the purple dye from these molluscs can lead to the tracing of the 'purple routes', analogous with the silk roads.

Precisely for the reasons outlined above, shell remains should be collected with great care, to achieve maximum recovery of this material. They are collected separately from each archaeological level and from rubbish pits, whole, broken, even in tiny fragments. Shells were also found as a filler in clay used for making bricks or vases, as material for consolidating floors, and elsewhere. Thus the importance of studying of this material from the modern archaeological perspective is obvious.

Earlier archaeological studies on molluscs and their shells are mainly of ethnographic content and concern population groups living in distant lands, such as the Solomon Islands, the Americas, East Africa etc. In the study of Aegean prehistory, evidence on the palaeoenvironment and on mollusc remains in particular, is to be found in the work of C. Tsountas on the Cyclades (Τσούντας 1898, 137-212, 1899, 134-173). Molluscs are mentioned, albeit superficially, in the publications of other Greek archaeologists, such as G. Mylonas (Mylonas 1929, 81). The first catalogues of

mollusc species found in excavations were prepared by N.G. Gejvall, who studied the material from Troy and Lerna (Gejvall 1937-38, 51-57, 1969).

The foundations for the study of molluscs as archaeological remains *per se*, were laid by N.J. Schackleton in his discussion of the marine molluscs from Knossos (Evans 1968) and from the Neolithic site of Saliagos off Antiparos (Evans - Renfrew 1968).

The first comprehensive review of the malacological material in the prehistoric Aegean was presented in the author's doctoral thesis (Karali 1979). Today, specialist scholars such as D. Reese, N.J. Shackleton, H. Chevallier, L. Karali and J. Powell are systematically studying the mollusc remains found in excavations in Greece, from prehistoric to later times. Through dissertations, articles and monographs on this material a rich data bank of archaeological importance is being compiled, essential for the conspectus of the past. Archaeologists now attach special weight to this avenue of research, as more and more facts become known, and it is now taking its rightful place in the examination and analysis of excavation data and testimonies that have survived to this day from time past.

Chapter II

Shells as Archaeological Material

The presence of malacological material in excavation assemblages

The number of shells brought to light in excavations varies according to the circumstances of their preservation while buried in the ground, the method of collecting them, the strategy of study, and the reasons they were used by man (Fig. 2).

a. Uses

Shells found in excavations provide information on the habits and everyday activities of the inhabitants of a settlement. For example, shells found in large quantities are associated with food residues, where it is reasonable to assume the consumption of large numbers of molluscs. On the contrary, those found in smaller quantities were normally used for making objects.

b. Conditions of preservation of the micro-environment

As with all archaeological finds, the state of preservation of molluscs varies, depending on the closer and wider environment of their discovery. In order to understand the more general relationship of mutual influence between mollusc remains and the deposition environment, that is the micro-environment, two factors should be taken into account:

1. The structure and the particular characteristics of the species of molluscs whose remains have been found.

2. The ability of these remains to resist the diverse processes of physical and chemical decay. The main structural material of molluscs, crustaceans and eggs is calcium carbonate ($CaCo_3$), which places them on the same scale of resistance to the forces of decay as bones, teeth and horns/antlers.

Decay is caused by both physical and chemical processes. Mechanical agents, rodents and humans, are responsible for the fragmentation or even the pulverization of even the most durable remains, both on the ground surface and a short depth below. However, the major causes of decay are small insects and micro-organisms. Most micro-organisms thrive in aerobic conditions, sufficient humidity being one of the parameters favourable to their action. Others are temperature and the great sensitivity of micro-organisms to the chemical properties of the environment. Most are unable to live in acid conditions, with the exception of some species of fungi that are adapted to soils with low pH (Davidson – Schackley 1976, 397-399)[2]. So the chemical behaviour of the environment can in fact curtail microbial action. Apart from acid conditions, the presence of toxic substances, such as copper and concentrations of salts, favour the preservation of various remains. Furthermore, extreme conditions, that is very dry or very wet soils, are ideal for the preservation of many classes of remains as for example wood, bones (Davidson - Shackley 1976). These same chemical conditions can, however, have a destructive effect on certain materials: acid conditions react on alkaline or calcareous materials such as bone, antlers and shells, destroying their mineral fractions. For example, the infiltration of acids to the inside of a grave ensemble decompose the bases of the structural elements so that only faint chemical traces of them remain, embodied in the soil horizon.

In general three classes of chemical agents should be taken into account for their particular role in the preservation regime:

1. Enzymes of remains and other chemical compounds (resins, tanins).
2. pH or acidity of the soil
3. Presence of metals and salts in the micro-environment of the deposits.

The effects of acid conditions on bones and shells have already been mentioned (Davidson - Shackley 1976, 137-143). Specifically, when the pH value is < 6.3 the mineral component of the material is destroyed. In contrast, in alkaline environments, though their organic

---

[2] The pH value measures the acidity or alkalinity of a soil and constitutes an important guide to the types of biological indicators expected to be preserved: the scale of measurement ranges from 0 to 14 with 7 as neutral. A pH value below 7 denotes acidity and above 7 alkalinity (or basicity). In general for soils and sediments the scale of values ranges from pH 3.5 (highly acidic peats) and pH 8 (alkaline chalk soils). Values over 8.5 are recorded in saline soils, while measurements below 3 are not uncommon. In basic soils (limestone, chalk, calcareous sediments) molluscs are the main biological material; in acid soils (poor deposits, sandstone strata, high rainfall) the main biological indicators are pollen and charcoal.

content is subject to the action of bacteria and other micro-organisms, the hard, external, skeletal elements retain their structure. On the other hand, a sufficiency of limestone is one of the preconditions for building the mollusc shell; lack of calcium results in a finer shell, less likely to be preserved, and limits the range of species.

Methods of collecting malacological material

Shells and heaps of shells are frequently uncovered at prehistoric sites in coastal zones, appearing in a variety of archaeological assemblages. In general, molluscs constitute a sensititive material and such finds should be treated, in the initial stages at least, in the same way as other categories of environmental remains of an archaeological nature. Any accumulation or deposit is recorded visually in photographs and drawings[3], measured in three dimensions (length, width and depth) and the nature of the immediate micro-environment or context described in detail. Where large deposits of shells are revealed these should be studied stratigraphically, to determine any possible succession of species (Καραλή 1992, 163-169).

The degree of preservation of the shells should be recorded, to be subsequently supplemented by comments on the condition of the individual specimens. Usually shells on the surface are more easily damaged and are thus found in fragments, while those buried in the ground are better preserved. On the other hand, because of filtering or other processes, shells at the nucleus of heaps receive excessive concentrations of calcium carbonate, creating a crystalline meshe on their surface (Meehan 1982, 162-7). In other instances the creation of crystals depends even more on the deposition environment.

A similar recording procedure is also followed in the case of storage pits, in which the relationship of the

molluscs to the other animal remains in the micro-environment of the pit is investigated. After these preliminaries, the mollusc remains are correlated with the wider macro- environment of the excavation, in an endeavour to understand the environment of the site, the way of life and the habits of its inhabitants.

The collection of shells and shell fragments must be thorough, for which reason fine tweezers are used. The finds are first classified according to their excavation provenance and placed in small plastic bags accompanied by the corresponding labels. In order to retrieve the smallest fragments the technique of sieving is employed. The type of sieving depends largely on the nature of the soil in each region (sandy soil-dry sieving, clay soil-water sieving etc.) (Shackley 1985, 22-23).

The first factor to be considered is the volume of the soil sample destined to be sieved, and the second the size of its particles - even the smallest particles are an indicator of what may have been lost.

Water sieving is a more complex process. Flotation is a relatively simple operation involving three stages:

a) The sediment enclosing the shells or their fragments is dissolved or removed with the greatest possible care (water sieving).
b) Paraffin is added to the acqueous suspension. It 'selectively' coats the organic components, which form larger aggregates of low density that rise to the surface through hydrostatic mechanisms.
c) A cleansing agent is then added and the mixture disturbed to create a foam. The paraffin-coated components that collect on the surface are then skimmed off, dried and classified.

Afterwards, those finds not collected by this method, because they remain as sediment, are separated out carefully in the laboratory.

The shells collected by dry sieving should be washed carefully with a soft brush. The mouth and apex of gastropods, as well as the serrations of bivalves, demand particularly delicate treatment because these points are in many cases critical for identifying the species and determining its use (Καραλή 1990, 14-16)[4].

---

[3] The depiction of shells both in photographs and drawings is particularly difficult since these are mainly small objects of diverse shape and volume with uneven surface. Shells found in excavations have lost their colour and nacre, for which reason their surface is dull and off-white. On account of their shape and colour special care must be taken when photographing them. They should be placed on a very dark background and a sensitive film should be used: magnification is often necessary in order to show traces of working or use.
On account of the difficulties in rendering the details in photographs, these should preferably be accompanied by drawings. Drawings should emphasize the way in which human action was exercised on the shell; they are, for example, the only means of showing such details as the section of a bead or the hole of a pendant. Though the range of species found in excavations is relatively small, it is useful to have illustrations, in photographs or drawings, of the basic ones.

[4] Conservation of shells
Collectors, archaeologists and museum personnel tend to believe that shells are not susceptible to damage during storage. The reality is quite different. At first a kind of dust appears on the shells' surface. In the next stage the surface becomes scaley and begins to break until it is totally fragmented and destroyed. This destructive process was first observed by L.G. Byne in 1899, for which reason it is called Byne's disease. Nowadays it is known that it is due to

Methods of studying malacological material

Once the shells have been cleaned they are ready for classification[5]. Primary morphological observations can be made directly with the aid of a magnifying glass. After separating the finds into groups, according to their special nature, taxonomic observations are made. In general the problems of identifying and interpreting such residues and more numerous and complex than would appear at first glance. Two basic factors govern the presence of species: a) the wider natural environment of the site and b) the native faunal populations. These dictate to a great degree the variety and the quantity of invertebrate remains brought to light in excavation. Difficulties in the identification of the species arise when shells are badly fragmented and/or have lost their colour and distinctive traits.

As with the classification of plants and vertebrates, the final identification of the species should be founded on comparison with reference collections that contain clearly defined species. The most important problem arising from the use of reference collection is that in most cases they comprise modern specimens, which do

not constitute a secure guide for comparisons and parallels with earlier species: there is a problem in identifying extinct species from earlier evolutionary phases. Consequently these collections should be used with circumspection particularly by scholars without much experience. Even when collections of earlier material are used, caution is counselled since minor taxonomic differences may exist among the shells, due to subtle deviations of form between species and sub-species, to a change in the name or to erroneous identification.

Wherever possible, it is interesting to present the variation in the local population so that the archaeologist studying shells can see whether the change of certain morphological features and the spread or reduction of certain species are due to human intervention in the biological cycle.

Molluscs as material for determining ancient environmental conditions

The species of mollusc provides information on its biotope, that is whether it lived in fresh or salt, deep or shallow water, in the sea, lake or river. So a picture is formed of the natural environment in the season of collecting the particular species. Even though terrestrial molluscs are outside the scope of the present work, it would be remiss not to mention their contribution to determining temperature and humidity (Evans 1972, 1973, 103-130, 1976, 397-399)[6].

The basic division in classifying molluscs is into terrestrial and marine. Terrestrial molluscs are important indicators of the natural conditions prevailing at the time of deposition. They enjoy wide distribution

---

the storage environment: wood and wood products (such as paper and cotton wool) produce organic acids that react with the shell to create calcium acetates and other products which corrode it. The situation is exarcebated when shells are stored in a closed box. Consequently wooden boxes or cases, even when lined with cotton wool and covered with glass, destroy the shells and shell objects they are supposed to protect. When signs of Byne's disease are noted the only course is to change the storage environment. Shells and shell objects should be placed in well ventilated containers such as plastic food bags or on acid-free paper such as that used in libraries. Even if a shell does not show signs of Byne's disease it should be removed from wood, paper or cotton wool and stored in a safer way. Shells found in quite good condition should first be washed in ion-free water or, if this is not possible, in salts-free water. Hard water, even sterilized, should not be used since its constituent elements do not dissolve the chemical compounds dangerous to the shell. After washing, shells should be left to dry thoroughly at a temperature not exceeding 40°C. In cases where other material adheres to the shell, it can be removed with a soft brush. The number of the object is marked with pen and Indian ink on a layer of clear varnish, as on pottery and other archaeological finds.

[5] Studying the material
The study of malacological material should be undertaken by a specialized archaeologist. A palaeozoologist who has no archaeological knowledge can only give the lists of species. Malacological material which has not been studied typologically or in association with the archaeological and environmental context results in the frequent phenomenon of the publication of simple catalogues. These cause confusions and generalizations. Basic precondition is to interpret the material collected from each site and then to correlate it with similar material from sites of the same chronological period. For example, a species of shell used for a specific purpose in one place, such as spondylus for jewellery, may be used differently in another: in some places it is consumed as food, in others its shell was used for making objects. For this reason a general presentation of the sites at which spondylus shells were found has little archaeological value unless it is followed by the determination of their uses and a typological presentation.

[6] Land snails
Land snails are frequently found in excavations but the reasons for their presence in archaeological assemblages is not always securely interpreted. Most of the species of land snails penetrate into the archaeological strata, depending on the depth of the deposit. The identification of species is particularly difficult on account of the external similarity of the shell. Shell preservation is likewise problematical on account of their delicate and fragile walls. In antiquity as today land snails were used for food. The presence or absence of snails in archaeological strata is an important indicator of environmental change and the degree of humidity. It can however reflect man's methods of collecting snails. The role of land snails in the diet can only be confirmed in a few cases, when these are found inside vessels, as at Dimitra in Macedonia (Karali 1997, 202), Lithares in Boeotia (Reese 1984, 199), in the large LM IB pithos in the Stratigraphical Museum at Knossos (Warren 1980, 16) and at Akrotiri Thera (Καραλή 1990, 4-12). A further trait that indicates the extraction of the snail from the shell by man is the irregular hole near the mouth, caused by introducing a pointed tool. From the condition of the shell of the edible land molluscs conclusions can be drawn on the way in which they were consumed, that is whether or not they were boiled. Very often remains of the elongated snail *Rumina sp.* are found. This is not edible and lives in dry open spaces or uncultivated tracts of scrub and on calcareous soils.

since they survive and are preserved in a variety of deposits. They occur in large numbers and in a way are free from human influences. They show a distinct preference for limestone environments, favourable to the better development of their shell. With the exception of acid conditions, their presence is expected in rivers, lakes, swamps, woods and open land. They are, however, also preserved in well-aerated oxidized deposits, although they then suffer catastrophic losses of their external surface, the structure of which constitutes an important diagnostic element. Moreover, the percolation of water into the interior of calcareous sediments, though not disturbing the shells, liberates calcium carbonated that covers them with a crust and disfigures their features. If these in the end survive their shape is in most cases preserved exactly on account of their rigid form.

Human intervention in the populations of terrestrial molluscs was more intense in the post-glacial period[7]. The reasons were cultivation and the general change in the earth's surface due to the increase in the human population. Even so, thanks to their adaptability, these molluscs resisted such changes and are consequently adequately represented in the fauna as a whole.

Terrestrial molluscs are important climatological indicators. Some species are characteristic of cold climates (e.g. *Columbella columbella)*), while others are limited to deposits of the interglacial periods or the warmer intervals of the post-glacial (e.g. the bivalve *Corbicula flumunalis)*. This evidence shows that criterion for reconstructing the climatic conditions is the absence or the presence of certain species, known for their adaptation to specific environments. In reality, however, there are very few data on the ability of terrestrial molluscs to adapt to warm conditions. In comparison with plant species we would expect them to be limited to specific parts, from which they will have

---

[7] Fossilized shells
Archaeologists usually study environmental remains, animal, plant or geological, but only rarely do they make laboratory studies of the fossils retrieved from archaeological sites. Mollusc fossils appear quite frequently. They occur in stones used for constructing buildings or are enclosed in rocks. They inform us firstly of the geological history of the site, but acquire a different importance if it is ascertained that they were brought there from elsewhere. For example, in the sanctuary complex at Kommos in Crete, in use from Geometric through to Early Roman times, fossilized shells were among the votive offerings.
Of particular significance is the correct identification of the fossilized species, since it may then be possible to determine their use and meaning. For example, fossilized oysters cannot be food residues, whereas a fossilized oyster with a hole can be an ornament: such objects are mentioned from Neolithic Cyprus and Jordan. The identification of fossilized species with specific use helps explain the reasons for and the manner of transfer from their original environment, and so their importance as trade goods or symbolic objects is more readily understood.

been displaced eventually by the spread of other more thermophile species, in the interglacial periods and the post-glacial period. So the fauna of terrestrial molluscs should be judged as a whole and not according to the reactions and behaviour of small groups representative of their adaptation to special conditions. Furthermore, all the hypotheses concerning the identification of certain species with specific conditions are based on the premise that their ecological needs do not change. In reality the varieties of terrestrial molluscs are able to provide climatological information when they are combined with corresponding volumes of soil samples, systematic microscopic examination of which may yield corroborative evidence. The contribution of other sources too, such as pollen, carbonized wood and the geological history of the site is considered equally necessary.

Bearing in mind the above, it seems that terrestrial molluscs express mainly microclimatic conditions and changes. The information they provide is considered more accurate when thick levels are examined. These are secure indicators of the evolution of the variety of species over time.

It is, however, feasible, on the basis of these data, to divide the species into groups of local distribution and to compile local ecological maps. It should be stressed that their distribution is somewhat asymmetrical to the dynamic of the climate, since it is dependent on the line of migration and the ability of various species to resist changing conditions. At the level of practical application, familiarity with the forms of distribution of species and co-evaluation of the parameters of their alteration, of the number of species, of the possible domination of one or more, as well as the ratios of land to water varieties, enable the specialist researcher to derive reliable information on the climate. Marine molluscs represent indictators of climatological conditions since they correspond to a specific depth, temperature or type of sediment (Dollfus 1978, 30-39, Shackelton - van Andel 1980, 357-359).

It is also important for the researcher to know whether the molluscs (marine or terrestrial) were collected alive or dead. For example, the volume of the exploitable live mollusc can be estimated by filling the inside of the shell with water. There are however certain species in which the soft organism does not occupy the whole of the shell's interior. Only by careful checking against controls (collections of living - already dead samples) is it possible to calculate the precise volume of flesh that corresponds to each mollusc shell.

Lastly, it is noted that all the marine molluscs correspond to specific depths in the sea. If the sea level is known the temperature can be determined through calculation of the oxygen isotopes (Shackleton 1970, 43-44). The temperature of the water depends on the general highest indices of temperature, changes in which are linked to the changes in the formation of the glaciers.

Consequently, since molluscs - land and sea – constitute archaeological material and the maximum possible amount of information should be extracted from them, it is imperative that the proper methods are applied for both their collection and study. Consistency in the application of a specific methodology is a basic precondition for extracting correct scientific results.

Molluscs as material for archaeological dating

Malacological material is not of primary importance for dating in archaeology. Nevertheless, indications can be deduced concerning the chronological period as well as the season of the year (Deith 1983, 423-440). On account of their nature, shells can be submitted to the laboratory method of C14 dating, which is in fact the most important method of dating them (Michael - Ralph (eds) 1971, 6). The samples must weigh at least 25 gr. The fundamental structural elements of mollusc shells are calcium carbonate ($CaCO_3$) and calcite or aragonite, which includes a small percentage of organic protein - of the order of 1 or 2% in modern shells.

However, one point merits attention: the carbon salt of old shells is susceptible to contamination by modern carbon compounds. This can be easily demonstrated if the external layers of the shell are separated from the internal (Karali forthcoming).

In general, local influences can adulterate the dates with deviations of a few hundred to a few thousand years. In order to avoid such phenomena about 30-50% of the exterior of the shell should be removed. For this reason it is preferable to select solid shells with thick walls.

Another method is that of seasonal dating, which is based on counting the daily growth line. It aims firstly at defining the period of deposition and then its subperiods, that is when exactly the shell was collected (September, July etc.). The method of seasonal dating is judged more accurate since it takes into consideration the constant features of shells. Moreover, it contributes to the better stratification of heaps of shells because it is based on the study of the distribution of the shells dated by this method, in the inside of the accumulations.

It emerges from the above that shells constitute a class of remains that helps absolute dating. They can also contribute to elucidating the seasonality of both activities and habitation, seasonal fishing or summer encampment (Deith 1983, 423-440).

Chapter III

Molluscs in the Life of Prehistoric Aegean Society

άγει δε παντοδαπά κογχύλια
λεπάδας, αστακούς, κραβύζουςς, κικιβάλους, τηθυνάκια,
... βαλάνους, πορφύρας, όστρεια συμμεμυκότα,
τά διελείν μεν εστι χαλεπά, καταφαγήμεν δ'ευμαρέα
μύας αναρίτας τε κάρυκάς τε καί σκιφύδρια
τά γλυκέα μέν εντ'επέσθειν, εμπαγήμεν δ'οξέα,
τούς τε μακρογογγύλους σωλήνας, α μέλαινα, τε
κόγχος, άπερ κογχοθηράν παισίν εστ'ισωνία
θάτεραι δέ γάιαι κόγχοι τε καμαθίτιδες,
ταί κακοδόκιμοι τε κηύωνοι, τάς ανδροφυκτίδας
πάντες άνθρωποι καλέονθ', αμές δέ λεύκας τοί θεοί.

Γάμος Ήβης, Επίχαρμος

The study of molluscs yields important information on the diet of ancient communities. This information concerns firstly the procurement - gathering and fishing - of living molluscs and secondly their place in the food chain. It can be deduced from the numerical and proportional presence of each species among the food residues as a whole, from traces on the shell - that is the way in which it was broken – and from the general archaeological assemblage/context. From the mollusc shells discovered at archaeological sites, and which are related to fishing activities and the diet, knowledge can be obtained about the ecological environment, the level of technological know-how, the economy and the way of life of the community.

Procurement of molluscs

In most cases it is possible to determine the way in which molluscs were procured, provided the species are identified. As has been mentioned several times already, each species is characteristic and therefore indicative of a particular biotope, because molluscs are highly sensitive to the salinity, the temperature and the composition of water in general. Certain species of molluscs inhabit the sea bed, others a rocky environment, others sandy areas. These habitats were all accessible to man, though some less easily than others. It is interesting to determine the technological means man used to reach them, as well as the tools used for procuring molluscs.

In most cases the environment of the zone in which an occupation site is situated explains the choice of resources for exploitation. Indeed this choice is confirmed by quantitative analysis of shells and by determining the ways and means the molluscs were procured (Fig. 3).

a. Quantitative analysis

This mainly concerns the ratio between the different species as this emerges from the size of shells and their nutritional value in the diet (Koike 1979, 63-74)[8]. The

---

[8] Valve-pairing technique
One of the latest methods of quantitative analysis, valve-pairing technique is applied to remains of bivalve molluscs, mainly for estimating the number of individuals in a shell population. It is characteristic that the two valves of a shell only fit together exactly if they belong to the same individual, and that every single shell has its own specific chromatic motif, very similar on both valves. These two facts, providing of course that the colour is preserved, permit the convincing reuniting of the separated valves.
The methodology of valve-pairing is as follows: the intact and coloured valves are selected from the material. They are then separated into groups, according to size and chromatic motif. The expected combinations are estimated on the basis of existing knowledge for each systematically classified species of mollusc. The pairs are formed by comparing successive right valves with a specific left valve until identity of colour is an achieved or a perfect pairing of the valves.
The population of shells can be estimated on the basis of the following probability equation (Feller 1968, 45): $Q(n)=nCin-ICKr$ $CKl/2nCk$, where k is the number of selected intact valves from a population of shells made up of pairs, i the number of pairs recognized in the population, kr and kl the numbers of unpaired right and left valves. $Q(n)$ is the possibility, the number of pairs in the sample of k valves chosen from the population to be equated with i pairs.
A schematic representation of the probability equation of estimating the size of the shell population by valve-pairing technique:

    n = the number of pairs in the population
    k = the number of valves in the sample
    i   = the number of recognizable pair-valves
    kr = the number of unpaired right valves
    kl = the number of unpaired left valves

In order to find its most probable value or the sequence $Q(n)/Q(n-1)$ is used in general and the most probable value of n emerges, when $Q(n)/Q(n-1)$ is almost equal to 1:
$Q(n)/Q(n-1)=[4n2-2n(2k+1)+k2+k]/[4n2-2n(2k-2i+1)=2k-2i]=1$
So the most probable value of n is the maximum intact of $(k2-k+2i)/4i$ that is $n+(k2-k+2i)/4i$.

9

comparative correspondences between the deposits of molluscs and the accumulations of other food residues are then recorded. The relationship between them reveals the degree of dependence of each human group on molluscs. Lastly, the various changes over time are noted. These are expressed by differentiation in choices, that is other sources or other species of molluscs (Brothwell 1969, 60-61, Meigham et al. 1958).

Such choices are due to environmental changes (creation of lagoons, temperature changes *inter alia*) or cultural preferences. They are either the consequence of previous situations (e.g. exhausting of natural stocks), or the result of changes in technology, the economy and the confrontation of the immediate ecological environment.

b. Ways and means of procurement

Despite all the attempted interpretations, it is not always easy to give the reasons for the presence of a smaller or larger percentage of shells in food residues. Ethnographic studies are a valuable aid in this respect, since they offer parallels for understanding ways of life in the past. Human groups whose mainstay is fishing tend to be conservative towards using new methods (Radcliffe 1921, 8, Powell 1993, 20, Buchholz - Johrens - Maule 1973, 137-155).

Though methods of procuring molluscs are diverse, they are governed by some basic principles and can be classified on the basis of three main parameters:

i. The cultural factor, on which the implementation of techniques appropriate to the natural conditions (currents, calm or stagnant water) depends.

ii. The natural environment, which to a certain extent determines the kind of methods used, through factors such as the depth and the salinity of the water.

iii. The effects of fishing methods on the living organism, which are clear from marks on the shell. Molluscs caught in nets or baskets do not suffer amputations, whereas those caught with a rod and line or other pointed objects receive severe wounds and disfigurations or specific damage to their shell (Orme 1981, Bailey - Parkington 1988).

In addition, the distance separating the valves of each pair provides information on the degree of disturbance of the deposit, bearing in mind the fact that before the valves were   parted they were joined by ligaments.

c. Procuring molluscs in the prehistoric Aegean

Most of the technical means of fishing in prehistoric times did not have a single but a multiple use (Fig. 4). Consequently it is important for the specialist scholar to determine the following:

i. Whether the molluscs were collected with a specific tool.

ii. Whether they were collected from deep or shallow waters.

iii. For those collected from deep waters, how this difficult operation was achieved.

Species living in deep waters were obtained by diving and by using a boat. At first molluscs were gathered by hand. Later the task was made easier by using tools, mainly pointed implements such as knives, for removing them from the rocky substrate to which they cling (e.g. limpets and oysters). A kind of two-pronged fork was used for molluscs living in the sand, tongs for mussels and pinnas, as well as a scoop or dip net for species living in shallow waters. In order to 'attract' and trap creatures such as the octopus bait was used (see indicatively Evans - Renfrew 1968, 122-138, Buchholz 1973, Branigan 1974, Persson 1931).

Some species of molluscs that could not be fished directly offshore could only be obtained by using boats. Boats made possible the procurement of more species from differing depths and consequently increased man's potential for exploiting the marine environment (Basch 1987).

The only special equipment the diver needed was a weight to help his submergence. In antiquity a stone could have been used for this purpose. He also required a knife and a bag, the use of which can be inferred from the objects found together with shells in the archaeological assemblage (e.g. sponges or species of molluscs that live at specific depths). Sponges are indicative of fishing activity by diving and the diver's special knowledge of the environment in which they live (Forsythe 1949, Perney - Follin 1985, 240).

Shells were collected and stored in objects such as baskets, which are known of from the seventh millennium BC (Nea Nikomedia, Carington Smith 1975, 163). These were particularly useful in food-producing and farming communities. Clay vases were also used for storing seafood, as for example at Akrotiri, Thera, where a vase containing sea urchin shells was found (Doumas 1983, pl. 85).

Baskets or wicker twigs were also used as traps, their shape and size depending on the species they were intended to catch. Even today similar baskets are used for fishing octopus, murex etc. Permanent traps were used to obtain fish in strong currents. Some were baited with cuttlefish, lobster and so on. Because they were made of perishable material, they have not survived.

At the Neolithic site of Kephala, Kea (Coy 1977, 133) a large number of limpets was discovered. From the state of the shells it is deduced that these had been smashed with a stone and their flesh probably used as bait. Similar finds at the Neolithic site of Aghios Petros in the Sporades (Ευστρατίου 1985) have been interpreted as food residues. There is information on fishing methods and techniques, on divers and on the ways of gathering certain species of molluscs such as octopus, *Pinna* and mussels, in the ancient sources (Homer, *Iliad* XXIV: 78-82, XXIX: 81, *Odyssey* XII:253).

Fishing requires knowledge of the habits and behaviour of the living organisms to be procured. It is of course particularly difficult to gain knowledge of creatures whose natural habitat is difficult of access.

Study of the equipment used for fishing reveals the general cultural infrastructure and helps the interpretation and understanding of a specific site (Karali 1979, 54-113, Shackley 1985, 52-76). However, before reaching conclusions the following should be taken into consideration:

1)   Several species of molluscs do not live at a strictly predetermined depth (e.g. *Murex trunculus* and *Murex brandaris* live at depths of from 4 to 40 metres).

2)   Remains of fish, octopus or fragments of molluscs were placed inside baskets or vases for the purpose of attracting other species. It is not easy to locate and recognize such an archaeological assemblage.

Consequently it is difficult to recognize the general use of molluscs as bait[9].

Even so, there are archaeological assemblages in which the use of molluscs as means of fishing can be

diagnosed. In these cases the procurement of food constitutes an important archaeological and environmental indicator.

---

[9] It is not always easy to pinpoint the shells of molluscs that were consumed as food, particularly when they are found mixed up with shells that were used in fishing activities (bait) or others that bear signs of natural erosion. Thus, though the way in which a shell has been opened is frequently indicative of its use, it is not always certain. The tables which present shell food residues are more indicative of species consumed than of quantities, since in many cases not all shells without signs of working are collected.
Consequently conclusions on people's preferences for specific species or generalizations about food residues characteristic of particular periods are hazardous unless all the malacological remains are collected.

Food

The participation of molluscs in the diet is proven from the earliest stages of human history. Bivalves, gastropods, cephalopods as well as many other fresh and salt water creatures featured in the diet of most prehistoric societies (Karali 1979, 54-56). Two factors contributed to this: the ease with which they were procured and their nutritional value.

It is known from modern research that the average net weight of flesh in each mollusc is 10 gr. Its solid components are 21.5% to 23% and its chemical composition is as follows: water 82.6%, nitrous substances 8.25%, inorganic constituents 1.79%, fats 1.72% and non-nitreous extractive substances 6.16%. The nutritional value of molluscs is particularly important even though their weight is small.

However, a large quantity of molluscs must be consumed to obtain the equivalent nutritional value to the meat of bigger animals (Karali 1979, 57-58).

Study of the food residues at prehistoric sites reveals the importance of molluscs. Shells of many species, and indeed in large quantities, are known from the Palaeolithic Age, in Europe, Africa, Asia and other parts of the world. Study of the shells reveals not only their variety and quantity but also man's awareness of the seasonal reproduction of the species. During the Upper Palaeolithic fishing and gathering of aquatic molluscs was restricted to lakes, rivers and accessible coasts. The diet of Neanderthal man in Gibraltar was rich in seafood, with a preference for limpets and mussels. The picture is similar for the Neanderthal populations of the Middle East, in particular the remains at the well-known excavation on Mount Carmel (Brothwell 1969, 59-64).

Cultural advances during the Mesolithic Age led to the improvement of ways and means of fishing. It seems that there was intensive and extensive exploitation of molluscs in some regions. The people who followed this way of life are known as 'strand loopers', that is foragers on the sea shore, and were to be found in many parts of the world: in the Americas (the Canaliniens in California), the Far East (the Hoabliniens and Toaliens), Africa (the Capsiens in North Africa), Europe (the Asturiens in Spain, the Tardenoisiens in Britain, the Larniens in northwestern France) and the people of the Ertbølle Culture in Denmark (Ucko - Dimbleby 1969, 479-488). 'Strand looping' was based mainly on collective activities (locating and exploiting large quantities of food) and characterized populations dwelling close to wetland habitats.

In Western Europe man became a 'strand looper' (Ucko - Dimbleby 1969, 479-488) after the end of the last Ice Age when sea food was plentiful on account of the change in sea level and the increase of the coastal zone due to isostatic and eustatic formations.

According to another theory the 'strand loopers' were forced to the coasts under the pressure of other human groups, and so installed themselves there.

In some cases the type of economy based on molluscs expresses a purely seasonal occupation. A familiar example of the importance of molluscs in the diet in Mesolithic Europe are the enormous heaps of shells (middens) in the Mugem region of Portugal. The, most frequent species in these are *Cerastoderma edule, Ostrea edulis, Triton nodiferus*, and *Ensis ensis*.

Heaps of shells, the so-called kitchen middens, have been located in Denmark. The species that appear most frequently are oysters (*Ostrea*), cockles (*Cardium*), mussels (*Mytilus*) and *Littorina* sp., all of which can be found on the modern coast, but less plentiful on account of over-consumption.

Molluscs continued to play a large part in the diet in many parts of the world during the Neolithic Age. Certainly, however, they did not enjoy the same wide diffusion as in the Mesolithic Age.

During the Neolithic Age and the succeeding Bronze Age, thanks to technological progress in ways and means of fishing (use of nets and boats), it became possible to catch big fish.

In most cases man is responsible for the vanishing of species. However, the reduced presence of certain species of molluscs within excavation assemblages may be due to other factors. For instance, different species are consumed at different times of the year. They are more numerous in the period of reproduction, because in that specific season their procurement is easier or their flesh is tastier. Moreover, environmental changes can affect the reproduction of certain species of molluscs. These changes are frequently due to human interventions in the environment or fluctuations in temperature.

In certain instances man succeeded in increasing the reproduction of some animal species with the aim of creating a series of individuals genetically differentiated from their wild ancestors. The 'domestication' of molluscs was impossible during prehistoric times. In fact, exploitation does not lead to domestication, but rather to the extinction of species. Even in the case of oysters, selective reproduction was not achieved; only intensive breeding to increase their quantity was successful. The earliest evidence of the 'cultivation' of molluscs is from Roman times (Brothwell 1969, 65-67).

From the foregoing discussion the relation of molluscs to the economy and the way of life of prehistoric communities is apparent. Three theoretical models can be proposed, that most probably correspond to specific forms and functions of inhabited settlements[10].

i.   Shell middens - hunter-gatherer sites

In these cases the mollusc remains usually represent a form of food reserve. Their place in the population's economy is supplementary. Nevertheless, they constitute a factor of stability: in contrast to other animal species and plant resources that are markedly seasonal in character, shells can be gathered all year round.

ii.   Heaps of shells - mixed economy

This is a model of economic organization in which agricultural production is clearly dominant but molluscs are used as an essential protein supplement.

iii.   Shell middens - towns, markets or semi-commercial employment in procuring molluscs

This class occurs in cultures with a mixed economy and a certain level of organization. The Arica region of Chile is cited as an example; there communities of fishermen in the Inca Empire exported fish and molluscs in exchange for agricultural produce.

As has been noted already, recognition of the type of the economy on the basis of the study of heaps of shells leads to one of these three theoretical models. However such an approach has been attempted at very few excavated sites. This fact makes it difficult to extract more general conclusions on account of the lack of sufficient evidence.

---

[10]   Shell fragments are also found in coprolites. No such material has been studied in Greece. Coprolite analysis from the Peruvian site of Avaka Prieta produced fragments of mussel shells (Callen 1969, 118-194), furnishing important information on the diet and the palaeoenvironment.

The Archaeological Evidence

Appendix I

α μέλαινα, τε κόγχος, άπερ κογχοθηράν παισίν εστ'ισωνία

Γάμος Ήβης, Επίχαρμος

Prevailing species in the diet

The archaeological evidence on molluscs in the diet of prehistoric man is incomplete because there are few full studies of the malacological material from sites. The number of specimens found by species are shown in Table 1.

As has been said already, molluscs were an important source of food for prehistoric man. Information from the Palaeolithic Age is limited because very few sites have been explored and published (Fig. 5). There are patchy data coming from the Petralona Cave, Chalkidiki and from the Kastritsa, Kokkinospilo and Kleidi caves in Epirus (Bailey 1984, 22, 1986, 16). Only the malacological material from Franchthi Cave, Argolid has been systematically studied and published. This shows that there was a preference for the species *Patella* and *Monodonta* which are easy to gather and common on rocky shores (Shackleton 1969, 379, Jacobsen 1973, 257-258, Shackleton - van Andel 1980, 357-359, Shackleton 1988, 11-27).

Equally limited is the information for the Mesolithic Age. Terrestrial and marine molluscs have been recovered from the sites of Sidari and the Airport on Corfu (Sordinas 1969, 393, Fig. 1). Characteristic of this period is the consumption of large quantities of land snails, as in the Cyclop's Cave on Youra in the Sporades, at Maroula on Kythnos and Franchthi in the Argolid, where land snails far outnumbered marine molluscs in the food residues. This picture is consistent with that from sites in Mesolithic Europe (Honea 1975, 277-279).

More is known about the consumption of molluscs as food in the Neolithic Age. Despite the development of stock-raising, molluscs were evidently an important dietary supplement, as borne out by the large quantities in which they are found. Mollusc remains are reported from most sites, especially coastal and riparian settlements.

At the Macedonian site of Nea Nikomedia a preference for *Cardium edule* and *Cerithium vulgatum* L. is observed in the Early Neolithic. These species are characteristic of two different environments, delta silt and rocky coasts respectively.

In Thessaly the prevailing species consumed in the Early Neolithic, at the sites of Pyrasos, Argisa and Soufli Magoula (Θεοχάρης 1959, 29-60, Milojčić - Boessneck - Hopf 1962), were *Monodonta, Triton Cardium* and *Unio*. These molluscs live in a variety of habitats: sand, rocks, rivers, lakes etc.

At Early Neolithic Nea Makri, Attica *Cardium* and *Patella* were the predominant species (Θεοχάρης 1956, 24-26).

The same species of molluscs were consumed during the Middle and Late Neolithic. In the final phases of the Neolithic Age, however, they are found in greater numbers.

At the sites of Dimitra, Dikili Tash, Sitagroi in Macedonia, in the Kitsos Cave, Attica and the Franchthi Cave, Argolid, there are species distinctive of diverse environments, such as *Cardium* sp. *Ostrea edulis L., Spondylus gaederopus L., Mytilus* sp., *Cerithium vulgatum Br., Glycimeris glycimeris L., Patella* sp. Particularly important is the presence and percentage of the riverine species, *Unio*, frequently found at Neolithic sites in Macedonia (Karali 1992, 153-157, Karali forthcoming, Shackleton forthcoming).

The differentiations observed during the Late Neolithic are in large part due to the increase in population, which is evident from the size and number of settlements, particularly in the Drama plain.

The malacological material has been studied from sites such as Sitagroi (Shackleton forthcoming), Dimitra (Karali 1997, 200-211), Olynthos (Mylonas 1928, 191), Dikili-Tash (Karali 1992, 153-157) in Macedonia, and Aghia Sophia and Dimini in Thessaly (Volos Museum, personal study by the author). The same species of molluscs are represented as in the preceding period: *Cardium sp., Ostrea edulis L., Glycimeris glycimeris L., Patella* and *Mytilus.*

In the Sporades, in the Cyclop's Cave on Youra (LN), marine species significantly outnumber terrestrial (Karali, study in progress).

The shells recovered from the Kitsos Cave in Attica and the Tharrounia Cave on Euboea are from the usual species of molluscs encountered at other sites during the Neolithic Age, that is *Patella* sp., *Cardium* sp., *Unio* sp. etc. Large quantities of shells were found in the Kitsos Cave on account of the continuous and intense habitation of the site, whereas far fewer were found at Tharrounia where occupation was seasonal. In both cases the species originate from diverse environments and indicate that the cave inhabitants sometimes travelled long distances to procure them.

In the Peloponnese there is evidence of the role of molluscs in the diet of the Late Neolithic communities at Corinth (Walker-Kosmopoulos 1948, 66) and Lerna, where in contrast to other sites *Murex* sp. predominates, followed by *Cerithium* sp. and *Glycimeris* sp. (Gejvall 1967, 50). Further south, in the Alepotrypa Cave in the Mani, species common on rocky coasts were mainly found, but in small quantities: *Patella* sp., *Monodonta* sp., *Gibulla* sp. and *Murex* sp. (Karali 1983, 229-232).

In the Cyclades a particularly important site for the study of molluscs is Saliagos, an islet offshore of Antiparos, where seafood played a major role in the diet. Indicative is the large number of mollusc species identified (35 species), the predominant ones being those characteristic of rocky, but also sandy, coasts. *Patella* sp. is the most numerous, followed by *Monodonta* sp., *Cardium* sp., *Mures* sp., *Pinna* sp., *Cerithium* sp. and *Spondylus* sp. (Shackleton 1968, 122-138).

From the Dodecanese there is information from the Aspri Petra Cave on Kos (LN) where *Patella* sp. and *Triton nodiferus L.* were the most abundant species (Levi 1926, 236-237).

On Crete, molluscs were an important dietary supplement at Neolithic Knossos (Shackleton 1968, 264-266). The species consumed were the same as at most Neolithic sites in the Aegean: *Cardium* sp., *Patella* sp. *Monodonta* sp. and *Glycimeris* sp..

During the transitional phase from the Neolithic to the Bronze Age, at Rachmani, Thessaly, some of the main species of molluscs encountered in the Neolithic Age continued to be a stable source of food: *Patella* sp., *Pecten* sp., *Ostrea* sp. and *Mytilus* sp. (Weishaar 1979, 385-392).

At Kephala, Kea during this same period the proportion of molluscs in the diet diminished in relation to other foodstuffs. *Patella* sp. heads the list, followed by *Triton*, *Murex*, *Charonia* and *Spondylus*, species characteristic of rocky coasts and the open sea.

From the beginning of the Early Bronze Age (EB I and EB II) at Pentapolis in Macedonia (prefecture of Serres), lacustrine and terrestrial species dominate

(*Unio* and *Helix*), as is to be expected from its close association with the lake (Καραλή 1981, 115-118).

Further south, at the coastal site of Aghios Kosmas, Attica, shells were found mainly inside the houses. They represent the known species of molluscs consumed in the prehistoric Aegean: *Ostrea*, *Pecten*, *Arca*, *Glycimeris*, *Mytilus*, and *Murex* species (Mylonas 1959, 191).

A similar picture emerges from Crete, particularly from Myrtos (EM II), where the same species of molluscs continued to be consumed, notably *Patella* and *Monodonta*, typical of rocky coasts (Warren 1972). The small percentage of organic remains found at Myrtos, as at corresponding Bronze Age sites, may be explained by the fact that the inhabitants removed their rubbish from the settlement.

In the Cyclades, the dominant species in the cemetery and settlement at Chalandriani, Syros, was *Patella*. The graves also contained small and large shells of the species *Cassis*, *Arca*, *Triton*, which come from diverse habitatis (Τσούντας 1898, 199-203). The shells reported from Korfi t'Aroniou, Naxos, are characteristic of rocky coasts: *Patella*, *Monodonta* (Ντούμας 1966, 41-64).

Patella sp. also dominates at sites in the northeast Aegean, such as Thermi, Lesbos, where large quantities of limpet shells were discovered along with other edible molluscs such as *Cardium* sp., *Glycimeris* sp., *Spondylus* sp., *Arca* sp., *Ostrea* sp. and others (Lamb 1936).

So in the Early Bronze Age Cyclades molluscs had an important place in the diet, dominant species being *Patella coerulea* and *Patella vulgata Linne*, which are native to the islands' rocky shores.

In Euboea a few shells were found at the Early Bronze Age site of Kaloyerovrisi. These include the species, *Arca*, *Spondylus*, *Glycimeris* and others (Καραλή 1993, 169-173). The small quantities are mainly due to the seasonal character of the occupation, while the species indicate the relations of this inland site with the coast.

Information of the consumption of molluscs in the Middle Bronze Age comes from Quartier Mu at Malia, Crete (MM III). Although rubbish was clearly removed from the site, there are remains of shells, predominant among them the familiar species *Patella*, *Cerithium*, *Monodonta*, *Charonia*, *Mytilus*, (Karali forthcoming).

In the Late Bronze Age at Akrotiri, Thera (LC I) the limpet (*Patella* sp.) prevailed, followed by *Monodonta*, *Murex*, *Glycimeris* and other species. The relatively large number of molluscs recovered from the town, despite indications that rubbish was removed from the houses, is easily explained by its coastal location and close ties with the sea (Karali 1990, 410-415) (Fig. 6a-k).

At Aghios Stephanos, Laconia (LH II) the species *Donax, Patella, Arca* and *Mactra* were located (Reese forthcoming).

Similar species are reported from Skala Sotiros, Thasos, again characteristic of rocky shores: *Patella* sp., *Solen* sp., *Gibbula* sp., *Monodonta* sp., *Pinna* sp., *Arca* sp., *Donax* sp., *Helix* sp., etc. (Καραλή 1993, 756-760).

The picture presented at Kommos, Crete is much the same, though the presence of tritons deserves attention, since these indicate the use of boats and nets for fishing them. The most important species are *Patella, Monodonta, Arcularia, Euthria, Charonia, Bittium* (Reese 1989).

At another Cretan site, Symi Viannou (LM III) the main species consumed were *Columbella, Conus, Patella, Charonia*, etc. (Reese - Lembessi 1986, 138-188).

There is no significant change in the species of molluscs found in excavations at Late Bronze Age sites. There is, however, a marked reduction in quantity, not only of those consumed as food but also of those used for other purposes.

The archaeological evidence for the consumption of molluscs in the prehistoric Aegean, resulting from the identification of species and the quantitative analyses of the material from excavated sites, may be summarized as follows:

There is very little information for the Palaeolithic Age. Future research will possibly help locate the sources of procurement.

For the Mesolithic Age the best documented evidence is from Franchthi in the Peloponnese, where marine species found near the shore were consumed. Significant and characteristic of the period is the proportionately large contribution of terrestrial molluscs to the diet, as evident from the Cyclop's Cave on Youra of Halonesos (Καραλή study in progress).

Though terrestrial molluscs seem to be a distinctive trait of the food-gathering (foraging) stage of the Mesolithic Age, they continued to be consumed throughout the Neolithic Age from Macedonia (e.g. Dimitra) to southern Greece (e.g. Lerna, Nea Makri).

At Nea Makri terrestrial molluscs were found on a LN hearth (Παντελίδου 1991, 86-87, Fig. 78).

Whereas at coastal Neolithic sites marine species were a basic source of food, at inland sites they merely constitute an occasional dietary supplement. At settlements situated near a river or lake, freshwater molluscs were also consumed, as is the case in Thessaly and Macedonia where *Unio* sp. is abundant.

Among the species preferred in the Neolithic Age *Patella* has precedence, followed by *Cardium, Murex, Pinna* primarily at Macedonian sites.

From the end of the Neolithic and during the Early Bronze Age the same species as in previous periods are encountered. However the proportion of shells found decreased considerably as the Bronze Age advanced. Increase in population, growth of settlements and division of labour led to further development of animal husbandry and agriculture. The diet was enriched and varied as a result of increased food-gathering and fishing. The same picture is observed in the Middle Bronze Age levels at settlements such as Malia, Phaistos and Knossos in Crete, Phylakopi in the Cyclades and elsewhere (Fig. 7). Dominant species are *Spondylus, Cardium, Mytilus, Cerithium, Murex, Ostrea, Patella* etc. and the land snail *Helix* in smaller percentage.

The contribution of molluscs to the diet of the inhabitants of the prehistoric Aegean is also attested by their preservation in jars, such as those found at Akrotiri, Thera (Καραλή forthcoming, Doumas 1983, pl. 85).

To summarize the above:

1) From the Palaeolithic Age to the Late Bronze Age molluscs constituted an important element in the diet.

2) There was a clear preference for particular species throughout the prehistoric era in the Aegean. In most cases these were species that exist today. They were either gathered (e.g *Patella*) or fished (e.g. *Triton*)

3) In Neolithic Macedonia, large quantities of molluscs were consumed at permanently occupied sites far from the coast (Fig. 8a-b-c). In contrast, smaller quantities are found in southern Greece (e.g. Tharrounia, Kaloyerovrysi), perhaps because of the seasonal nature of habitation at some of these sites, such as Tharrounia.

4) During the Bronze Age there is a fall off in the consumption of molluscs throughout the Aegean. This is probably due to the rise in the standard of living and the change in dietary

preferences (cephalopods, whose remains are difficult to detect).

5)   At the sites cited above, molluscs appear in the following order of preference (see Table 1):

         Patella
         Cardium edule L.
         Monodonta turbinata L.
         Cerithium vulgatum Br.
         Mytilus galloprovincialis L.
         Murex sp.
         Conus mediterraneus Br.
         Arca noae L.
         Triton sp.
         Spondylus gaederopus L.

Vessels and Tools

a. Research methodology

The study of shell remains characterized as tools in each case follows some model of systematic analysis (Leroy-Prost 1978, 179-184, Moundrea-Agrafioti 1975, 124, Payne 1973, 253-254, Leroi-Gourhan 1943). First comes the precise description of the excavated area and the recording of the material brought to light. These data are accompanied by further information on the location of the site, the circumstances of discovery of the finds, the stratigraphy, the possible existence of workshops or work floors for shells, the other categories of remains (floral, faunal etc.) as well as evidence of practical activities. The last are, of course, associated with the diverse utilitarian functions of the various tool types (Kourtessi-Philippakis 1986).

Next the assemblage of data is assessed by the researcher, with the aim of formulating feasible hypotheses concerning the environment, the economic framework, the 'industrial' units and the chronological classification. The objective is to present a synthesis covering the maximum possible amount of data.

The conclusions drawn from such a study, in turn pose specific questions. Of course there is leeway for doubt and for redefining the data. The quality of the conclusions reached depends on the choice of analytical criteria; these are related to the location, the organization of the exploitation and the distribution of the raw material.

The transition from the description of the finds to the extraction of conclusions would not be possible without the intervention of typological examination (Taborin 1974, 108). Typology contributes definitively to the clear distinction of the partial assemblages composing a homogeneous body of remains, such as shell tools. A series of problems must be confronted. The source of the raw material must be ascertained (systematic classification by mollusc species) as well as the degree of human intervention (worked or unworked shells).

There are of course extreme cases; the absence of even minimal intervention on the shell or man's alteration of its original form beyond recognition. These in their turn set a host of constraints which should be taken into account. On the one hand, the discovery of totally unworked shells does not automatically mean that they were not used as tools - there are specific signs (traces) which permit recognition of different uses. On the other hand, worked shells frequently lose the diagnostic traits of the species from which they were fashioned. Study of traces of working can provide information on the methods and techniques applied by the human

group as well as on the utilitarian value of the object (Flamand 1901, 729-734). It should also be borne in mind that natural erosion caused by time distorts the external features of the finds, to a greater or lesser degree (Taborin 1974, 108).

The description of the finds leads to their taxonomic analysis, and investigation of the internal relations between them leads to conclusions of a general nature. Such a study is more effective when other data are implicated too, such as the fauna, flora, climate and terrain, as well as the surviving species, natural erosion of the remains, traces of working etc. The more evidence taken into account, the closer to reality are the conclusions.

b. The singularity of Greece

Pottery, stoneworking and metalworking in the prehistoric Aegean display a clearly superior development, in some cases (particularly pottery) attaining unexpected levels of technical and artistic perfection. This phenomenon is partly explained by the geological substrate of Greece, in whose earth there is an abundance and diversity of raw materials.

The marriage of environmental imperatives and cultural criteria led to the dominance of artifacts of stone and clay. Those of bone and even more so of shell appeared on only a limited scale.

The existence of shell artifacts presupposes the development of special practices and methods for procuring molluscs and, of course, the existence of settlements involved in these activities in the coastal zones. The use of shell tools was always temporary in character. Only thanks to some of their exceptional properties did molluscs enjoy a wider distribution, as is the case with murex from which purple dye is produced. This phenomenon, however, has nothing to do with specific uses as tools. Agricultural production and all it entailed at a technological level gave steady precedence to clay and stone.

c. Traces of working

One of the most important observations made when examining shells is whether the molluscs were procured alive or when the organism was already dead (Karali 1979, 113-135).

Shells gathered when empty frequently bear holes, but careful study can distinguish between those caused by natural agents and those by human hand. Holes were deliberately opened by friction, i.e. rubbing the shell on a flat stone, or by piercing with the sharp end of a stone tool (e.g. Saliagos) or an obsidian blade with retouch.

Holes in shells may also be due to damage suffered while the shell was buried in the ground or during the process of excavation (Poplin 1976).

For example, because of its crystalline structure the limpet shell is vulnerable to detachment of the lower ring, parallel to the base of the cone, resulting in a smaller cone and a separate ring. However, limpets may have been used as scrapers, with the same consequences for the shell, while it is also possible that such a break was due simply to their removal from the rocks.

d. Shell tools

Shells used as tools appear on many excavated sites. It is obvious that for such purposes largish shells, distinguished for their resistance and thickness, were selected (for these very reasons shell tools are usual and expected in regions of the Pacific where there are very large shells). In general shell tools are of two kinds, unworked and worked (Fig. 9a).

Unworked shells

Many molluscs had 'dual-purpose': after the flesh had been consumed as food, the shell was used as a tool, in its natural state, without any intervention.

Such tools are extremely difficult to recognize, unless they are found in a context which corroborates their characterization, as for example in houses and in rubbish pits (middens).

In many cases shells were probably used as a tool only once, perhaps for opening other shells or for 'imprinting' a pattern on the surface of mouldable material (e.g. on the wet clay of a vase). When the task was over they were discarded, so that in the majority of cases there are no specific traces of use-wear. In such cases the excavation context is the only clue to the possible use of these shells.

Unworked shells of *Cardium* sp. were used by prehistoric man for decorating vases: indeed a distinctive ceramic class is known as Cardium Ware[11].

---

[11] Cardium ware
This type of pottery is named after the tool used for incising the pattern (Fig. 12b). It is impossible to recognize the Cardium shell used as a tool when found together with other shells because it has not been worked in any way. What can be studied by the archaeologist is the clay on which the incision was made with the specific tool. The group of vases decorated with incisions from *Cardium* shell constitute a well-known ceramic class in Neolithic Europe, known as Cardium ware (Θεοχάρης 1959, 39-49, Milojčić 1971, Χουρμουζιάδης 1969, 169).
In Greece this group of vases is subsumed under the wider class of incised pottery; it is Tsountas's second goup. For the non-specialist it is not always easy to recognize the tool used for incising. The

The species *Spondylus gaederopus Linne*, mainly known because it was chosen for making jewellery, was also used in diverse activities on account of its hardness and durability.

Worked shells

Shells in this category display either limited interventions or substantial alterations that often obliterate their original form. Most of the shells used were very resistant and as a raw material have many of the properties of bone, thus their transformation into diverse objects for manifold uses was possible.

The following classes of worked shells can be distinguished:

1) Small shells of indeterminate use.
2) Small spoon-shaped shells, of which three sub-types can be recognized: a) Ovoid-hollow spoon, b) Ovoid-flat spoon, c) Round spoon. This class also includes, on account of the shape, shells used as scoops and lamps.
3) Shells of various sizes used as: a) spatulas, b) burnishers, c) seals, d) containers, e) spools.

e. Typology of shell vessels and tools

Indeterminate use

At several Neolithic sites in Greece a significant number of shells were used for fashioning spoons or spoon-shaped objects. Among their uses was the transfer of liquids from larger to smaller vessels (e.g. tritons). In most cases minimal interventions were made to the original shape of the shell. The following species of molluscs belong in this class: *Patella coerulea L., Mytilus galloprovincialis L., Spondylus gaederopus L., Charonia lampas L., Venerupis aureus Gmelin.*

---

typology of incision on clay with Cardium or other related shell differs from that executed with a comb, finger nail or other pointed tools in the following respects:
- the incision is not double or treble as with a comb
- there is no variety of shapes as when a pointed tool is used
- traces from use of the finger nail are deeper, which fact facilitates recognition of the means of incision.
Incision with shell takes place as follows:
The *Cardium* shell is placed vertically to the vase, creating broad rectilinear incisions. More rarely the shells are imprinted along the entire length of their periphery on the surface of the vase, creating continuous and undulating incisions (Karali 1979, 128-141).

Cardium ware has mainly been found in Thessaly. The clay fabric of the vases contains numerous inclusions. The decorative motifs consist of a combination of horizontal, vertical and semicircular lines. Many scholars have studied Cardium ware, both with regard to its provenance and its relationship to pottery types displaying affinity (Tringham 1971, Philipps 1975).

Of the shells collected at most Neolithic sites, the majority are of the species *Patella coerulea L.* or *Patella lusitanica Gmelin.* Unfortunately their state of preservation is generally poor. These species were also widely used as food, exemplifying a phenomenon of dual use.

After consumption of the flesh, the shell could be used as a spoon, on account of its hollow shape. In some cases, careful attempts were made to sharpen the blunter edges by abrading the entire periphery of the shell.

Even so, such finds are usually classed as food residues, while only rarely a secondary use is being attributed. This is because the dietary value of these molluscs is well known and their shell is particularly fragile.

Specific use

i. Spoons (Fig. 10)

Ovoid-hollow spoons

Sometimes shells of *Mytilus galloprovincialis Lamarck* (the common mussel) were used as spoons. On Saliagos 144 shells of this mollusc were counted, 47 of which were worked (the largest number so far known from an excavated site). These shells were chosen even when small in size and difficult to work. The exterior is reddish brown and the interior covered by a layer of nacre. The periphery of the shell was rubbed on a hard flat surface in order to sharpen the edges. The abraded area near the top of the valve may be 1 to 2 cm wide and the layers of nacre markedly exposed. Usually the shape of the shell is retained and only the edge sharpened: any extra intervention was to facilitate the object's use for particular tasks. The object thus formed has both functional and aesthetic value.

The delicacy of these objects does not rule out their function as tools. Even those that are very small could have been used as spoons. It is obvious that these are not *ad hoc* tools but, on the contrary, shells gathered and shaped for quite specific purposes. In general this kind of spoon is ovoid and elongated in shape, with a sharp edge. Because spoons of this type appear in Middle and Late Neolithic horizons they can be used by the archaeologist as evidence for dating.

Ovoid-hollow spoons of *Patella* sp. were also made in this way as can be seen on a few shells from Cyclop's cave (Fig. 11).

Ovoid-flat spoons

The stratigraphy at Saliagos, where shell vessels and tools were studied for the first time, offers the possibility of tracing the development of spoon types. The unworked or roughly worked shell gave way to an entirely different type of tool, a deliberately fashioned object.

This fact is also evident from the species of molluscs chosen for working: *Charonia lampas Linne* and *Charonia variegata Lamarck.* The spoons were shaped from the thickest part of the shell (4-8 cm thick) and in some cases were additionally worked by abrasion on a flat stone.

Round spoons

The use of an unworked or a roughly worked shell of *Spondylus gaederopus Linne* as a small, shallow palette has been ascertained. However, this type can be adapted to a host of different uses on account of the durability of the shell and its multiple layers of nacre. Even so, shells with the periphery smoothed by abrasion on a stone surface are rarely found.

Spoons of *Charonia variegata L.* were made in this way, as can be seen on one shell from Saliagos (no. 122) which had been rubbed on a flat stone so that its edges are precisely formed (Shackleton 1968, 68-69).

ii Spatulas (Fig. 12)

These are small objects used for transferring-storing small quantities of products or pigments or medicinal substances. Spatulas are usually longer than spoon-shaped objects and are rare, mainly because of the difficulty both of discovering and conserving shells. They were usually fashioned from the shell of the mollusc *Pinna nobilis Linne* which is exceptionally beautiful but very fragile. For this reason only fragments of the thicker sections of the shell are found in excavations. On the basis of existing information it is difficult to ascertain how widespread was the use of shell spatulas.

iii Burnishers

It is taken for granted that shells used for burnishing pottery also represent a specific category of tools. Examples of this type have been discovered at several sites and are made from different species.

In general their function is deduced from their form. Sometimes there are natural signs of wear on a shell, caused by the action of water and wind and not by intentional smoothing. When the traces of wear are not natural they are the result of the shell's contact with the surface to be smoothed, polished or burnished. Such traces of wear are localized at certain points and do not appear over the entire surface of the shell. Characteristic is the erosion along its length, distinguished by a medial line from the remaining unworked and unused surface.

It is sometimes possible to recognize from the traces of wear on the shell tool the material smoothed by it. Shell of the species *Cymatium parthenopium* was frequently used for burnishing vases, rubbing leather and other materials. Other species used were *Cardium* sp., *Patella* sp., *Spondylus* sp., *Cerithium* sp., *Glycimeris* sp.

iv. Lamps

To date no shells that were used as lamps have been found in Greece.

At Troy I (Gejvall 1937-38, 52) (EBA), shell valves were found (the species are not mentioned in the publication), with a hole in the interior hollow. In some case there are traces of grey from burning around the hole. These shells may have been used as spoons or as lamps. In the first case, the spoon handle will have been inserted in the hole in the shell. However, such a use presupposes the blunting of the edges of the hole, in which case the shell is in danger of destruction because it shakes when the perforation is made upon the medial axis of the valve. In the second case, if the shell was used as a lamp, then the hole was to receive the 'wick'. This hypothesis is reinforced by the presence of traces of burning substances suitable for lighting (Fig. 12a D).

v. Spools - cylindrical pestles

Pestles constitute a further class of small tools whose function has been doubted or overlooked. Marble and hard stone are cited as the main materials of manufacture.

Some of them, however, were produced from shells of *Spondylus gaederopus Linne*. They constitute a class of minor objects rarely exceeding 5 to 6 cm in length, with two circular bases united by a cylinder of smaller diameter. Sometimes they are in the form of two united regular truncated cones. Spools - pestles mainly occur in the Neolithic and the Early Bronze Age. Their form remains the same, the dimensions do not vary appreciably and only the profile displays marked tendencies to change. It seems they were mainly used for preparing pigments and cosmetics.

vi. Vases

Shell vases were used quite widely. Such objects demanded sizeable, durable shells of suitable shape that could be transformed into vessels with only minor interventions. On account of the nature of shell it was difficult to add attachments to the vases. By removing the internal spiral of gastropod shells a large free space was opened and whole shell was transformed into a vase with fine walls of porcelain-like quality.

On the basis of shape two vessel types are distinguished: flat open and high closed. The first type is represented by small palettes or open vases made from wide valves of large bivalve molluscs. In some cases these were used even without interventions. When the shell was worked the aim was to create a small flat disc, on the circumference of which the natural anomalies of the periphery of the shell remain. In some cases the discs bear a small protuberance which perhaps constituted a handle. Though similar in shape to the corresponding spoon, flat open vases are wider. They are domestic objects that are recognized fairly easily.

The species *Pecten jacobaeus L.* was commonly used during the Cycladic period as a palette or a pyxide containing cosmetics and is found among the offering in the graves. Unic is the small pecten pyxide from L.C. Akrotiri in Santorini (Fig. 13b).

High closed vases are known from the beginning of the Neolithic Age at Khirokitia in Cyprus and were formed by removing the collumela (internal spiral) from large conical shells (Fig. 13a).

In many lands of the Mediterranean basin such vessels were used for drinking. Shell of *Charonia* sp. was selected for making both vases and trumpets. In the latter case the pointed apex of the shell was removed but not the central internal axis, so that the object could produce sounds. In addition, those shells used as trumpets generally bear signs of wear at the edge from which it is supposed the users blew into them.

Important criteria for the scholar with regard to distinguishing between vessels and trumpets are the removal of the internal axis and the detachment of the pointed apex of the shell.

vii. Weapons

Very few examples of shell 'weapons' are mentioned in the bibliography. Some mollusc species, such as spondylus, whose shell is as hard as stone, were used for aggressive activities such as hunting. These are objects directly related to attack, such as the mace-head, or that were used as shafts/hafts of other tools mainly of metal.

viii. Triton shells (trumpets)[12]

A particularly important class of objects from triton shell are the trumpets (table 3). This name was adopted with analogous meaning to the wind instrument (Karali 1979, 130-135, Darque 1983, 59-73, Reese 1990, 7-14) (Fig. 14).

Several species of triton, belonging to the *Cymatiidae* family, live in the Mediterranean. The commonest are *Charonia sequaenzae* and *Charonia nodifera*. The shell of the first is up to 30 cm long and has an almost smooth surface, while that of the second is up to 40 cm long and has a nodular exterior and strongly relief interior.

These molluscs live at great depths in pebble or gravel habitats. Carnivorous, they secrete strong acids that break down the shell of their prey which they swallow whole (fish, crustaceans, bivalves, echinoderms). Noteworthy is the fact that a further two species of the same family live in Aegean waters, *Cymathium parthenopium*, up to 15 cm long, and *Cymathium cutaceum*, up to 9 cm long.

The species of shell often selected for fashioning a trumpet is *Tritonium nodiferum Lamarck*. One of the most robust species of molluscs in European seas, it is carnivorous, preying on starfish, crustaceans, even fish. Its thick-walled shell forms a large cone, consisting of 8 to 9 whorls, and attains a length of 30 cm. Its surface is white, yellow or light brown, reminiscent of marble, bearing radial grooves of brownish hue and numerous excrescences, of varying width, intersected by deep, criss-crossing, radial grooves.

Typology of trumpets

Only minimal interventions were made to the triton shell because it is very resistant and its shape lends itself to the production of a distinctive sound. The apex was removed to create a small hole and the cut surface smoothed. The primitive form of wind instrument, known as the trumpet, is a widely distributed object of ancient provenance still used today in regions with a traditional character.

---

[12] Triton shells have been associated with religious - symbolic 'acts'. In addition to ritual and ceremonial use, this shell featured in everyday activities too. For this reason tritons should be studied with caution, on the basis of their typology and especially the archaeological context.
For example, at Akrotiri, Thera objects traditionally regarded as having symbolic importance (including tritons) were found in buildings that are not characterized as sacred.

The Archaeological Evidence

Appendix 2

Presence of objects of triton shell

Since most of the tritons found in excavations bear no traces of working, their use and significance can only be understood from their context. Triton vases were used for everyday tasks, as scoops for skimming oil and other products, and in ritual activities, as evident from the libation vessel represented on the Mariani seal (Mosso 1910, 365) (Fig. 15c).

Worked tritons with a variety of functions are found at sites from the Neolithic to the Late Bronze Age. From the dawn of the Neolithic Age, at Khirokitia in Cyprus (Dikaios 1953, 439), there are whole and fragmentary shells of *Charonia lampas Linne*. It is not possible to determine the use of these particular shells because the material found is largely fragmentary. A plausible interpretation is that they were used as vessels. The most important piece is a big concave fragment of triton (l. 9.5 cm, w. 3.8 cm, th. 5 cm), but because no clear traces of working can be detected it is difficult to ascertain whether this is raw material or a formed object (Chevallier 1981, 611-32).

The same applies to shells of the same species found in Crete. At Neolithic Knossos 9 fragments of *Charonia lampas Linne* or *Charonia variegata Lamarck* were found. Their use as trumpets cannot be confirmed (Shackleton 1968, 264-66).

Fragments of *Charonia nodifera* were found in the Kitsos Cave, Attica.

Two large similar shells were found in the deeper Neolithic level of the east sector of the settlement known as 'Tou Papa to Choma', east of Chora on Skyros, together with vase sherds, a flint blade, a broken bone needle and some obsidian blades. Though the mouth of the shells bears signs of working it is still difficult to determine their exact role (Θεοχάρης 1945-47, 1-12).

In general it is difficult to determine the use of tritons in the Neolithic Age. On the contrary, in the succeeding Bronze Age there is more information on these shells, which have been found at both mainland and island sites. A shell of *Triton tritonis L.* was recovered from the Early Bronze Age cemetery at Chalandriani on Syros (EC II). Its use is not clear since the state of its preservation does not permit confirmation of traces of

working (Τσούντας 1898, 78). Another triton, with no traces of working, was discovered in the Panaghia cemetery on Paros (grave no. 56) together with other grave goods (figurines, pottery etc.).

It is difficult to draw conclusions on the use of the tritons recovered at Myrtos, Crete (EM III) because of their poor condition. Some 27 tritons - fragments and whole shells of *Charonia nodifera* - were found in all (Warren 1972, 324). The apex had been intentionally removed, except on one of the intact examples which has a broken end (level I, below room 28), while another bears a hole in the ventral area, probably due to erosion.

Three large tritons found at Malia, in two adjacent rooms (6 and 7) of sector XIV of Quartier Mu (MM III), could have been used as trumpets because the apex has been cut off (Karali, forthcoming). Similar finds are reported from the palaces of Knossos and Phaistos (LM IA), but their exact number is unknown.

A *Charonia sequenzae*, 19.5 cm long was found in LM I context on the islet of Pseira (Room 1e). Of the same period (LM I) are the triton found in the lustral basin of room LVIII at the palace of Zakros and at Gypsades where a *Charonia* with carefully cut off tip was found in a domestic shrine (Πλάτων 1974).

A broken *Charonia,* l. 15.5 cm, was found at Kommos (LM IIA). At a Minoan site on Kythera tritons with both ends cut off were unearthed.

In a Minoan house (room 12) at Knossos (LM III) shells were found together with coarse ware. Among these was a triton with worked apex. In room 4 of the same house there was another triton with cut off end (Reese, forthcoming). A triton was also found in a burial at Knossos (Reese, forthcoming).

Tritons with diverse uses are also known from Cycladic sites. From Phylakopi on Melos (NAM case 65) there is a triton (no. 1 2015) with broken lower end (approx. l. 12 cm). Some 30 tritons, in quite good condition, have been found at Akrotiri, Thera (LC I). The majority do not bear traces of working (Καραλή 1990, 410-415) and were probably for domestic use (scoops, decanting vessels).

In Mycenaean Greece, a triton was found at the

entrance to a tomb at Peristeria, Pylos (Κορρές 1977). At Traganas, near the palace at Eglianos, Pylos, 12 intact tritons and fragments of others were found together with 200 large vases in a room of the Late Helladic I period (Μαρινάτος 1962, 786).

The archaeological evidence strongly suggests that the use of tritons as trumpets was unknown in the Neolithic Age. This use is clearer during the Bronze Age. Many are known from the palatial centres of Minoan Crete as well as from tombs. Their interpretation as trumpets is more secure in the Late Bronze Age when they are found in areas of particular archaeological importance, such as the rock-cut tomb at Poros, Herakleion (Reese 1992, 181).

Presence of shell tools (table 2)

The archaeological evidence for shell tools comes from different parts of Greece, although the actual number of objects is small. The most important class includes shells of different types and sizes that were probably used as spoons. These objects are found from Macedonia to the Cyclades and the Peloponnese. At Franchthi in the Argolid (Reese 1987, 128), not only were *Mytilus* shells used as spoons, but also *Spondylus* shells (LN).

At Saliagos different types of spoons were discovered. In the earliest habitation levels spoons of *Mytilus* shell were found. In the upper levels an evolution of the type is observed and the use of a different shell. So the round spoon of *Charonia* constitutes a development of the ovoid-hollow shape in *Mytilus* of the preceding phase (Shackleton 1968, 122-138). Among the 178 examples located at Saliagos it is difficult to distinguish those that were used as spoons without any working of the shell. Four other examples from Saliagos (nos 438, 436, 434, 442) belong to another category, rounded, slightly modified or smoothed but without particular care.

Unique are the first 'true' spoons made out of patella sp., found recently in the Cyclop's Cave on Youra, Halonnisos (Karali, forthcoming), from the Early Neolithic levels. They were found together with a spatula made out of Ostrea sp. Spoon-shaped objects are also known from the Late Neolithic sites of Paradeisos, Nea Nikomedia, Tharrounia Euboea, the Kitsos Cave Attica and the Alepotrypa Cave Mani.

Two worked shells from Saliagos have been described as spatulas. The first has a natural curve at the centre of the valve that was shaped into a narrow spatula. The second is cut from a wider point, but because it is broken its original shape and function are a matter for speculation. A similar object has been found in

Macedonia among other minor objects from the Greek excavation at Dikili Tash (LN). It is a *Mytilus* shell, deep reddish brown in colour (Καραλή 1992, 157). At Dimitra two spoons of this type have been discovered, one in quite good condition. The first is dark brown on the outside with nacre deposit on the inside. The second is much lighter in colour, almost yellowish green (Karali, forthcoming). Unique is a chisel of spondylus from Franchthi cave (LN).

Triangular objects of *Mytilus* shell, smoothed on two sides, were found at both Late Neolithic Paradeisos and Sitagroi. Some shells found at Lithares in Boeotia (EH I-II) have been identified as burnishers. No other use of shells for tools has been noted to date.

A rare use of shell is to fashion an offensive weapon (mace). So far only four such objects have been found, from different periods and geographical regions. The earliest comes from Dikili-Tash (LN). It has a cylindrical hole 3.4 cm in diameter and the two edges broken (Καραλή 1992, 157). A small object of this kind is known from Syros (Kastri, EC II-III) and from Poliochni, Lemnos (NAM case 41, 7278). Of ovoid shape, one edge is broken while the other is pierced by a cylindrical hole 3.4 cm in diameter. A second 'mace' from Poliochni, probably of spondylus, is broken at the height of the hole into which the haft was inserted.

Spools, though rare, are characteristic of the Early Bronze Age, particularly in southern Greece. Such objects have been found at Lerna (EH II) and Franchthi (Reese 1987, 128), as well as at Zygouries (EH) (Blegen 1928, pl. 22, Buchholz - Karageorghis 1971, 256), Ayia Irini Kea (EC III) (Caskey 1979, 340) and in the Trapeza Cave Lastihi (EM I-MM I) (Pendlebury et al. 1935-36, 124, 126, pl. 19). Other kindred objects are mentioned, that are considered to be of spondylus, but further examination is necessary to confirm the material of manufacture (Jacobsen 1969, 343-381, Shackleton 1988, 105). The archaeological evidence for the use of shells as tools is limited in the prehistoric period in the Aegean, mainly on account of the fact of their fragility. Shells of the species *Spondylus*, *Mytilus* and *Charonia* were mainly used, primarily to form 'spoons', objects common in the Neolithic Age, from Macedonia (Sitagroi) to the Cyclades (Saliagos) and the Peloponnese (Franchthi). Spoon-shaped objects were also made of other materials such as bone and clay (e.g Dikili-Tash). Ovoid-hollow spoons appear to be the development of flat spoons of *Charonia* shell. Spoons of spondylus shell are more perfect in form and more durable. However, 'real spoons' were made out of patella.

Other uses of shells after the Neolithic Age are isolated and rare, since more resistant raw materials came into wider use, such as metals for example. Offensive weapons of shell are rare.

Lastly, some shell tools are very difficult to recognize, such as those used for burnishing pottery.

Ornaments

a. General remarks on shell ornaments

Συν μαργαριτόρριζες εστι καλλωπισμένον.
Παΐσιος Ρόδου, τελ. 19ου αι.

Shell ornaments are encountered from the Palaeolithic Age to the present day. Various terms are used indiscriminately for different groups of objects that were sometimes used for personal adornment, and sometimes for the arrangement of objects of adornment or the disposition of decoration, and sometimes in other contexts. So confusion reigns concerning their use, making it difficult to recognize the significance of the finds (Taborin 1974, 104-105, Sargon 1987).

There is, however, a way of differentiating and classifying the ornaments found in excavations. Since man defines the role and the function of every object, ornaments should be studied in relation to their probable place on the human body or to the space in which man lived (room, house, settlement), as well as to the general archaeological environment.

The interpretation of ornaments becomes more complex in the case of burials. A new factor intrudes that contributes to the characterization of the objects accompanying and adorning the dead. The concepts expressed by this context are religious or symbolic (Κουκούλη-Χρυσανθάκη-Καραλή 1993, 756-760).

Shell ornaments can be divided into objects of adornment or of decoration, according to the following scheme:
a. Objects to adorn the human body
b. Objects to adorn garments, hairstyle etc.
c. Decorative objects found in man's immediate living space (inlays from pyxides, furniture etc.).

Thus the term 'ornaments' is directly associated with the human environment. When referring to archaeological finds, the term describes both the objects worn by the individual on his body and the individual's more general desire for adornment, for enhancing his personality, ideas and inner propensities.

Ornaments are either found directly associated with the skeleton (graves) or dispersed in other places (e.g. jewellery-making workshops at Neolithic sites in Macedonia). Their recognition is difficult unless they are definitely formed objects belonging to specific types.

Ornaments constitute a wide field of study, implicating social anthropology and modern archaeological concepts. Scholars are increasingly concerned with determining the actual value and the wider significance of these objects in the archaeological context.

The archaeological evidence shows that ornaments were related to social, psychological and symbolic factors. Consequently their systematic study and understanding furnishes valuable information on unknown aspects of man's life and thought. Each individual's choice of the ornaments for his adornment depends on his rank, social origin and economic status. Lastly, the ornaments and the manner of adornment are determined by gender and age. For example, cowries are usually associated with the female gender, dentalia with the male and cockles with children. The personality of each individual is another factor to be considered and the modifications in each case may reflect a particular aesthetic perception or the desire for distinction in the context of the social group.

Since the beginning of the history of mankind shells have held an important place as ornaments. They were chosen for their shape and colour as well as for the nature of their material which lends itself to working. Shell ornaments are still encountered today in both advanced and preliterate societies. The study of ethnographic parallels is the only living source of information for the modern scholar (Johnson 1952, 20-21)[13].

---

[13] Ancient societies, and contemporary ones too, attribute certain qualities/properties to shells. Information on these is derived from excavations, historical-literary sources and ethnographic-anthropological studies.

The attributing of specific qualities/properties to shell jewellery and other kinds of objects in the prehistoric period is hazardous and speculative, on account of the fragmentary nature of the finds. More reliable information is provided by grave assemblages when the decorative objects are associated with human skeletal remains.
Certain species of shells are attributed with the same qualities / properties in different regions and periods, presumably because of their particular characteristics. On the contrary, others acquire different value analogous with the chronological era and the geographical area.
There are archaeological indications on the significance of shells already from the Palaeolithic Age, at sites in Central and Eastern Europe and the Middle East (e.g Brno in Czech Republic, Mount Carmel in Palestine and elsewhere). At all these sites skeletons were found decorated with Dentalium shell, believed to symbolize the male gender (Joleaud 1935, 495-500).
In Greece archaeological indications exist for the Late Helladic period; in the Perati cemetery (LH III) Cardium sp. was associated with child burials (Ιακωβίδης 1970). In the Roman period shells of Cypraea sp. were associated with fertility (Brothwell 1969, 65-67).
Ethnographic studies note the special significance of shells of Dentalium sp., Cypraea sp. (Fischer 1949, 82-83, 149-157) and Spondylus sp. (Levi-Strauss 1991).
Narratives and myths of natives of the Pacific islands associate shells of Dentalium sp. with the male gender and of Haliotis sp. with the female (Levi-Strauss 1991). The use of Dentalium sp. is more widespread spatially and temporally because it is common in most sandy regions and is easily collected.

The basic intervention made to create shell ornaments is perforation, when this is necessary to create a hole. Some shells (e.g. *Haliotis sp.*) bear natural holes, while others acquire holes through the action of external agents (lithophages, natural erosion etc.).

Very important for the study of this material is knowledge of the fashioning and the function of analogous minor objects of shell (Fig. 15).

b. Provenance of material

Ornaments are made from the shells of gastropods, scaphopods and bivalve molluscs. The shells belong to two basic groups: those gathered when the organism was already dead and those procured when the organism was still alive. In the first group the effect of natural factors on the shell surface is obvious and results in a smoothed, porous surface. These are features of dead molluscs whose shell has been exposed to unfavourable environmental conditions. After the shell has been worked by man it is more carefully smoothed and without traces of damage or pores on its surface.

Particularly interesting are the shells of molluscs that live in limited habitats, since these indicate that despite the difficulties (great depth, dangerous waters etc.) a

With regard to the shell of the *Cypraea* sp., there is ethnographic evidence from Africa - in particular Guinea - that it has an exchange value, that is, it is used as a kind of currency. Indeed it is to this use that it owes its name: *Cypraea postularia (monetaria) moneta Linne* (Jackson 1916, 8-9, Labador 1971, 5-13). This species lives in the Indian and the Pacific Ocean and can be easily collected from the beaches where it is brought ashore by the large breakers. It is also associated with diverse other activities and was even used as a medicine.
Archaeological and ethnographic data from Latin America indicate that another species of shell, *Spondylus princeps* was used as an exchange commodity from the Neolithic Age till the Spanish Conquest. Regarded as a food of the gods, it was offered to the deities that protected the harvest, as well as being used in rain-making ceremonies. Moreover, it constituted a significant trade good in the regions of Central and South America (Peru, Colombia, Ecuador, Guatemala and elsewhere (Lavallée 1985, 366). Especially important is the area on La Plata island in Ecuador where large quantities of spondylus shell were worked and from where spondylus objects were exported to Mexico (Levi-Strauss 1991).
In Oceania another, related, species of spondylus, together with shells of *Conus* sp. constituted exchange objects (Garanger 1979, 147-161, Malinowski 1963). In the Solomon Islands and New Guinea there was an exchange of bracelets of *Conus mellapunctatus* and necklaces of small discs fashioned from spondylus shell. There was also the belief that these ornaments endowed their owners with status/prestige. They were inherited down the generations and according to local myths their first owners were the tribal heroes (Seferiades 1995, 44-45).
The subject of ethnographic parallels for the use and importance of shells is not exhausted here. We have selected the species *Dentalium*, *Cypraea*, *Spondylus*, *Conus* and *Haliotis*, which are frequently found at prehistoric sites in the Aegean.

special effort was made to acquire them, because of the special importance accorded to them.

c. Form, Working, Treatment

The way in which shells are worked depends on the quality and shape of the material (Taborin 1974, 123-128) as well as on the desired form of the object the craftsman endeavours to create. The shell's thickness and shape are decisive for the manner and methods of working it and consequently of the objects that can be formed from it. The limpet (*Patella* sp.), for example, round in shape and with a fine shell, is suitable for limited working and thus limited uses. Only the central cone can be removed and in rare cases its periphery smoothed. Further working would shatter the shell. In contrast, *Spondylus* sp., with its thick, resistant shell, is an ideal raw material for creating minor objects. Likewise the triton, conical in shape, was frequently used as a rhyton.

The basic methods of working shell are perforation and shaping. They are encountered separately or combined. For example, shells already bearing a hole are then shaped. In other cases the shell is perforated to create a hole and then shaped to render the final form.

I. Perforation

Shells are perforated in three possible ways:
1. Natural erosion (Fig. 17a)
2. Action of lithophages
3. Human intervention

Natural erosion

The shells of dead molluscs are susceptible to natural erosion. The continuous action of sea water, in conjunction with other environmental factors (wind action), gradually destroys the empty shell, creating a surface liable to perforation. Very often holes caused by natural erosion are used without further modifications or corrections. The rim of the hole is smoothed at the point of contact with the thread on which the shell is strung. Shells of *Cardium* sp. and *Patella* sp. are frequently selected, because holes on these shells are frequently created by the action of natural agents.

Action of lithophages

Some molluscs, such as those of *Murex* sp., are equipped with an organ that penetrates the shell of other molluscs like a drill. In their effort to locate the living organism in the shell they select either the intermediate zone of the entrance or the middle of the penultimate whorl of the gastropod. The diagnostic traits of this kind of hole are its position, its vertical section and its shape. Varying in diameter from 0.2 to 0.5 cm, such holes are cylindrical and terminate in a regular rim of the same internal and external diameter.

Perforation by lithophages usually occurs in shells of the species *Murex, Callista chione* etc. However, because this type of hole is extremely small such shells were rarely used as ornaments.

Human intervention

Five techniques of perforating shells by man can be distinguished. These same techniques were applied to other materials of comparable hardness (Fig. 18).

Direct percussion

This is a 'brutal' technique, which is intended to create a hole. Direct percussion frequently leads to cracking or breaking of the shell and is rarely completely successful, especially on shells that do not have a flat surface. This method was used for creating a hole in the upper section of the valve in bivalves and in the ventral area of gastropods. The hole has an irregular, polygonal rim since percussion creates cracks that follow the line of minimal resistance on the surface of the shell. It varies in size from 0.1 to 0.6 cm and is characterized by a graduated mouth. It is usually found in shells of the species *Cardium edule Linne* and *Luria lurida Linne*

Abrasion of convex zone

This method involves the abrasion of the convex face of the shell on a hard surface until the shell is perforated. This technique can only be used on those parts of the shell where there is strong relief. This type of hole can be recognized from its eroded, wide, smooth surround, which has a slight gradient. The internal zone is untouched and the bevelled rim is visible on the vertical section of the mouth, unless the thread has left traces of wear. In the case of perforation by abrasion the section of the hole is acute-angled. Holes of this type are mainly encountered on shells of *Glycimeris glycimeris Linne*.

Sawing

This method involves the abrasion of a limited area on the shell surface so that the smoothing corresponds to the width of the tool. It is mainly applied to gastropods, from which the top whorls were removed to create a hole and to form a pendant. This type of hole is characterized by its narrow elongated shape. The species of shells usually selected are *Luria lurida Linne* and *Columbella rustica Linne*.

Abrasion and direct percussion

Abrasion and direct percussion can be combined to create a hole. The shell is first abraded to create a small flat surface on the convex zone and then a hole is opened by direct percussion. This is the commonest technique used for perforating the valves of bivalve molluscs. Usually the dorsal section of the shell is selected, near the point where the valves join. There the shell is thick, markedly curved and the surface limited. Holes of this type are characterized by smoothing of their surround. They are oval in section and have pronounced traces of abrasion around the mouth. The usual shells selected are *Cardium edule Linne* and *Glycimeris glycimeris Linne*.

Drilling

This method involves the use of a perforating tool to create a hole. A sophisticated technique, it results in a carefully formed hole without damaging the shell surface. It is encountered on bivalves's and gastropods's most resistant points. When the shell is quite thin the hole is of conical section, whereas when it is thick it is biconical because it is drilled in two stages: first from the outside and then from the inside.

This is the commonest method for perforating schematic ornaments, especially those of spondylus shell, such as button-shaped pendants.

The above techniques for perforating and shaping shells are encountered from the Palaeolithic Age through to the end of the Bronze Age. A gradual development of these methods is observed over time, with a preference for the last two at the end of the Neolithic and the beginning of the Bronze Age.

d. Shell objects (Fig. 19)

Morphological classification

Ω φιλτάτη πατρικία, μάργαρον ες χείρας τας εμάς τη προτεραία εμπέπτωκεν...

Προκόπιος

Shell objects can be classified according to their shape and their use. The scheme adopted for the classification of shell ornaments has been adapted on the one hand to the properties of the material and on the other to the peculiarities of the general geographical and cultural environment of the Aegean. Ornaments are divided into the following classes: pendants, beads, annular objects, inlays.

I. Pendants

There are several types of pendants which are distinguished by shape and the degree of working the shell.

a) Unworked perforated shells with minimal interventions. These are objects of shell perforated by natural agents or human action. They are usually flat, spherical or oblong.

b) Worked shells. These ornaments fall into two sub-classes:

    i) Schematic: Major interventions on the shell result in the creation of geometric ornaments, usually square, trapezoid, oval or circular in shape.

    ii) Zoomorphic: Products of careful working of the shell, these ornaments represent animal figures inspired by nature.

II. Beads

There are numerous classes of beads, which are distinguished according to their shape and the degree of working of the shell.

a) Unworked perforated shells with minimal interventions. These are objects of shell perforated by natural agents or human action. They are usually flat, spherical, oblong or fusiform in shape.

b) Worked shells. Major interventions on the shell result in the creation of geometric ornaments, usually disc-shaped, annular, cylindrical, tubular of round or square section, polygonal or trefoil in shape.

III. Annular ornaments (bracelets - rings)

Objects of carefully worked shells, usually elliptical in shape, two sub-classes are distinguishable:

a) bracelets - of diameter approx. 5 to 9 cm.

b) rings - of diameter approx. 1.3 to 2.5 cm.

IV. Inlays

Worked shells with important interventions in both their shape and surface. Inlays are usually flat and rectangular, square or polygonal in shape with two or more holes (see appendix on ornaments).

Typological Analysis

I. Pendants (Fig. 20)

Particularly significant for the typological classification of shell ornaments is the distinction of the pendant from

the bead, which is not always easy. In some cases the pendant closely resembles a bead but is distinguished because it is the central element of a necklace, and is frequently larger than the beads. For example a shell of *Cardium* sp. can be a pendant at the centre of a necklace of smaller shells, and can also be a bead in a necklace of *Cardium* shells.

This class includes unworked perforated shells with makeshift interventions to their form and shape. A further division into sub-classes is based on the shape and the position of the pendant when hanging from the thread:

a) elongated pendant (height greater than width)

b) flattened pendant (width greater than height)

c) spherical pendant (height and width more or less equal)

The morphological analysis of each class is difficult however because of the considerable variety of shapes. Their typology can be determined on the basis of the number and the shape of the sides (straight, concave, convex), and the number of perforations. With regard to the position of the holes, it is known that each object was orientated along its axis of suspension.

These typological criteria are useful for the classification of large numbers of pendants. However, numerous intermediary shapes exist that mainly result from perforating the shell by direct percussion. The efficacy of this method varies depending on the reaction of the shell and the skill of the craftsman.

Very interesting is the cross-shaped pendant from MN Salonica (Παππα 1993, f 7). In addition to geometric pendants, other types are encountered that have been formed with considerable care and skill, such as button-shaped ornaments. Very rare and of special aesthetic value are the zoomorphic pendants such as the bear from the Kitsos Cave (N.N), Attica (Vialou 1974, 794), and a duck from Ayia Irini, Kea (EC III) (Crzyskzowska 1990, pl. 32).

Shell pendants hold an important place in the jewellery of the Neolithic Age. In contrast to those made of stone or bone, they are characterized by a stability and homogeneity of form. This is due to the limitations of working shell to produce ornaments. Unlike other materials, shell does not lend itself to the creation of angular outlines, the fact that perhaps explains why 'geometric' pendants are quite common in stone, while shell ones are rare (Taborin 1974, 141-144).

II. Beads

Beads are usually the component elements of a necklace, normally distinguished from pendants by their small size and large numbers. Beads are made of shells of various shapes and sizes by simple perforation or shaping (Taborin 1974, 152-153) (Fig. 21).

They are made in exactly the same way as pendants. In some cases beads are found that are the same size as pendants but they are so numerous that the existence of a necklace is assumed, which was of course strung on a perishable thread. However, in general, as has been said before, beads are characteristically smaller than other suspended ornaments. The excavation context also helps in their identification by providing additional information.

The typological examination of beads is carried out on the basis of the shape of the sides and the type of perforation (straight or curved sides, natural or man-made hole etc.). For example, there are elongated beads with natural holes, such as those made from shells of *Dentalium* sp., or spherical ones with one natural and one man-made hole, such as those of *Nassa* sp. Lastly, beads fashioned from large thick shells are encountered in diverse shapes.

The bibliography on worked shell beads is remarkably scant. This is probably due to two factors: their smallness and the erroneous identification of the material.

On account of their size they may well have disappeared from ancient deposits leaving no trace (at Dikili-Tash, for instance, only 42 shell beads were found). Very often they are mistakenly classed as marble or bone objects. The following types of worked shell beads are encountered: annular, cylindrical (fusiform, barrel-shaped), tubular (of square or circular section), stellar, trefoil (Fig. 23).

Of particular interest in the morphological classification of beads is the study of traces of use-wear that appear on the rim of the hole. The weight of the bead exercised pressure on the thread, causing tiny cuts on the edges of the inner and outer mouth of each hole.

In the Aegean there is a clear preference for beads of unworked shell and annular beads, of various sizes.

Annular beads - disc ornaments

On the basis of typological criteria these constitute an independent group of objects. In aesthetic terms their shape is the most perfect.

In general they are fashioned from shells with a smooth, slightly convex surface (Fig. 22). Their shape and size vary according to the species of shell. Common choices are *Cardium, Unio* and *Spondylus*.

The ornament is first given a roughly circular shape. Then the interior and the exterior surface are abraded. Such objects with holes have been found half finished, indicating that they were first perforated and then given their final shape. The perforation was executed from the inside to the outside or from both sides.

The largest of these beads are generally geometric in shape. In 90% of cases the hole is exactly at the centre. Dimensions vary but mainly correspond to medium-size shells such as those of *Cardium* sp (Fig. 24a).

Disc ornaments of shell are known, the existence of which seems to be related to the use of nacre (mother-of-pearl) rather than to the shell *per se*. This raises the problem of use, however, since when such beads are strung on a necklace the nacre is only visible on the inside face and the greyish side shows. It is of course possible that the discs were sewn onto garments, with the opalescent surface outwards.

Some large shells of this species (e.g. *Unio margaritanea*) are particularly suitable for working on account of their bulk, but the majority of ornaments found so far come from delicate shells with flat surfaces. However, the nacre layers of *Unio* sp. are easily separated and some sections examined may come from the flaking of more bulky shells. These pieces can often be identified from their two pearly surfaces.

Most of these objects have been badly fragmented; that is why it is impossible to estimate their quantity and frequency of appearance. It is believed that the inhabitants of Macedonia used ornaments of this type towards the end of the Neolithic Age, since many fragments of worked *Unio* sp. have been discovered at certain sites (Dimitra, Dikili-Tash).

Such disc-shaped objects are rather rare in the Aegean, mainly occurring in Thessaly and Macedonia. Beads have also been found made of various materials, such as white stones, e.g. limestone, steatite and marble, that resemble shell ornaments in shape and size. Their form tends to be more globular, however, and their edges more curved. Sometimes the object's thickness between the two holes is greater.

IV. Annular ornaments (bracelets and rings)

Bracelets

Annular ornaments were common in prehistoric and protohistoric times, especially during the Middle and Late Neolithic, and the Early Bronze Age (Καραλή 1979, 143-189).

Ethnographic parallels provide information on a

multiplicity of uses for such objects. They were not only worn on the wrist but higher up on the arm, as well as on other parts of the body and the head. The Papuans of New Guinea use them to adorn their arms and nose, and suspend them on poles together with other objects of ornamental and symbolic significance. Characteristic is the abundance of bracelets per person, sometimes 10 on each arm (Johnson 1952, 20-21, Joleaud 1935, 495-500, Piette 1896, 385-427). Such bracelets are known from southeast Asia, as well; there they are worn by the women to bring good luck or to protect them from falls or injury (oral information).

A large number of annular ornaments have been found in excavations in Greece and further North in the Danubian lands. Only in the Varna cemetery in Bulgaria (Černica) were the bracelets discovered in direct association with the human skeleton (Cantacusino 1970, 449). In Greece no site has been reported where bracelets were found on the human body.

Archaeological data show that these ornaments were widely distributed throughout Greece. However, they were evidently important in prehistoric Macedonia, where there is a relative abundance (Karali forthcoming).

Sites such as Nea Nikomedeia, Dikili-Tash, Sitagroi, Servia, Dimitra appear to have been places of production and supply of shell ornaments.

The objects characterized as bracelets are in most cases made from shells of the mollusc *Spondylus gaederopus Linne*. Less often bracelets were made of *Glycimeris glycimeris* and *Charonia nodifera Lamarck*.

Spondylus is a bivalve mollusc that is encountered in many varieties. Annular ornaments produced from it varied in shape depending on the part of the body for which they were intended. The making of spondylus bracelets involved different techniques. First the exterior of the valve was abraded. Then the central cone was removed and the periphery of the ring thus formed was smoothed. An oval object was obtained, visually resembling a bracelet, which was further treated until it acquired a polished surface (Taborin 1974, 152-153, figs. 24, 25, 26).

It is difficult for a non-specialist to distinguish such an object from an analogous one made of stone, and indeed marble. The white colour and the similar texture of both materials is often the cause of confusion in the publications. The same is true for other objects of spondylus shell, such as beads, pendants etc.

The exterior of shells of *Spondylus* sp. is red and although the surface of bracelets - rings is quite flat and perfectly polished, some minute pits of reddish colour remain, depending on the conditions of preservation and working. The objects are white, off-white and shades ranging from red to brownish red. They turn grey or black when burnt.

Bracelets are of average internal diameter 6.5 cm and external 9 cm. Their final shape depends very much on the structure of the shell. On the side of the hinge of the valves the bracelet is quite thick, of more or less rectangular section. On the opposite side it is thinner and the hoop is about 0.3 cm (Fig. 29).

The craftsman adapted the hoop according to the resistance and the thickness of each shell. In the case of the lower edge of the valve the object is wider to avoid breaking.

Of the ensemble of items of shell jewellery, spondylus bracelets are considered the most important. They are frequently mentioned in the bibliography because they constitute concrete evidence of contacts between the inhabitants of the Aegean and cultures that developed further North (Karali 1979, 143-189, Karali 1992, 57-61, Rodden 1996, 411-413, Tringham 1971, 186-240).

Rings

No true finger rings of shell have been found in the wider region of the Balkans, Greece included. Although shells of *Monodonta* sp. found at some Late Bronze Age sites have been considered to be rings, neither the archaeological context nor the typological study provide sufficient information for recognizing this class of objects in Greece. Indicatively the list of *Monodonta* shells characterized as rings and coming from Chania, Kommos, Mycenae and Koukounaries on Paros is included in the appendix on jewellery (Reese 1984, 237-238).

According to Reese's descriptions only four *Monodonta* shells from the aforementioned sites are abraded and with the central cone missing.

These shells range in diameter from 1.3 cm to 4.5 cm. Given the durability of the material and on account of the diameter (very small or very large) of the hole, it is highly unlikely that these objects were worn as finger rings. This view is bolstered by the fact that none was found in association with human remains. So there is no substantial indication of such a use.

Other proposals concerning the use of ring-shaped objects of *Monodonta* sp. are numerous but in the absence of archaeological evidence they are no more than speculation. For example they could have been used as inlays, as the finials of small tools such as awls etc.

V. Inlays

These are small ornaments that were affixed to larger objects (e.g. furniture, containers etc.) (Taborin 1974).

Inlay is a technique of decorating objects which demands specialist skill and does not seem to have been applied before the Bronze Age, from which the earliest examples date.

The shells used for this type of decoration were carefully worked to produce shapes completely different from the original. The lustrous layers of nacre were preferred. This fact poses insurmountable problems for identifying the species of mollusc from which the worked shell comes. There is only a limited bibliography on this subject which remains essentially unknown.

As a whole the shell ornaments in the Aegean are characterized by the predominance of shells with holes of natural origin. Examples of these may be traced to the Palaeolithic Age. The working and shaping of shell ornaments appears in later phases, particularly the Late Neolithic and the Early Bronze Age.

The Archaeological Evidence

Appendix 3

I. Presence of pendants (table 4)

Pierced shells with minimal interventions

Very little is known about shell jewellery in Greece during the Palaeolithic Age. A few ornaments of *Dentalium* species and *Cyclope* are mentioned from Palaeolithic sites in Epirus, notably Kleidi (Bailey *et al.* 1986). It is generally accepted that shell jewellery existed during the Mesolithic Age. Pierced shells of the species *Patella* and *Cerithium* are cited in excavation reports on the Franchthi cave (Jacobsen 1969, 343-381, Shackleton 1988, 105). Due to the dearth of archaeological evidence it is impossible to form a clear picture of the types of shell pendants in the Palaeolithic and Mesolithic Ages.

In the Early Neolithic period at Sesklo (Θεοχάρης 1958, Fig. 2). *Cardium* and *Cypraea* shells with cuts in their upper section were found together with minor artifacts of flint and obsidian. Similar shell objects are also known from other sites.

A shell of *Cardium* species with a hole in its upper section was found in Early Neolithic context at Argisa Magoula. Two pierced shells, one *Cypraea* and one *Cardium* edule, are known from Tsangli (Wace and Thompson 1912). The Neolithic levels in the Franchthi cave in the Argolid are particularly rich in shells; an accumulation of 900 shells of *Donax trunculus* is reported.

The Neolithic levels at Knossos, Crete (Shackleton 1968, 265) yielded numerous *Cardium* and *Patella* shells from which the central section had been removed. The *Patella* shells may have been used as ornaments but because the state of preservation is poor no secure conclusions can be drawn, especially as their apex is susceptible to breakage.

N.J. Shackleton mentions 130 pierced cockle shells (*Cerastoderma edule*) from Knossos, 1/4 of which had been perforated by direct percussion and 2/3 by drilling. In the latter case the shells were pierced from the inside, which in fact is indicative of their use as ornaments since the intervention was not made to remove the mollusc but to create a specific object. Certainly the majority of these molluscs had a dual function - dietary and decorative. A significant number of *Patella* shells was found, few of which bear holes. Some holes were perhaps created by chance, while at least one is due to percussion. The only example of *Venerupis aureus* (*Gmelin*) identified has two holes. Sixteen intact shells and fragments of the species *Glycimeris* were recovered, one of which has a hole at the top and a smoothed periphery. This is a common type of pendant in Neolithic Greece. Of the gastropods a pierced shell of *Conus mediterraneus Bruguiere* was found. There are five examples of the small shell *Luria lurida L.*, all pierced. Three of them have a regular cut made by sawing along the upper edge (Evans - Renfrew 1968, pl. ix a cone shell with similar cut), while the remaining ones have perforations of less clear provenance.

Of the shells recovered from the Late Neolithic site of Saliagos in the Cyclades (Shackleton 1968, 127, Fig. 49) the most important examples are two of *Haliotis lamellosa Lamarck*. These are particularly impressive shells with a thick layer of nacre on the inside and natural decoration with a row of holes. It is very possible they were used as ornaments without any intervention to the original shape, though there is no indication of this on Saliagos, where worked shells were also found. Shells of *Columbella decollata* may also have been used as ornaments (this particular species is quite common in excavation assemblages in the East).

Three shells of *Cypraea achatidea Sowerby*, perforated by the method of sawing, were evidently collected while alive since their surface is in relatively good condition (their colour and lustre are preserved). Of two only the mouth and one side are preserved, while the third has a cut perpendicular to its horizontal axis. These examples are comparable to corresponding shells of *Cypraea lurida* found at Jericho, in which the cut was horizontal to the lengthwise axis of the shell. It is not known which of these were used as pendants. It should also be noted that beads and stone pendants were found nearby, which fact argues in favour of these shells being used as jewellery.

Neolithic Macedonia, and specifically Servia (LN) (Heurtley 1939), is the provenance of a *Cardium* shell with an irregular hole (from violent percussion applied directly to the surface of the shell), considered to be a pendant.

Numerous shells are reported from Olynthos (LN) (Μυλωνάς 1929, 81). The majority however were evidently food residues, though the existence of pendants or even the phenomenon of dual use cannot be ruled out (more will be known in a forthcoming publication of this material).

At Dikili Tash (LN) a deposit of 35 intact pierced shells of *Cerastoderma edule Linne* (Deshayes 1970, 161-172) and fragments of *Trunculariopsis trunculus* shells was found. A thread for suspension probably passed through the interval between the opening of the mouth and the hole created by removing the apex. Also found at the same site were four shells of *Glycimeris glycimeris* with a drilled hole at the top. There are also shells of *Nassa neritea* with a clumsily made hole as well as *Conus ventricosus* shells with two holes, one at the apex and the other beside it.

At most of the Neolithic sites in Macedonia pierced shells of *Cardium* and *Glycimeris* species have been found. The corresponding *Cardium* shells from Nea Nikomedeia (Shackleton, forthcoming) also bear a hole in the upper section of the valve.

At Sitagroi (LN) (Renfrew 1973a, Shackleton, forthcoming) the five stratigraphical phases have produced several shells of *Glycimeris glycimeris* (phases II, III, IV), pierced by the technique of abrading and drilling. Shells of *Lurida lurida L.* were also found, pierced in a different manner. Some have two parallel holes near the bottom edge, while on others the dorsal section has been cut away and they bear a hole made by sawing. A roughly shaped fragment of *Trunculariopsis (Murex) trunculus* may have been a pendant (phase IV). Pierced shells of the species *Nassa, Murex, Cerithium* and *Arca* were also found.

A Late Neolithic vase found in the Cave of Pan in Attica, on the north side of the hill on which ancient Oinoe was located, contained a necklace of beads of assorted sizes, two stone celts and five perforated *Cypraea* shells, four of which were about the same size, while the fifth was smaller. The square holes were opened by direct percussion (Παπαδημητρίου 1959, 587-589).

The finds from the Kitsos Cave (LN) (Chevallier 1970, 732-735) bear witness to the specialized skills of the cave's inhabitants: the shells have perfectly formed holes. The following species were used as pendants: *Naticarius dillwyni* (two perforated shells), *Conus mediterraneus* (four shells, three pierced and one intact), *Arcularia gibbosula* (three objects smoothed by rubbing vertical to the axis) and one *Columbella rustica*. Other perforated shells and fragments of shells were very possibly used for making pendants. Sometimes the holes were due to natural agents e.g. water action, as seen in one *Murex* and one *Cerithium*

vulgatum). There is an artificial hole in the valve of a *Glycimeris glycimeris* and in three valves of *Cerastoderma edule*. Shells of *Lurida lurida L.* were also found (see reference for ethnographic parallels). Shells and ventral fragments bear no clear traces of working.

Shells continued to be used as pendants in the Bronze Age. At Poliochni (EB II) (Bernabo-Brea 1964, 51-52) *Cypraea* pierced by sawing were used. A pierced valve of *Ostrea edulis* is also mentioned. Of particular interest are some fragments of *Pinna nobilis* which bore holes.

A small cone shell pendant from Troy I (EB) has a hole at its apex (Gejvall 1937-38, 51-57).

Similar ornaments from small shells of *Pectunculus* and *Cardium* species are known from Malthi in the Peloponnese (MH). Found both in graves and houses, they are all pierced at the top and were most probably used as pendants or necklace elements (Valmin 1938, 359). The distance of the site from the sea meant that the inhabitants went a long way to the coast in order to obtain molluscs which were consumed for food and the shells used for adornment.

At Kirra (MH) in Phocis, in Central Greece, the skeleton of a young child wearing a necklace of seashells was found in a pithos burial (Jarronay - van Effenterre 1969, 44).

A particularly important Late Bronze Age site is the cemetery at Perati in Attica (Ιακωβίδης 1970). Three *Cypraea* shells and one shell of *Haliotis* species were recovered from grave 74. Among the grave goods in grave 100, which contained three adult burials and one child, was a *Cypraea* shell 3.7 cm long, with a cut at its narrowest end. Close to the hand of the single burial in chamber tomb 109 were *Cypraea* and *Conus* shells, 0.4 cm and 0.21 cm long respectively. Near the entrance to grave 116, which contained a child burial, were a broken vase and a *Cypraea* shell with a cut at its top end (length of shell 0.41 cm).

In Crete pierced shells continued to be used as pendants, as is evident from the pithos burial at Vrysses, Kydonia. The dead infant was inhumed wearing a necklace of thirty-four shell beads (Ζωης 1976, pl. 40).

Pierced shells of various species (*Littorina littorea, Cypraea* and *Patella*) were found at Late Minoan Tylissos (Hatzidakis 1912, 232-233).

More or less contemporary is the small shell of *Cypraea* species (0.24 x 0.13 cm) with a cut at the top found in grave XX in the Prosymna cemetery (LH III) in the Peloponnese (Blegen 1937, 458, 464-5). Numerous *Cardium edule* shells (62) with a cut at the upper edge were also found in this grave and in grave XVII. It is interesting that in the same Late Bronze Age horizon several species of shells were found. In all 61 shells were recovered from eleven graves. Of these the only possible ornaments are one small spiny *Fasciolaria* and a fragment of another (0.24 cm and 0.12 cm) (grave XXXVIII).

Evidence of ornaments from perforated unworked shells during the Palaeolithic and the Mesolithic Age in the Aegean is minimal.

In the Neolithic Age pendants of pierced unworked shells are numerous. They are particularly frequent in the Middle and the Late Neolithic.

The lustrous nacre of the shells, the variety of natural shapes and colours as well as the ease of collecting and working them explain their wide diffusion during these periods. Small and medium-size shells were used, such as the species *Nassa, Columbella* and others. *Cardium* and *Glycimeris* are commonest in the earlier phases however, while *Cypraea* is more characteristic of the Late Neolithic and the Bronze Age.

Throughout the Bronze Age the methods, techniques and traditions of the past for pierced unworked shell ornaments were preserved. The presence of such jewellery in graves attests that it continued to be used. There are no obvious regional preferences for particular species.

In general the perforations are more carefully executed. In the Middle and the Late Bronze Age unworked shell ornaments were combined with other materials. In the graves at Mycenae and Perati there is a distinct predilection for *Conus, Cypraea* and *Cardium* shells, the last being more frequently associated with female and child burials.

Worked Shells

a. Schematic pendants

Fully worked shell pendants occur far less frequently in excavations than unworked ones, due to the difficulty in working most shells. The considerable diversity in both choice of species and methods of working the shells available endows these objects with a special quality. Thus perhaps a more general group of 'luxury' artifacts is created, consisting of worked shell ornaments.

Known types of schematic shell pendants of the Late Neolithic period are horn-shaped, triangular and oval, fashioned from *Spondylus gaederopus L.* or *Glycimeris glycimeris L.*

A pendant with pointed tip and of triangular section (maximum width 7.7 cm), and another of crescentic shape were found at Dikili Tash (Karali 1993, 157-164).

From Sitagroi (phase III) there are oval pendants of *Glycimeris* shell, the central section of which had been removed by sawing. A hole at the top of the valve was opened by the combined techniques of abrasion and drilling (Shackleton, forthcoming). Similar objects in private collections are reported as coming from Thessaly.

Other known types of schematic shell pendants are plaques and discs (button-shaped).

Fragments of nacre from shells of *Pinna nobilis L.* were found in the Kitsos Cave, Attica (LN). The largest (6.5 cm), quadrilateral in shape, bears traces of working. Perforated plaques of *Spondylus gaederopus L.* were found in the same place. Two of these (3.9 - 2.9 - 0.4 cm) have a biconical hole at the centre. On a third there are clear signs of attempted perforation from both sides. Another two plaques are irregular parallelograms. There are other quadrilateral plaques without holes. Similar but larger objects are known from Crete.

Among the worked shells from the site of Poliochni on Lemnos (EB II), in the northeast Aegean, are fragments of *Pinna nobilis*, some with smoothed sides, and a quadrilateral plaque with curved corners and a central hole.

These objects are classed as pendants but could have been sewn onto garments or affixed to furniture or other objects, a use known from later periods (Krzyskowska 1990). There are occasional references to shell inlays from the palace of Knossos (MM IB,

Room of the Basins), while pictorial shell inlays have been found at Phaistos (Hood 1978, 140. P.M. 11, 45 Fig. 21 a,b).

Another type of schematic shell pendant is the disc or button-shaped, for which the entire valve of *Spondylus* was used. The centre was first smoothed and then two small symmetrical cuts were made, through which the cord passed. Similar objects are known in bone, stone and other materials.

Button-shaped shell pendants mainly occur in northern and central Greece. Very interesting is the cross-shaped pendant from Salonica (M.N.), discovered in the area of the International Fair (Παππα 1993, f. 7). A button-shaped pendant (external diameter 2.8 cm, internal diameter 0.31 cm) with two parallel holes on the central axis and bearing clear signs of wear was found at Dimitra (LN) in Macedonia (Karali, forthcoming). An analogous pendant from the Rhodochori Cave (LN) bears four holes (Rodden 1964, 114-124).

A series of similar objects from Thessaly have been interpreted as buttons. Many are in private collections and a few unpublished pieces are in the Volos Museum. A disc pendant is also known from Franchthi (LN).

b) Zoomorphic pendants

A few zoomorphic pendants fashioned from spondylus shell have been found. Among the most interesting are the following: schematic 'bear' and a 'goose'. The first was discovered in the Kitsos Cave (LN) (Fig. 19). The parts of the animal are clearly distinguishable: the limbs and the belly are indicated by alternating hollows and protuberances. Balance is ensured by the correct placement of the biconical suspension hole. The second is from Ayia Irini on Kea (Caskey 1970, Krzyszkowska 1990, pl. 32b) and represents a 'goose' (EC III) (w. 0.5 cm, h. 0.32 cm).

In summary, worked shell pendants, primarily of spondylus shell, enjoyed a wide distribution during the Middle and Late Neolithic periods, in Thessaly, Macedonia and southern Greece. They are usually quadrilateral, disc-shaped, horn-shaped, oval or zoomorphic. Similar decorative objects were made of other materials such as bone. They are located mainly in Thessaly and are indicative of advanced technological knowledge (Karali 1996, 165-166).

II. Presence of Beads

a. Unworked shell beads

As has been mentioned already, unworked shell ornaments are common in the prehistoric Aegean. It is difficult to assign them to a specific category - pendant or bead - because they are rarely found in sufficient quantities to characterize them confidently as necklace elements. Shells of various shapes, depending on the species - flattened (*Cardium - Glycimeris*), elongated (*Dentalium*), spherical (*Nassa - Monodonta*) - are also classed as beads.

Beads of small shells of *Cerastoderma edule Linne* and *Venerupis decussata Linne* are mentioned from Franchthi in the Peloponnese (Palaeolithic - LN) (Jacobsen 1969, 343-381, Shackleton 1988, 133-157).

Cardium beads were discovered at Nea Nikomedeia (LN) (Rodden 1964, 114-124). Fifteen small pierced shells of *Glycimeris glycimeris L.* and four of *Cardium edule L.*, varying in size from 1.2 cm long to 2 cm wide, were found at the Macedonian site of Dimitra (Karali, forthcoming).

At Dikili Tash (LN) the same species of shells, always small, constitute a common category of objects, as is the case at Paradeisos (Reese 1987, 119-134).

Beads of the elongated shell of *Dentalium vulgare da Costa* and of small conical shells of *Conus* and *Columbella* species are found at Neolithic sites all over Greece.

At Khirokitia on Cyprus (LN) *Dentalium* beads were used in combination with semi-precious stones to form necklaces. Of particular interest is a plaque for linking the ends of a necklace composed of sard and *Dentalium* beads. The cord passed through one hole then over a groove along the middle of the plaque and through a second hole, and so did not touch the wearer's skin.

Another six comparable necklaces are known (Fig. 25). In two of them groups of sard beads alternate with groups of *Dentalium* beads. Three others, almost identical, consist of picrolite or limestone beads and *Dentalium* beads (Dikaios 1953, 438-440, pls LXVIIIA, XCIC, Fig. 54, no. 928a).

Noteworthy is the fact that five of these necklaces accompanied female burials. Entire necklaces are extremely rare in the Neolithic Aegean.

Numerous *Dentalium* beads were found at Neolithic Knossos. None however were discovered on Saliagos (Shackleton 1968, 265, Reese 1987, 207-211). In contrast they are rather common in northern Greece, examples are known from Dimitra (Karali 1991, 318), Sitagroi phase II (Shackleton, forthcoming), Dikili Tash (LN) (Karali 1992, 157) and Vassilika (Γραμμένος – Καραλή 1991, pl. 32, 27, 64).

Dentalium beads occur further south too, in Thessaly, and specifically at Achilleion (phase III) (Gimbutas 1989, 252-253, pl. 8).

Beads of *Conus* shell were recovered from the Kitsos Cave in Attica and the Alepotrypa Cave in the Mani (LN) (Καραλή, forthcoming).

A pierced *Cardium* shell was found at Spedhos on Naxos (EC I-II) (NAM case 71, no. 8811) and a necklace of Patella shells, from which the central cone has been removed by abrasion, at Phylakopi on Melos (NAM no. 121107).

Beads of the species *Conus ventricosus Gmelin, Columbella rustica Linne* and *Monodonta turbinata Born* have also been found in Early Cycladic graves. In grave 103 in the Pyrgos cemetery (EC I-II) on Paros small shells of *Monodonta turbinata* and *Conus ventricosus*, pierced on one side, were found. Necklaces of pierced cone shells are known from the Mycenaean period. In grave no. 343 of the same cemetery small pierced shells of *Littorina littorea L.*, beads of a necklace, were found (Τσούντας 1898, 160).

Two necklaces were found in EC II graves on Syros (NAM case 60). The first (no. 12459) consists of 72 *Dentalium* beads, while the second (no. 12458) combines *Dentalium* and *Spondylus* beads. Two *Dentalium* necklaces were found at Kastri (EC III) on Syros (NAM case 70) (Fig. 30a).

From Malia in Crete (Pelon 1970) come numerous small shells of *Columbella rustica* with a regular circular hole at the apex, which were probably necklace beads (MM II). *Dentalium* and *Glycimeris* beads were found at Kommos (MM III). Pierced *Conus* shells and an *Acanthodardia* shell were found at Symi Viannou (MM III - LM I). Late Minoan levels at this same Cretan site have produced pierced shells of *Glycimeris* and *Columbella* species (Reese 1984, 257, 1990, 185).

At the central Macedonian site of Assiros (LH) beads of *Natica* and *Fasciolaria* shells were found (Halstead - Jones 1980, 265-267).

The Palace of Nestor at Pylos (LH I) produced one shell with hole at the apex. At Knossos a few *Conus* shells with a hole at the side were found on the site of the Stratigraphical Museum (LM IIIC) and of the Royal Road (Blegen *et al.* 1973, 203).

Similar beads were found in Late Helladic I and Late Helladic III excavation assemblages. Quite large *Conus* beads are reported from the hamber tombs at Mycenae (burial I, no. 235), while a small necklace of *Dentalium* beads was associated with burial II.

Necklaces of *Dentalium* beads were found with burials in Cyprus in Neolithic Chirokitia (Fig. 29 b-c-d). *Dentalium* beads with traces of red pigment found in Messenia, at the site of Nichoria date to the Late Helladic I-IIIA period (McDonald - Reese 1992, 770-778). A possible parallel for these is the bead from room 27 in the palace of Pylos.

Pierced and abraded shells of *Glycimeris*, as well as beads of *Conus*, *Natica* and *Fasciolaria* have been found at Aghios Stephanos in Laconia (LH II - LH IIIA) (Reese, forthcoming).

From the Late Bronze Age site of Kastri on Thasos (LH IIIB) come beads of *Dentalium*, *Monodonta* and *Glycimeris*. A necklace of 75 *Dentalium* beads was found in the Tsiganadika cemetery (Καραλή 1992, 756-760).

At Lefkandi on Euboea (LH IIIC) pierced *Conus* shells were found inside a vase (Popham - Sackett 1968). In room B of the workshop at Thebes there were pierced shells of *Nassa*, *Murex* and *Conus* species. Lastly, small pierced *Conus* shells were recovered from a LH I-IIIC grave at Vromousa (Chalkida) in Euboea.

Much rarer is the use of the operculum of the *Murex* species, the disc-shaped covering of the mouth of the shell, for making beads. Ten pierced *Murex* opercula were found in grave 468 of the Chalandriani cemetery (EC II) on Syros, together with jewellery of other materials (two bone rings and six stone beads) (Τσούντας 1898, 164).

In the Neolithic Age unworked beads of *Cardium edule L.*, *Glycimeris glycimeris L.* and *Dentalium* predominate. The last species was also used throughout the Bronze Age, along with *Conus* and *Monodonta*. Interesting is the parallelism and continuity in piercing the same shells for adornment in primitive societies and in coastal regions generally where these are accessible. The same shells are encountered used in similar ways in many cultures.

b. Worked shell beads

The following types of beads are also known in materials such as stone, bone, clay and others.

1. Ring type

Ring beads are the most frequent in the Neolithic Age. They are of small dimensions, average diameter 0.4 cm (rarely reaching 2 cm) and have a biconical hole. Shell ring beads are known from Knossos, the Kitsos Cave, the Franchthi Cave, Nea Nikomedeia, Dikili Tash, Dimitra and elsewhere, mainly in Late Neolithic levels.

2. Disc type

Disc beads are also common in the Neolithic Age. They are distinguished from ring beads in that they are flatter in shape.

Disc beads are made from shells with a slightly curved and smooth surface. The shape and size of the discs vary according to the species of shell chosen, usually *Cardium*, *Unio* and *Spondylus*. The circular outline of the bead is smoothed on the inside and the outside.

Shell disc beads are known from the Early Neolithic levels at Knossos: two small ones from level X and a burnt fragment of a third. The first is 0.8 cm in diameter and 0.1 cm thick, the second 0.11 cm in diameter and 0.15 cm thick, while the third is 0.1 cm in diameter and 0.1 cm thick. Two more beads made of spondylus (0.05 x 0.07 and 0.03 x 0.01 cm) come from the Aceramic and Late Neolithic levels of Cyclop's Cave (Καραλή, forthcoming)

There is a marked increase in the quantity of shell disc beads in the Middle Neolithic at Knossos (Evans's level III). White disc beads, somewhat elliptical in shape and of mean maximum diameter 0.28 cm, predominate. In the transitional phase to the Late Neolithic (Evans's level II) a considerable number of white circular beads of maximum diameter 0.15 cm was found (Shackleton 1968, 264-266). The large quantity has been interpreted as indicating the prevalence of a particular type of adornment.

At the Macedonian site of Dimitra (LN) a large number of similar beads of *Spondylus gaederopus L.* and *Unio pictorum L.* has been found. Their external diameter ranges from 0.5 to 0.4 cm, and the internal from 0.3 to 0.2 cm (Καραλή, forthcoming).

There is a distinct decline in the use of shell disc beads in the Bronze Age. Very few are cited, most of them from Poliochni on Lemnos (EB I), where two such beads with biconical hole were found in the area of the defensive works on the west side of the hill. A disc bead of *Ostrea edulis Linne* (external diameter 2.5 cm, internal diameter 2 cm) recovered from megaron 832 is dated to the second phase of the Early Bronze Age (EB II). A second bead (diam. 2.2 cm, th. 0.4 cm) was recovered from the same horizon (Bernabo-Brea 1964, pl. XCVIII nos 2-8, Pl. CLXXIX no. 23).

Shell disc ornaments are widely distributed throughout the Aegean during the Neolithic Age. At Neolithic Knossos with its undisturbed habitation levels these are more frequent in Middle and Late Neolithic contexts.

Disc beads also occur at sites in Macedonia. In the Early Bronze Age the presence of shell ring beads is limited. Shells used for the production of ring and disc beads are *Spondylus* and *Cardium* and secondarily *Dentalium* and *Unio*. The riverine species *Unio* and objects made from it are dominant at inland Macedonian sites.

3. Elongated 'olive-shaped' beads

These bear biconical perforations and since the natural ridges of the shell are clearly visible the species is easily identifiable. Very few beads of this kind are cited in the bibliography. In Macedonia one was discovered at Dimitra (LN) and another at Sitagroi (phase V - Early Bronze Age) (Καραλή, forthcoming, Shackleton, forthcoming). Both are fashioned from *Spondylus gaederopus L.* and belong to a more general group of ornaments that were disseminated into northern and western Europe.

4. Tubular beads

The most common of these are cylindrical in shape. Some examples are known from the Kitsos Cave in Attica (LN) and Franchthi Cave in the Argolid. One was found at Dikili Tash (LN) and another at Sitagroi phase V (EBA). Beads of this type exhibited in the National Archaeological Museum, Athens are from Paros and dated to the Early Bronze Age. Drop-shaped beads mainly occur at Early Bronze Age sites in the Cyclades, those from grave 135 at Zoumbaria, Paros (EC I) (NAM no. 4882) are characteristic.

Two tubular beads of square section are known: one from Dikili Tash (M446) and the other from Dimitra (LN) (Karali 1992, 157-164).

5. Stellar bead

Just one star-shaped bead is known, from Sitagroi phase II (LN). It has a central hole and is of particularly careful workmanship (exhibited in the Philippi Museum).

6. Trefoil bead

One such bead has been found at Dimitra (LN). The periphery is polygonal (diameter 0.2 - 1.3 cm) and the hole central.

Beads of these last two types occur occasionally during the Early Bronze Age.

It seems that virtually all the worked shell beads were fashioned from *Spondylus gaederopus Linne* (Karali forthcoming).

Shell beads of types 1, 2 and 3 occur during the Late Neolithic, while drop-shaped beads are distinctive of the Early Bronze Age Cyclades.

Annular ornaments (bracelets - rings)

The shells of *Spondylus gaederopus Linne* and *Glycimeris glycimeris Lamarck* were used for making oval objects conventionally known as bracelets but whose specific use, particularly those of small diameter, is unknown. These artifacts are found throughout Greece, and especially in Macedonia, during the Neolithic and the Bronze Age. In all probability they were exchange commodities used in transactions with the Danubian lands and Central Europe. Their size and thickness varies according to the type of shell used as raw material.

Excavation reports and surface finds indicate that 'bracelets' are most common in Macedonia and northern Greece generally during the Middle and Late Neolithic periods (Καραλή 1992, 57-62, Karali 1993, 163-164).

However, 'bracelet' fragments are known from earlier phases of the Neolithic in Thessaly. At least two fragments are reported from Sesklo (Θεοχάρης 1958, 70) and some from Halai in Boeotia (EN) (Walker-Kosmopoulos 1948, 66).

Fragments are also published from the Middle Neolithic period at Tsangli (Wace - Thompson 1912, 125, pl. 78a). Eighty-seven fragments are reported from Late Neolithic Dimini (Wace - Thompson 1912, 83, pl. 46, Tsuneki 1989, 8), and fifteen from Aghia Sophia (Milojčić 1976, 12-13, pl. 21,Tsuneki, forthcoming).

In Macedonia numerous fragments were found at Nea Nikomedeia (Shackleton, forthcoming), while the 89 fragments from Dikili Tash, varying in diameter from 6.3 to 7 cm (internal) and 8 to 9.5 cm (external), represent the largest amount known from any Neolithic site (Karali 1992, pl. 166, 207 g,h).

Some 30 'bracelets' were recovered at Dimitra. Oval-elliptical in shape, their thickness varies and the diameter ranges from 7 to 4.5 cm (Karali, forthcoming). Many 'bracelets' of *Spondylus* and *Glycimeris* shell were found at Sitagroi (MN-LN), with a marked increase in phases II and III (about 13 objects). The exact number of finds is not known since they await final publication (Shackleton, forthcoming). At Vasilika bracelets of *Glycimeris* shell were found in trench I, and of *Glycimeris* and *Spondylus* in trench II. Analogous finds are reported from Paradeisos (Reese 1987, 119-134). One of the most interesting *Spondylus* bracelets was discovered at Olynthos (Mylonas 1929, 81, dawing 93). Elliptical in shape, its surface is grooved due to the veins of the shell and the edges are broken. Two holes are discernible on one side and a third at the opposite edge. The perforations were clearly made so that the bracelet, worn singly or with another, could be secured on the wrist or arm with the help of a cord or leather thong. A small fragment of a bracelet with grooved convex surface was found at Servia (Heurtley 1939, 78-248, Fig. 35 h, Ridley - Wardle 1979, 212, pl. 26 c).

Shell bracelets are also known from further south in the Aegean region. Three fragments of *Spondylus* 'bracelets' were found in Late Neolithic context in the Kitsos Cave, Attica (Vialou 1981, 410-413, drawing 282, pl. 50). In the Peloponnese, three pieces are reported from the Alepotrypa Cave (Karali, forthcoming) and twenty from Franchthi (Jacobsen 1973, 258, Fig. 48b).

In the Sporades two fragments are known from (EN – MN) Cyclop's Cave. In the Cyclades such finds are only known from Saliagos (MN-LN). Two very similar elliptical fragments are published, one of oval section and the other of square (Shackleton 1968, 127). Other fragments have also been identified (personal observation during a visit to the site).

Evidence exists of the production of shell 'bracelets' in the Early Bronze Age. A fragment of *Spondylus* shell, probably part of a bracelet, was found in grave 325 in the Chalandriani cemetery on Syros (EC II).

Only a small number of *Spondylus* objects is known from Bronze Age Crete. From Early Minoan Myrtos (EM II) there is just one 'bracelet' fragment bearing traces of burning and in very poor condition, while another *Spondylus* fragment is so badly preserved that its typological classification is impossible (Shackleton 1972, 321-325).

Shell bracelets are characteristic ornaments of the Neolithic Age. They appear sporadically in the Early Neolithic and enjoy a wider distribution in the Middle and Late Neolithic periods. 'Bracelets' predominate at sites in Macedonia but also occur in the southern Aegean (Cyclades, Attica, Peloponnese). Their presence falls off in the Early Bronze Age, or so the few examples known suggest. These objects were fashioned primarily of *Spondylus* shell and secondarily of *Glycimeris*, the choice of species determining their dimensions.

Presence of rings

Shells of the species *Monodonta* that were perhaps used as rings have been found in the Neolithic levels of Franchthi Cave (Jacobsen 1973, pl. 48d).

A section of a ring-shaped *Monodonta* shell is known from the Unexplored Mansion at Knossos, Crete (LM IIA2) (personal communication by D. Reese based on his analysis).

Two ring-shaped fragments of *Monodonta* (int. diam. 0.13cm, w. 0.19 cm) were found in room 15 of the palace at Mycenae (personal communication by D. Reese based on his analysis) in a LH IIIC context. A ring of the same species was found at Aghios Stephanos in Laconia (personal communication by D. Reese based on his analysis). A similar ring of *Monodonta* and a *Monodonta* shell with a large, carefully worked opening at the top were found at Chania, Crete. Lastly, two *Monodonta* rings have been published from Koukounaries on Paros (LH III) (Reese 1984, 237-238).

If the rings of *Monodonta* shell were indeed used as ornaments then they, together with *Conus* shell beads, are characteristic of the Late Bronze Age.

* * *

To recapitulate, shell jewellery (pendants, beads, bracelets) was used throughout the prehistoric era in the Aegean. There are indications of shell adornments, *Dentalium* and *Nassa* beads, even in the Palaeolithic Age (e.g. Kleidi, Epirus).

Such finds dating from the Mesolithic Age are equally limited. The most important information is from Franchthi Cave where *Patella* and *Cerithium* shells were used.

Shell jewellery is particularly abundant during the Neolithic Age. No significant differences are noted between periods. Predominant species are *Cardium, Glycimeris, Cypraea, Cymatium, Dentalium* and *Spondylus*. A distinct preference for *Spondylus* is observed in Thessaly and Macedonia during the Middle and the Late Neolithic.

No changes are noted in the types of shell jewellery produced in the Early Bronze Age, with the exception of the appearance of the drop-shaped bead. However, there is a marked decline in the quantity of shell ornaments. This trend continued in the Middle and the Late Bronze Age, when shell ornaments are very restricted, the most characteristic being *Conus* beads.

Figurines

Representations of humans and animals were made in a variety of materials, including shell. Indeed it is not always easy to distinguish at first glance between marble, bone and shell. Furthermore in references to shell figurines no attempt has been made to determine the species from which they were fashioned, since they have not been studied by specialists (Χουρμουζιαδης 1994, 24-31).

Shell figurines mainly date from the Neolithic and the Early Bronze Age (Fig. 31). Although shell objects are quite common in the Neolithic Age, there are very few shell figurines. This may be an erroneous impression, however, judging from the number of unpublished pieces, particularly in private collections.

Craftsmen mainly carved figures to be used as prominent necklace elements, such as the zoomorphic pendants (see p. 36). Miniature anthropomorphic representations will have had an analogous use. The absence of a suspension hole does not preclude use as a pendant since a cord or thong could have been tied round the cruciform shape created by the neck and arms of the figure (Χουρμουζιαδης 1994, 243, par. 13, Ασλάνης 1992, 211-212, Gimbutas 1986, figs 9, 12). A factor in favour of their use as pendants is that shell figurines are light and small.

In the majority of cases spondylus shell was used, particularly suitable for carving figurines on account of its thickness and resilience. On the anthropomorphic figurines the head is normally rendered in detail and the limbs schematically. The few figurines known are from Crete, Thessaly, Euboea and the Cyclades.

D. Theocharis reported a *Spondylus* figurine from Sesklo. A shell figurine (h. 1.3 cm, w. 0.4-0.5 cm, th. 0.1 cm), perhaps of *Tridacna* species, was found in Early Neolithic deposits at Knossos. The arms are placed horizontal and parallel below the breast, the face is schematic and the lower legs formed separately (Ucko 1968, 256, pl. 39).

Another shell figurine now in the Ashmolean Museum, Oxford, is said to come from central Crete and is dated to the Neolithic Age. Of length 2.1 cm, width 1.0-1.1 cm and thickness 0.2 cm, it resembles the Knossos piece, except that the facial features (eyes, nose, mouth) are denoted (Evans 1921, drawing 13, 20, Evans 1935, drawing 352b). A third anthropomorphic figurine of about the same type, probably of spondylus shell, is known from Aegina (Welter 1938, drawing 8) (Fig. 31).

There are occasional references to shell figurines in the Bronze Age, from the Cyclades (Μαραγκού 1990, figs 86, 87, 100, 101), as well as from Manika in Euboea (Sakellarakis 1978, 233-264).

Any interpretation of the meaning attached to these objects, or to the choice of shell for their creation, is purely speculative. Some scholars maintain that shells were among the first materials from which figurines were made, on account of the aptness of their curvaceous forms. Shell figurines will have had a limited life span, on account of the fragility of the material and the effects of wear from the cord or thong from which they hung.

Information on shell figurines is scant because of the small number of finds and the lack of systematic study. It is not known whether the rarity of shell figurines in excavations reflects the limited use of this particular material for such objects. If this is shown to be the case it could be due to the limitations of working shell, on account of its natural shape, in contrast to stone and even moreso clay, in which materials details could be more accurately rendered. No significant differences are observed between Neolithic shell figurines and Early Bronze Age ones: all are characterized by total abstraction.

Toys - game-pieces (the use of *Conus* shells) (table 5)

Shells of the *Conus* species are characterized by certain interventions that place them in a different class from other worked shells (Ιακωβίδης 1970, 364-366, Karali 1979, 272-279).

Cone shells with a smoothed ventral side and filled with lead can be considered as game-pieces. Quite often the smoothing or abrasion led to the creation of a hole (Fig.32).

Experiment has shown that smoothed and lead-filled cone shells when rolled on a horizontal surface stop after a short distance. It seems that such shells were used in a kind of game in which several shells were thrown to control and restrict the movement of some. The actual rules of course elude us, but it may well have been like knuckle-bones played in historical times or marbles played today.

Conus shell objects of this kind were found in the Perati cemetery, where 64% of them were grave goods associated with child burials. The use of these shells as amulets can be ruled out, since on the one hand they were found in large quantities and on the other many of them display a trait revealing their use; they have been intentionally smoothed on one side in order to create a flat surface, which imparted stability and checked their roll (Ιακωβίδης 1970, pl. 56β).

In general outline the basic problem is to determine whether the abrasion on the *Conus* shell was in order to create a hole for a bead or represents the failed effort to make a game-piece. Only after careful study of the traces of wear on the rim of the hole (friction from the suspension cord/thong) is it possible to make this distinction. It has also been suggested that cone shells were used as net weights in fishing or as loom weights in weaving (Reese 1982, 125-129). These are mainly cone shells without special preparation which could also have been used as buttons or beads. Similar objects for purely decorative use are known from prehistoric cemeteries in the Cyclades (Doumas 1977, NAM cases 54, 55, 56, 57, 58, 59, 60, 61, 65, 68, 69, 71), as well as from Late Bronze Age deposits. At Mycenae many pierced cone shells (55 in all) were found in room 83, in the northwest corner of the so-called Cult Centre (Τσούντας 1889, 136-180, Μυλωνάς 1975, 611-612). Pierced cone shells filled with lead have been found, in addition to the Perati cemetery, at Mycenae, Argos, Prosymna, Olympia, Dorion, Athens, Chalkida, Thebes, on Naxos, at Ialyssos, Kamiros and on Kos (Τσούντας 1889, 136-180, Blegen 1937, 464-465, figs 143, no. 20, 463, no. 11-13, 492, no. 4-5, 116, no. 9, 212, 263, no. 1, 276, no. 4, 310, no. 5, Valmin 1938, 359, pl. XXVI, M5-8, Thompson 1952, 107, Hankey 1952, 95, Κεραμόπουλος 1917, 182, Deshayes 1966, 9, 48, 99).

Other uses (Fig. 34)

a. Seals[14]

Shell seals are essentially unknown; so far only one has been discovered, at Poliochni on Lemnos (EBA). This object needs further examination in order to ascertain whether it is really fashioned from a thick shell *Spondylus gaederopus* or of ivory. It is truncated pyramidal in shape with an irregular squarish base on which is engraved a linear sphragistic device: four lines round the periphery, a cross with radial hatching in the quadrants. At the centre, from which the engraved lines arise, is a tiny depression; a second smaller depression near the margin is probably accidental. The seal is 2.7 cm high, 2.4 and 2.2 cm wide (Bernabo-Brea 1964, pl. LXXXVI, Fig. 33).

The rarity of such objects in sea shell is probably due to the fact that the majority of seals were made of semiprecious stones. It is not unlikely that other shell seals exist which have been erroneously classified as stone, bone or ivory, as is the case with many minor objects (Karali 1979, 125-129).

b. Filler (temper) - Building material

Broken sea shells are often present in other materials, such as the fabric of clay vases and the beaten earth of house floors. This is due to the abundance of shells in the Aegean region and the coastal location of many settlements (Fig. 35).

Microscopic examination of clay samples, both from vases and bricks, reveals the proportion of shells used as filler, but hardly ever the species since the fragments are extremely small (Guest-Papamanoli 1978, 3-24, Milojčić 1971, 16, Θεοχάρης 1959, 38-39, Evans 1964, 144, Χουρμουζιάδης 1979, 128, Caskey 1957, 156). Crushed shells were added to pottery clay intentionally, in order to create more durable vessels - just as other materials were used (grit, straw, grog etc.).

The use of broken shells in the construction of floors is a rare phenomenon, of which there are examples at Akrotiri, Thera (Doumas 1983, Karali 1990, 414, Fig. 28). The floors occur in different buildings and in rooms with different functions, and there is insufficient data to explain their purpose. The lack of references in the literature does not necessarily mean that such floors did not exist elsewhere. They may have been destroyed in the course of excavation since the shell layer is extremely thin. Only future research will show whether particular species were preferred and whether floors in particular rooms were laid with shells.

c. Purple (purpura)

Purple is widely known as the dye used for colouring the garments of kings and prelates, for which reason it was highly esteemed in antiquity - and indeed in later times - being associated with power and authority. The production of purple dye was a laborious process and the final product was literally worth its weight in gold. According to historical testimonies, in the reign of Diocletian it cost the equivalent of 2500 pounds a pound. The English poet Robert Browning speaks of purple as the 'dye of dyes'. It is characterized by a variety of epithets: royal, Tyrian, imperial etc. Purple dye was regularly used into the twelfth century AD[15].

The chemical composition of purple was determined and studied by Fried Leander in 1909, who showed it to be 6,6'-dibromindigotin: $C_{16}HB Br_2 O_2 N_2$. It was also synthesized by the reaction of alkalis on a mixture of π-bromo-nitro-benzaldehyde and acetone (Forbes 1956, 112-144). Purple is prepared from the hypobranchial gland in the mantle cavity of the living mollusc. In the Mediterranean three species of mollusc were used for its production, *Murex trunculus. Murex brandaris* and *Thais (Purpura) haemastoma*.

All are edible molluscs, also used as bait, for making shell ornaments etc. They live in slightly different habitats and produce dye of different hues (Karali 1988, 41-43, Resse 1985a, 1987b, 205-206) (Fig. 33).

The best description of the production of purple is given by Pliny the Elder, writing in the first-century AD (*Natural History* IX 62, 127, 142, X 3, 4, 12, XXXI 130-131). The molluscs were caught in baited wicker baskets. The flesh was then removed from the shells

[14] In addition to their obvious use, seals were also decorative objects, that is items of jewellery - rings, bracelets, pendants - and as such belong to category I. So far only one seal of shell has been found, at Poliochni (Bernabo-Brea 1949). A large number of seals of semi-precious stones bear representations of shells or molluscs: these are examined separately.

[15] The use of purple is also mentioned in the Homeric epics, indeed it is regarded as the noble and sacred colour. In Greek mythology, Perseus was cast into the sea in a chest and was rescued by Zeus who recognized him thanks to his purple garments. Likewise Theseus, when asked by Minos to prove his divine origin, dived into the sea and then emerged wearing a purple garment given to him by Amphitrite. The production of purple is attested archaeologically in Greece from the Geometric period onwards. Processing installations have been revealed at several coastal sites (e.g. Kythera). The importance of purple in ancient Greece is well known. In Rome purple was a symbol of sacerdotal, political and military authority. In Byzantium it continued to distinguish princes of the Realm and of the Church, and to this day it is considered a royal colour.
Purple was not just used for dyeing garments but also as a pigment for painting, for colouring buildings, statues, books and other objects, as well as in female cosmetics (rouging cheeks and lips).

and collected in shallow pits opened in the ground, where it was left to rot for three days. The smell from the decaying molluscs was particularly pungent and noxious. The dried remains were then placed in vats of stone or lead, water added and the mixture warmed. The whole operation lasted ten days and the end product was a viscous dye (Karali 1990, 413).

The equivalent of 3637 litres of mollusc flesh is required to extract 2.38 mgr of dye. In a study by Leander (1948, 425) it was shown that each mollusc contains only 6.8-12 mgr of purple and consequently 12,000 *Murex brandaris* were required to obtain 1.5 mgr of purple, just enough to dye the hem of a simple garment. The colour of the dye varied from blue to mauve, dark red, deep purple and so on, depending on the species and the quantity of molluscs used. Other factors affecting the shade of the dye are the type of cloth and the type of mordant. In Pliny's view the most desirable shade was that which gave the impression of dried blood (deep crimson).

Ugaritic and Hittite documents dated to the first half of the fourteenth century BC refer to the value of purple textiles. The Egyptian holmiensis papyrus (14th century BC) mentions purple and substances used for dyeing wool. There are indications of the production of purple at Sarepta on the Lebanese coast in the thirteenth century BC. At this site large numbers of crushed *Murex trunculus* shells were found in a hollow in the ground (Pritchard 1970, 126-127), as well as a small jug containing the earliest sample of purple - long before the spread of its systematic production by the Phoenicians in the Early Iron Age (1000 BC, Tyre - Sidon).

In Greece there is information on the production of purple from very early on. Four Linear B tablets from Knossos (LBA) mention purple dye and purple cloth [Palaima 1992, list L (7) 474].

The text on the Knossos tablets, in conjunction with the presence of *Murex* shells in the area, generated the view that purple was produced locally. However the quantities of shells are very small and the distance from the coast quite far. Moreover, no corresponding installations have been found.

Surface surveys on Kouphonisi (Bosanquet 1904, 321, Papadakis 1983, 58-65) mention sherds of Late Minoan vases in connection with installations for purple production and crushed shells. However, the results of a surface survey cannot be considered as definitive archaeological evidence. The Minoans' close relationship with nature and with the sea is well-known, but the degree to which these were exploited is a matter for speculation. In the case of purple dye there are

conditions and constraints which should be taken into account; the technical know-how certainly existed but the organization of this activity is not known. The available evidence is as follows:
- small quantity of shells
- mixture of *Murex* with other irrelevant species (making it difficult to characterize the assemblage)
- lack of description in the bibliography of the state in which *Murex* shells were found (i.e. intact, crushed etc.), a trait indicative of their use.

The characterization of the supposed installations is hazardous. In most cases these are shallow hollows in rocks by the sea (Quartier Mu at Malia), the few shells found in which could be due to a variety of reasons, (Chevallier 1975, 156-159, Karali, forthcoming), such as broken shells for baits, food residues and generally instances of shells coexisting with fishing tackle.

When *Murex* shells are found in an inhabited area the relationship between space and finds should be investigated. At Akrotiri, Thera for example, *Murex* shells were found both inside and outside the West House (Karali 1990, 413). Their presence cannot be considered proof of the extraction of purple on the spot, since this particular building is a lavish residence decorated with wall-paintings and provided with a sophisticated drainage system, features that indicate a concern for cleanliness and sanitation, hardly consistent with such a malodorous activity as purple dye production. However, the production of purple elsewhere in the settlement cannot be ruled out. Logically we would expect to find such installations on the outskirts, far away from the inhabited area[16].

The use and importance of purple is confirmed archaeologically in the Geometric period and in Classical times. The substance was particularly prized in the Roman Age. This precious colouring agent

[16] The study of purple is a subject that has occupied and still occupies many archaeologists. Before characterizing a site as a place of purple production the time frame must be clearly defined. This leads also to the type of installations as well as the area of the settlement in which these are found. Auxilliary evidence is the manner of crushing the shell, which is indicative of the specific use. Sites characterized by D. Reese, R.R. Stieglitz (surface survey) and S. Muller as places of purple production in prehistoric times, do not provide sufficient evidence to support this claim. For example, in the area of Malia small natural hollows in the rock which is nowadays beside the sea and is submerged by the winter tide, were regarded as installations for extracting purple dye because crushed murex shells were found there together with sherds. However, the quantities of murex shells are too small to justify such an activity, while the hollows are very shallow. It is more likely, given the amount of shells and the presence of pottery, that this was a locus of fishing activities. Modern research demands conclusive rather than circumstantial evidence.

continued its journey through time as a symbol of power and authority.

It is deduced from the excavation data that the beginning of purple production should be dated in the end on Middle Mionan – beginning of Late Minoan period, as the Knossos tablets testify. The problem of the nature and extent of its production remains unresolved.

Sites of purple production from Antiquity onwards

Important centres of purple production were established in Phoenicia, to whose inhabitants its discovery was attributed. It was to this industry that the cities of Tyre and Sidon owed their development and prosperity, and even after their decline purple continued to be produced there for many centuries. Other places renowned for purple production were Caesareia, Naples, Lydda, Cyprus and Phoenician colonies in Egypt.

In time 'industrial' centres appeared in the wider area of the Middle East, the Aegean islands, southern Greece and Macedonia.

During the Antonine dynasty the purple-dyers of Phocaea in Lydia and of Hierapolis in Phrygia were organized in a guild that founded a workshop - the *'Ergasia Thremmatike'* - for training indigent youths in this skill. Of the Aegean islands Rhodes, Kos, Amorgos, Chios and Nisyros were famed for their purple, indeed the last was formerly known as Porphyris. There was a guild of purple-dyers in Thessalonike. In the rest of Greece the most important centres for purple dye were the coastal areas of Laconia and the Corinthia - the coins of the latter bore the emblem of a murex shell -, the east coast of Euboea and the coast of the Argolid. The textiles in Darius' treasure at Susa, later possessed by Alexander the Great, had been produced in Hermione.

Important purple-dye workshops existed in Calabria, Dalmatia, Sicily and Istria. The merchants who traded the dye were known as *'porphyropolai'*. According to Athenaeus Asian purple cost its weight in silver, while Plutarch relates that the aforesaid textiles in Darius's treasure were worth the sum of 5000 talents.

The Archaeological Evidence

Appendix 4

Noted below are the archaeological sites at which some quantities of shells of the molluscs from which the precious dye is extracted have been found. This does not constitute evidence that these were centres of purple dye production and the presence of such shells should be treated with circumspection. Most of the sites are in Crete. Shells of *Murex trunculus* and *Murex brandaris* have been recovered from the Neolithic and the Early Minoan horizons at Knossos (Evans 1964a, 132-240), as well as from Middle Minoan levels in the Royal Road and the Unexplored Mansion at the same site (Evely1984, 296-297).

Some shells of *Murex* species were found in Middle Minoan context at Zakros, along with Kamares ware.

Murex trunculus shells from the same period were discovered at Makrygialo and *Murex* and *Thais* at Myrtos (Reese 1987, 206).

At Palaikastro (MM III - LM IA) 144 fragments of *Murex trunculus* shells were found. Both Bosanquet (Bosanquet 1904, 321) and Hood mention two heaps of these shells, dated on the basis of associated pottery to the earliest phase of MM II. All three species from which purple was extracted were found at Tylissos and Youktas (Reese 1987, 201-206). Shells of 400 *Murex trunculus*, 13 *Murex brandaris* and 10 *Thais* have been identified from LM Komos (Reese, forthcoming). The Greek-Swedish excavation at Chania brought to light both species of *Murex*, while fragments of these shells were found under LM I floors (Reese, forthcoming).

Large numbers of *Murex* shells have been located at Akrotiri, Thera (LC I), many of which were used as raw material for the construction of house floors (Karali 1990, 413).

Asine in the Argolid yielded 224 fragments of *Murex trunculus* (MH III), most of which are from graves and thus not connected with dye production (Reese 1982, 139-141).

Murex shells have also been found on Aegina (1650-1600 BC) (Walter and Felten 1981, 179, pl. 128 no. 529, X), at Aghios Kosmas in Attica (LH) (Μυλωνάς 1959, 58, 100, 148, Fig. 37 nos 1-3, 4-9) and at Troy (1400-1300 BC) (Gejvall, 1937-8, 51-57).

In the wider area of the eastern Mediterranean, fragments of *Murex* were found at the sites of Minet el-

Beidha, Ugarit (northern Syria) (1500-1400 BC). Items dyed with purple, sent by King Tusnath of the Mittani to Pharaoh Amenophis IV (1417-1379 BC), are mentioned in the Tel el Amarna correspondence.

Trade goods

Shells provide information on yet another of prehistoric man's activities: Trade. Much has been written on trade in prehistoric societies but little is in fact known (Renfrew 1984, 86-135), not least because many of the goods involved were perishable and have left no traces in the archaeological record. It is the imperishable materials that survive, such as minerals and inorganic remains in general, among them the shells of molluscs.

Trade exists in primitive societies but differs from that in advanced societies in form and dynamic. In the former societies goods are exchanged between friends or small trading associations on the basis of reciprocity. There is no specific locus of buying and selling or bartering, i.e. no market place. The simplest/earliest form of trade is the exchange of gifts or other objects. The following parameters should be taken into account when considering trade:

1.   the existence of an exchangeable commodity
2.   the existence of a potential 'purchaser / customer'
3.   the value (i.e. the 'price') of the commodity, which depends on the need/desire to acquire it.

Trade in a prehistoric society is also an indicator of cultural contacts and communication with other societies close at hand or further afield. The dynamic of trade, that is a society's degree of dependence on the import or export of goods, is affected by the evolution of that society.

In the Palaeolithic Age minimal trading activity is noted since the possibility of communication was limited and needs were covered by existing goods. In contrast, in the Bronze Age means of communication facilitated and fostered contacts with other sources of raw materials with the consequent growth of trade. So trade evolved from a chance event to a significant economic factor in society.

Shell remains from the Palaeolithic Age in Greece are scant. It is impossible to tell whether the few shells present at Kokinospilia in Epirus are the result of exchange or of food-collecting activity (Dakaris - Higgs - Hey 1964, 199-244, Higgs - Vita Finzi 1967, 1-29). Consequently on the present data from Palaeolithic sites in Greece no inferences can be drawn concerning trade of shells.

Both the excavation data and the finds from the Mesolithic Age are insufficient to change this picture.

In the Neolithic Age food production led to the accumulation of a surplus and to permanent settlement, presenting a picture of a self-sufficient society. For this reason it was originally believed that the dominant economic form was that of local production and consumption (domestic economy).   Trade in the Neolithic Age should not be considered separately from the way of life of the community/group. Depending on the way of life followed   (sedentary, nomadic, transhumant etc.) each group came into contact with others, resulting in the diffusion of goods, techniques and ideas (Renfrew 1973, 179, 191, Reese 1991, 160-180). It is unlikely that molluscs per se were traded in Neolithic societies because they can only be kept fresh in special conditions (e.g. on ice). Their shells on the other hand were attractive objects on account of their colour, surface texture and lustrous nacre.

Throughout the Neolithic Age in Greece shells do not seem to have reached remote regions of the hinterland. Sites which nowadays lay inland (Sitagroi, Nea Nikomedeia etc.) were close to the shore in Neolithic times (Shackleton - Renfrew 1970, 1062, 1065, Rodden 1970, 411-413). Consequently the shells found there were accessible in the immediate vicinity. In the Middle and Late Neolithic periods there are signs of trade of worked shells from northern Greece into the Balkans. This activity focused on ornaments fashioned from *Glycimeris* and *Spondylus* shells, mainly beads and bracelets, and more rarely pendants.

The presence of *Spondylus* ornaments at a site does not *ipso facto* signify trade, however.   Such objects recovered from the Skoteini Cave at Tharrounia, Euboea (MN and LN) (Karali 1993, 370-377) and the Alepotrypa Cave, Mani (LN) (Karali, forthcoming) were almost certainly produced locally, since this species is also included among the food residues of the cave dwellers and was native on the nearby coast. Furthermore, the general cultural context indicates a cultural substratum and technological level in common with the rest of the Neolithic sites in the Aegean from which worked shells are known.

Two factors point to the existence of trading activity in northern Greece:

a)   the location of 'workshops' for the production of jewellery of *Spondylus* and *Glycimeris* shell at the sites of Dikili Tash, Dimitra, Sitagroi *inter alia* (Καραλή, forthcoming)
b)   laboratory examination of worked *Spondylus* shells found at sites in Bulgaria and the former Yugoslavia has shown their provenance to be the north Aegean (Shackleton - Renfrew 1970, 1062-1065).

So it appears that *Spondylus* shell was worked in northern Greece and thence disseminated into the

Balkans and Central and northeastern Europe (Bulgaria, Romania, Hungary, Czech Republic, Slovakia and the Caucasus). The objects reached these regions along the river valleys, most probably in a series of exchange transactions of northern regions with more southerly ones.[17]

During the final period of the Neolithic and the succeeding Bronze Age, trade acquired other dimensions, as the wealth of finds from excavations indicates. There is abundant evidence of craft specialization and the import and working of new materials (metals, semi-precious stone etc.).

In the Late Bronze Age the first imported shell species in the Aegean appeared (Lindos, Kamiros and Vroulia on Rhodes, site of the Stratigraphical Museum at Knossos): *Tridacna*.

The largest species is 137 cm long and weighs 230.5 kilos, while the smallest is just 5 cm long. *Tridacna* was mainly imported from the Indian Ocean and is associated with the burgeoning of trade at this time, particularly in exotic raw materials such as elephant ivory, ostrich eggs etc., that were fashioned into luxury and prestige items characteristic of the important Late Bronze Age sites (Reese 1991, 170-171).

In the majority of cases *Tridacna* was found in graves and the rarity of its presence underlines the special status of this import.

To summarize, two phases of trading activity in shells can be distinguished:

a)   export of worked shells from northern Greece to the Balkans and Central and northern Europe, mainly during the Late Neolithic.

b)   import of *Tridacna* shell from more southerly seas, in the latter years of the Late Bronze Age.

There may well have been exchange on a smaller scale between settlements in Greece, but this is extremely difficult to pinpoint.

---

[17] Shells of the species *Spondylus gaederopus L.* as well as ornaments fashioned from it have been found at most Neolithic sites in Greece, in the Peloponnese (e.g. Alepotrypa Mani, Franchthi Hermionida), Central Greece (e.g. Kitsos cave), Thessaly (e.g. Sesklo, Dimini), Macedonia and Thrace (e.g. Sitagroi, Dikili-Tash and elsewhere). As can be seen in the table in the chapter on jewellery, spondylus shell ornaments are more numerous in the area of Macedonia during the Middle and mainly the Late Neolithic. From there they diffused to Central and Eastern Europe, following the axis of the rivers Axios-Morava and that of the rivers Strymon, Nestos and Hebros (Evros) to the East.

Objects of spondylus have come to light in Bulgaria, Romania and Serbia (Gulmenica and Cucuteni culture: Varna cemetery, Duran-Kulak near the Black Sea, Anza, Boian, Hamangia cultures in Oltenia, Vinča). Similar objects have also been located in Moravia, specifically at the sites of Moravsky, Krumlov and Zabrdovice. Spondylus shells seem to have 'travelled' even further North, since they have been found in Slovakia at Nitra, in Austria at Eggenbourg, Emmersdorff, Poysdorf and elsewhere. There are references to worked spondylus shells from the sites of Flombom, Elsloo, Bernbury, Rheingewann in the Rhine vally, and from burials at Zofipole and Szcotowice in Southern Poland (Karali 1979, 299-302). Along with spondylus other shells were circulated in much smaller quantities, mainly *Cardium* sp. and *Glycimeris* sp.

Ornaments of spondylus shell display morphological differences depending on the place where they are found. This differentiation perhaps means that spondylus shell was distributed as raw material and then worked locally (*in situ*). Distinctive objects at Neolithic sites in Central and Northern Europe are a kind of horseshoe-shaped pendant not found anywhere else (pendentif en fer a cheval, hüfformiger).

Molluscs in Aegean art

Molluscs are represented in Aegean art in a variety of media and techniques, either as the central theme or as filling motifs. They are painted in wall-paintings and on pottery (Darque - Poursat 1985, 63-81) (Fig. 40), incised or engraved primarily on sealstones (table 6) (Fig. 38), and modelled or sculpted in clay (Zervos 1956, drawing 97, pl. 30d) and stone (marble, alabaster etc.) (table 3).

Molluscs are represented in three aesthetic modes:
   a) naturalistic,
   b) abstract
   c) symbolic.

Depictions of molluscs on pottery should be considered in relation to the Minoan Marine Style that prevailed in Late Bronze Age Crete (Bulié 1925, 149-151, Zervos 1956, 1957, Karali 1979, 194-209).

Molluscs are represented in decorative groups in their natural environment, under the sea - the motion of which is indicated - on rocks between seaweed and other marine creatures (Mountjoy 1984, 161-169). They are often painted in such detail they give the impression that the artist had personal knowledge of them.

The Aegean sea played a seminal role in moulding the personality and especially the aesthetic perceptions of the peoples living on the islands and in the coastal areas. This familiarity with the sea naturally and understandably influenced their art: the sea is represented with its waves, its flora and fauna, the men and means that plied the watery element.

Molluscs evidently played an important role in the life of the Aegean islander, since they are frequently represented in art. Moreover, some species are easily recognizable.

In most cases their depiction on pottery and in wall-paintings is naturalistic. The same is true of molluscs rendered in relief in clay or faience, carved in stone etc. On the contrary, on sealstones both naturalistic and schematic-abstract representations occur; the latter are mainly distinctive of the Late Bronze Age (Kenna 1960, 1966, 1967, 1972, 1974).

In the Early Minoan period the decorative motifs are essentially geometric (Betancourt 1985, 144-145). Towards the end of this period the decoration diversifies and the thematic repertoire evolves, even though its subjects do not change. In the Middle Minoan period there are depictions of sea creatures in wall-paintings, on vases and on sealstones. The Marine Style commences in the early phases of the Late Minoan period (LM IB).

A common motif in Minoan art is the octopus (*Octopus vulgaris*), in some cases framed by rocks, seaweed, triton shells and sea anemones. The argonaut is likewise popular, though depicted in an environment different from its natural one its coloration is by contrast realistic (Boyd-Hawes 1908, pl. 3, BM A718). Frequent too is the crab (*Carcinus mediterraneus G.*) which is usually not rendered realistically (*PM* IV Fig. 215, CMS II.5, no. 301 and CMS XII.1 no. 246, Marinatos - Hirmer 1960, Fig. 85). Occasionally the artist paints the squid (*Loliga vulgaris L.*)

Careful examination of the representations of molluscs, excepting cephalopods, in Minoan art reveals that the living organism is rarely shown but usually the empty shell (*PM* I Fig. 379).

Of the gastropods the most popular is the Triton (*Triton tritonis L.*), though the topshell (*Monodonta articulata Lamarck*) has been recognized in a few cases, as well as argonauts and murex (*Murex brandaris L*).

Of the bivalves the best known are the clam (*Glycimeris glycimeris L.*) and cockle (*Cardium edule L.*).

Other marine invertebrates encountered are the starfish (*Asterias paracentrotus lividus Lamarck*) and sea urchin (*Echinus esculenus*) (Fig. 36,37,38).

Characteristic examples of depictions of molluscs in Bronze Age art are:

- The Early Minoan vase with zone of argonauts, from Gournia (Boyd-Hawes 1908 pl. 5).
- The Middle Minoan representations on seals, wall-paintings and vases. Sepias and bivalves dominate. Of particular interest is a series of vases from Phaistos with relief *Cardium* shell ornaments (*PM* IV, Fig. 83). The shell was imprinted on clay, as can be seen from the fragments found in the 'Kouloures' (pits) at Knossos (*PM* I, 521-522, Fig. 380) and Malia (Karali, forthcoming). Shells of *Patella* and *Pecten* were imprinted too, and in one instance the shell of a species of crab (*PM* IV, Fig. 69, Zervos 1956, Fig. 331) (Fig. 39).

Larger compositions with marine themes were created in the Middle Minoan period, particularly on large vases. The pithoi fragments from Pachyammos are a case in point (Evans 1921, 133).

Molluscs are represented in wall-paintings and on stone

vessels, as well as being modelled in clay and faience (M.P. I, figs 379-381, IV, Fig. 27, pl. 30 d).

Towards the end of the Middle Minoan period themes from the marine world are rendered in repoussé technique on metal objects, sometimes realistically and sometimes schematically.

The most familiar marine motifs in the Late Minoan period are the octopus and the argonaut. The type of octopus representation that held sway in this period had already appeared in the Middle Minoan. Characteristic is the vase from the Kamares cave on which an octopus is shown with its tentacles extended in all directions (*PM* IV, Fig. 215, 635, *PM* II, Fig. 312 c, d). The argonaut is usually rendered schematically (*PM* IV, 889-891, figs 870, 871), as can be seen in the Knossos wall-paintings (*PM* IV, Fig. 870). The starfish (*Asterias* sp.) features on a series of conical rhytons (Bosanquet 1904-1905, figs 38-41, pl. 20). The triton is invariably placed vertically at the centre of an underwater setting, both in vase-painting and glyptics. Its representation is quite naturalistic, as exemplified by a vase from Palaikastro (Bosanquet 1924, pl. XIX, Fig. 116) and a sealstone from the Idaian Cave (Mariani 1985, 178, Fig.12).

On the Palatial Style pottery the most popular motifs of the preceding periods are repeated, but flora predominates.

- During the Mycenaean period on the Greek mainland the thematic repertoire of pottery decoration is overtly influenced by Minoan art. The species *Octopus* and *Murex brandaris L.* are represented schematically. *Murex* (whorl shell) is frequent in the Late Helladic period particularly on cups, kraters and kylikes. Characteristic examples come from Perati (Ιακωβίδης 1970, figs 89, 90) and Argos (Deshayes 1969, Fig. 72).

In the palaces of Mycenae and Tiryns some floors were of stucco painted with representations of octopus and other marine creatures. A frieze of argonauts decorated the interior of the House of the Sphinxes at Mycenae (Schliemann 1895, Fig. XXIIc, Blegen - Rawson 1966).

From comparative analysis of the aforementioned iconographic themes conclusions may be drawn on the relations and reciprocal influences between geographical regions and societies.

In Minoan art dominant species are the cephalopods (*Octopus* sp., *Sepia* sp. etc.) and secondarily the gastropods (*Murex* sp., *Triton* sp.). Their frequent depiction in the Middle and Late Bronze Age is most probably associated with their role in everyday life or other activities (e.g. cult). For example, the representation of the *Triton* species is perhaps related to the use of this shell as a trumpet or a libation vessel.

More or less the same species are represented in Mycenaean art, albeit less frequently, bespeaking a continuity in ideas and decorative motifs. A few marine species such as *Murex* and *Octopus* are represented throughout most of the Late Bronze Age, perhaps indicating the importance attached not only to the motif but also to the animal itself.

Lastly, noteworthy is the fact that through iconography in art information is preserved on both the marine fauna of the Aegean and the importance of species of which no traces are found in excavations (e.g. cephalopods).

Chapter IV

Conclusions

In his struggle to adapt to the environment man endeavoured to satisfy that triad of basic needs defined by Plato and Aristotle (*Politics*, A8, 1256a, 18 - 1256b, 7): food, shelter and clothing (της τροφής της οικήσεως και της εσθήτος). The contribution to archaeology of the study of palaeoenvironmental remains - among them those of molluscs - lies in the interpretation of these three needs (without of course neglecting the interpretation also of concepts and beliefs).

Examination of the malacological material brought to light in excavation is not confined to identifying and classifying the species, and to compiling quantitative and statistical tables showing their frequency of occurrence. Its importance lies in the scholar's attempt to place man in his actual space of action. The most laborious but the most significant phase in the study of environmental evidence is the interpretative, the explanation of the particular material's essential significance in the life of the past inhabitants of an archaeological site. There are many situations and relations that are difficult to detect, such as the relations governing the individual activities of a group (e.g. food collecting-foraging, hunting, stock-raising); the way in which these activities were combined with other activities and concepts (everyday life - art); the relationship between man and his environment, and in particular the animal kingdom, in each chronological phase; the degree and manner of man's intervention in the environment; the reasons for one choice or another at a given time. So it is obvious that in order to determine the uses of shells, when the data permit, these should be examined in relation to the excavation context and the evidence emerging from it.

There is abundant malacological material in Greece, mainly on account of its geographical location. The findings from its study constitute important information on man's way of life and facilitate the archaeological interpretation of diverse sectors, such as fishing, diet, tools, jewellery, building material, fillers/tempers, burial habits, toys/games, symbolism, artistic representation.

The Aegean people's involvement with the sea has a long and fascinating history. As far as fishing is concerned, study of the aggregate of remains provides valuable information on man's technological progress, choices and conceptions. Since the equipment required for fishing or collecting molluscs depends on the habits and habitat of each species, an assemblage of fishing tackle (e.g. special vases, tools such as harpoons, blades, knives) and shells of molluscs which live in deep waters (e.g. triton), indicates the use of a boat. Thus the stage of cultural development and man's relations with the sea and seafaring are revealed.

Even shell fragments without trace of working are important because they provide information on man's diet. Crushed shells were also used as building or insulating material (as in the floors of rooms at Akrotiri, Thera), and as filler or temper in clay for pottery and bricks.

The methods and means of working shells are indicative of technical advances and innovations, as well as of the general cultural level.

Information on cultural uniformity or local diversity emerges from dated material with clear signs of working and use, such as button-shaped pendants and *Spondylus* bracelets. In this case it is possible to correlate sites belonging to the same chronological phases.

The archaeological context is also a clue to the role of shells. For example, those found in remains of fires or sacrifices are interpreted according to the traces and degree of burning. If their presence near the fire is not accidental then it is possible to determine a specific choice of species (food).

Shells occur as grave goods throughout the Bronze Age (Doumas 1977, Ιακωβίδης1970).

Shells covered a broad spectrum of uses in the Aegean from the Palaeolithic to the Late Bronze Age. In the Palaeolithic Age the changes in climate and landscape largely determined man's relations with animals and plants. Molluscs were a part of this complex nexus of relations, and were mainly used for food and as ornaments. The same species are still found today on the coasts of Greece. No full study of the malacological material from the Palaeolithic sites of Greece has yet been published. Sea shells have been reported from sites in Epirus, while at Apidima in the Mani pierced shells were found in the same context as a human skeleton. The main species consumed were *Patella* and *Cardium*. *Nassa* shells were found at most Palaeolithic sites and seem to have been used for adornment (e.g. Apidima Cave, Mani).

Though little is known of the Mesolithic Age, it is generally characterized by food-gathering activities, that is man's parasitic rather than productive relationship with the environment, and the accumulation of middens containing large quantities of shells. The few finds and limited knowledge of the Mesolithic Age in Greece preclude the drawing of general conclusions. Nevertheless, the earliest finds from the Franchthi Cave and the latest from the Theopetra Cave, and very possibly from the Cyclops Cave on Youra, indicate a considerable consumption of land snails. The most frequent marine species are *Patella coerulea, Cerithium vulgatum* and *Nassa neritea*.

During the Neolithic Age, with the development of agriculture and animal husbandry, and the application of new techniques, man's relationship with the environment became more dynamic. He intervened directly in order to exploit those resources necessary not only for survival but also for improving his living conditions. So fluctuations in the curve of mollusc consumption and the selection of species correspond to the degree of development of the farming economy and the level of production.

Molluscs continued to play an important role in the life of Neolithic man as food and as bait, as ornaments and as tools. Shell tools occur throughout the Neolithic Age, but mainly in the Middle Neolithic and markedly in the Late Neolithic when many worked shells are noted. In Macedonia in particular large quantities of *Cardium* sp., *Spondylus gaederopus, Glycimeris glycimeris* and the freshwater *Unio* sp. have been located. The species *Cerithium* continued to be consumed. The same molluscs predominate in Thessaly. In southern Greece the principal species found at sites are *Patella, Monodonta, Murex, Pinna, Glycimeris* and *Cardium*, while the presence of land snails is important, as seen from Franchthi Cave in the Peloponnese, Kitsos Cave in Attica and elsewhere. In the Aegean islands the contribution of molluscs to the diet was particularly significant: primarily *Patella, Monodonta turbinata* and *Cerastoderma edule*, followed by *Venerupis aureus, Murex trunculus, Pinna nobilis, Cerithium vulgatum* and others.

Worked and unworked shells are the main items of jewellery in Neolithic Macedonia and Thessaly. They are beads, pendants and bracelets, primarily of *Spondylus gaederopus* and *Glycimeris glycimeris*, and secondarily of *Cardium edule L., Conus ventricosus Gmelin, Nassa neritea L., Dentalium dentalis da Costa* and *Luria lurida L.*

The shells used as tools in the Neolithic Age are more difficult to distinguish than other categories of objects. Mainly of *Patella coerulea L., Cardium edule L., Mytilus galloprovincialis L., Spondylus gaederopus L.* and *Charonia tritonis L.*, they are spoons, burnishers and palettes.

A few figurines of spondylus have been reported from Thessaly.

Noteworthy is the fact that the shells found at sites in the Danube valley had the same uses as those in Greece, particularly northern Greece, while certain of the worked objects were evidently imported from the Aegean via some network of barter trade or exchange. In settlements in the South too there are obvious similarities in the use and working of shell, which seem to extend as far as Cyprus (see Reese on Cyprus).

The rise in living standards during the Bronze Age is possibly responsible for the smaller quantities of shells found in excavations. Conversely there is a proliferation of representations of shells on sealstones, in wall-paintings and in materials such as stone and metal. It was in this period that man discovered how to extract pigments from molluscs and to prepare purple dye from *Murex* sp.

In the Bronze Age shells from the Aegean area were not objects of commercial transactions with alien ecological environments. This applies to all molluscs, whether they were consumed as food or used for jewellery or had ritual significance (graves, pyres, sacrifices). The only import was *Tridacna* sp.

There is a clear fall in the percentage of *Cardium* sp. at Bronze Age sites and a rise in that of *Patella coerulea L., Murex trunculus L., Murex brandaris L.* as well as *Triton tritonis L.* Shell tools are rare, while there are a few instances of spool-shaped objects of *Spondylus* and trumpets of *Triton tritons L.* (mainly at Mycenaean sites).

The use of shells in jewellery decreases appreciably, though beads of *Dentalium* and *Conus* have been found at sites in the Peloponnese, the Cyclades and Central Greece.

The most important species of molluscs represented in Bronze Age art are the cephalopods, while *Murex, Triton* and *Cardium* also feature.

A few shell figurines of Cycladic provenance are of Early Bronze Age date.

The production of purple dye from *Murex* sp. probably began in the Middle Bronze Age and is well attested in the Late Bronze Age.

Conus shells interpreted as 'game pieces' have come to light at Late Bronze Age sites on the Greek mainland (Perati, Mycenae).

The relatively low frequency of shells at sites dated to the closing years of the Bronze Age is notable but not inexplicable. Possible reasons are:

a)   the location of sites excavated, the methods and aims of the excavation. That is sites that do not seem to have had contact with the coast or at which malacological material was collected only by sampling or not at all in the course of their excavation.

b)   change in dietary preferences on account of sufficiency of agricultural and stock-raising produce.

c)   probable provision for refuse clearance/disposal at sites where the standard of living was evidently high, such as Quartier Mu at Malia, the West House at Akrotiri.

d)   Some species of molluscs, such as cephalopods, are hardly ever detected in the archaeological record.

Consequently the picture presented by the malacological remains does not necessarily reflect the true relationship between man and molluscs in the Bronze Age.

The manifold uses of shells ascertained by the archaeologist, and their establishment as a material that can contribute to dating confirms their importance in the prehistory of the Aegean. Problems and gaps in our knowledge still exist, many of which are due to lack of interest hitherto in malacological remains. Modern excavations with the detailed stratigraphical study and recording of the archaeological and the environmental evidence constitute the data base for an integrated and proper approach to shells in the prehistoric Aegean.

It is possible to determine the role molluscs played in the life of the Aegean people according to the cultural phase. Their presence, both qualitative and quantitative, convinces the modern archaeologist of the necessity of studying them. It is ascertained from our knowledge of the material so far that molluscs played a role in both the base of the social structure and the superstructure. That is they feature in the economic relations and as cultural products that are the consequence of the content of the base.

Epilogue

According to the present level of scientific knowledge and the existing archaeological material the sources of information have been exhausted. The approaches to the malacological material give the archaeologist the opportunity of understanding the finds better and of placing them in a more general environmental-anthropological context. Where remains of shells exist they play their part in reconstructing man's life and action in different phases of his history.

Questions that remain unanswered are mainly to the quantity in which shells are discovered in and recovered from excavations, in which many factors are implicated: a) excavation methods, b) different chronological periods, c) subjective interpretation of material according to the personal views and the theoretical background of the researcher.

The future possibilities and prospects are apparent from the above. Further aims are to extend the study of shells not only in excavations of the prehistoric period but also of other periods, to set up a data base, to form reference collections, to recognize diachronic uses, and last, to promote fuller interdisciplinary treatment of the material with laboratory study.

TABLE 1. Diet

NEOLITHIC AGE

SITE	DATE	Cerithium	Tritonium	Cerastoderma	Tonna	Cyclope	Gibbula	Monodonta	Cypraea	Patella	Arca	Ostrea	Dentalium	Cardium	Glycimeris	Mytilus	Donax	Pinna	Thais	Spondylus	Chlamys
Prodromos, Thessaly	EN	-	-	-	-	-	-	-	-	-	-	-	-	-	-	-	-	-	1	-	-
Franchthi	MN-LN	44	-	-	-	-	-	-	-	-	-	-	-	-	-	-	-	-	-	-	-
Malia, Crete	EN	-	-	3	-	25	3	31	-	70	16	240	-	8	3	26	-	3	-	9	-
Paradeisos	EN	-	-	-	-	-	-	-	-	-	-	-	-	-	-	-	-	-	-	-	-
Partheni, Leros	EN	-	-	-	-	-	-	-	-	-	-	-	-	-	-	-	-	-	-	-	-
Koumelo, Archangelos	EN	148	-	-	-	-	-	20	6	18	111	-	-	-	-	-	-	-	-	-	-
Dimitra, Macedonia	EN	90	-	-	-	-	24	-	-	52	6	27	6	587	54	26	-	-	19	17	6
Alepotrypa, Mani	EN	-	-	-	-	-	11	317	-	749	-	-	-	-	-	-	-	-	-	-	-
Tharrounia, Euboea	EN I-II	-	-	-	-	-	-	1	-	10	-	-	-	7	1	2	-	2	-	1	-
Dikili-Tash	EN	26	-	-	-	-	4	8	2	64	10	3	-	93	16	4	-	-	-	26	-

SITE	DATE	Venerupis	Venus	Cassis	Chama	Charonia	Columbella	Conus	Euthria	Murex	Nassa	Pisania	Purpura	Ensis	Luria	Unio	Helix	Bittium	Callista	Pecten	Chlamys
Prodromos, Thessaly	EN	-	-	-	-	-	-	-	-	-	-	-	-	-	-	-	-	-	-	-	-
Franchthi	MN-LN	-	-	-	-	-	-	-	-	-	-	-	-	-	-	-	-	-	-	-	-
Malia, Crete	EN	9	1	3	2	-	3	3	10	214	4	1	3	-	-	-	-	-	-	-	-
Paradeisos	EN	-	-	-	-	-	-	-	-	-	-	-	-	-	-	-	-	-	-	-	-
Partheni, Leros	EN	-	-	-	-	-	-	-	-	-	-	-	-	-	-	-	-	-	-	-	-
Koumelo, Archangelos	EN	148	-	-	-	-	-	-	-	-	-	-	-	-	-	3594	252	149	-	-	-
Dimitra, Macedonia	EN	-	-	-	-	-	-	-	-	-	-	-	-	-	-	-	-	-	-	-	-
Alepotrypa, Mani	EN	-	2	-	-	-	-	-	-	-	-	-	-	-	-	-	-	-	-	-	-
Tharrounia, Euboea	EN I-II	-	-	-	-	-	-	-	-	-	-	-	-	-	-	91	-	-	-	-	-
Dikili-Tash	EN	-	-	1	-	-	-	-	-	19	2	-	-	-	-	154	8	-	-	3	-

EARLY BRONZE AGE

SITE	DATE	Cerithium	Tritonium	Cerastoderma	Tonna	Cyclope	Gibbula	Monodonta	Cypraea	Patella	Arca	Ostrea	Dentalium	Cardium	Glycimeris	Mytilus	Donax	Pinna	Thais	Spondylus	Chlamys
Lithares	EH I-II	3	1	13	1	-	-	1	-	5	53	1	1	-	-	1	-	-	-	23	-
Pentapolis, Macedonia	EH II	-	-	-	-	-	-	-	-	-	-	-	-	10	-	1	-	-	-	-	-
Zygouries, Argolid	EH II	-	-	-	-	-	-	-	-	-	-	-	-	-	-	-	-	-	-	-	-
Kastri	EH I-II	1	3	-	-	-	2	135	-	2568	19	1	-	108	9	26	-	4	-	17	-

SITE	DATE	Venerupis	Venus	Cassis	Chama	Charonia	Columbella	Conus	Euthria	Murex	Nassa	Pisania	Purpura	Ensis	Luria	Unio	Helix	Bittium	Callista	Pecten	Chlamys
Lithares	EH I-II	1	-	-	-	-	-	-	-	-	-	-	-	-	-	-	223	-	-	-	-
Pentapolis, Macedonia	EH II	-	4	-	-	-	-	-	-	-	-	-	-	-	-	524	13	-	-	-	1
Zygouries, Argolid	EH II	-	-	-	-	-	-	-	-	-	-	-	-	-	-	-	-	-	-	-	-
Kastri	EH I-II	1	-	3	-	-	-	-	-	81	1	-	-	-	-	76	-	1	-	-	-

TABLE 1 continued

MIDDLE-LATE BRONZE AGE

SITE	DATE	Cerithium	Tritonium	Cerastoderma	Tonna	Cyclope	Gibbula	Monodonta	Cypraea	Patella	Arca	Ostrea	Dentalium	Cardium	Glycimeris	Mytilus	Donax	Pinna	Thais	Spondylus
Lerna, Argolid	EH-LH III	163	1	-	-	-	-	11	-	224	441	-	-	3416	149	4	926	171	28	1908
Malia, Crete	MH III-LH III	-	-	-	-	-	-	-	-	-	1	10	-	126	-	-	-	-	-	2
Symi Viannou, Crete	MH III-LH III	3	-	-	-	-	1	-	-	6	1	-	-	-	55	-	-	-	-	2
Akrotiri, Thera	LC I	8	31	-	-	-	6	81	-	739	3	-	-	3	49	-	-	23	-	6
Asine	LH III	6	-	4	1	-	-	-	-	-	1	-	-	-	5	-	-	1	-	15
Agh. Stephanos, Laconia	LH III	-	-	-	4	-	-	28	-	27	2	1	-	-	42	-	-	-	-	-
Skala Sotiros, Thasos	LH III	63	-	1	55	-	2415	1790	36	18005	153	7	-	-	5	1	196	174	140	163
Kommos, Crete	LH III	6	46	16	-	-	-	-	-	-	-	-	-	-	-	-	-	-	-	-

SITE	DATE	Venerupis	Venus	Cassis	Chama	Charonia	Columbella	Conus	Euthria	Murex	Nassa	Pisania	Purpura	Ensis	Luria	Unio	Helix	Bittium	Callista	Pecten	Chlamys
Lerna, Argolid	EH-LH III	-	17	-	-	-	-	15	1	2080	-	-	-	-	-	82	-	-	-	-	-
Malia, Crete	MH III-LH III	-	-	-	-	-	32	-	-	3	-	-	-	-	-	5	-	-	5	3	-
Symi Viannou, Crete	MH III-LH III	-	-	-	-	6	-	23	-	-	-	-	-	-	-	-	-	-	1	1	-
Akrotiri, Thera	LC I	-	-	-	-	-	13	-	4	1108	2	-	-	-	8	-	196	-	-	16	-
Asine	LH III	-	-	-	-	-	-	-	-	9	-	-	-	-	-	-	-	-	-	-	-
Agh. Stephanos, Laconia	LH III	-	85	-	-	-	-	-	-	-	-	-	-	-	-	-	-	-	12	-	-
Skala Sotiros, Thasos	LH III	-	-	-	-	-	15	-	-	351	-	-	-	12	3	117	-	-	-	-	-
Kommos, Crete	LH III	-	-	-	-	-	-	-	-	-	-	-	-	-	-	-	-	-	-	-	-

TABLE 2. Tools

Neolithic Age	Date	Spoons	Spatulas	Burnishers	Triangles	Other shapes	Vases	Mace heads	Spools-Pestles
N. Nikomedeia	EN	1 Mytilus	1 Unio		1 Mytilus				
Saliagos	MN-LN	48 Mytilus	1 Unio	27 Cerastoderma 1 Ostrea				1 Spondylus	
Paradeisos	EN				13 Mytilus	1 Unio			
Dikili-Tash	EN	2 Mytilus	1 Unio		16 Mytilus			1 Spondylus	
Kitsos	EN	9 Mytilus			26 Mytilus				
Dimitra	EN			Glycimeris					
Alepotrypa	EN	1 Mytilus							
Tharrounia	EN	2 Mytilus							
Sitagroi	EN								
Franchthi	EN	5 Mytilus			16 Mytilus				
Cyclop's Cave	EN	5 Patella	1 Ostrea						

Early Bronze Age

	Date	Spoons	Spatulas	Burnishers	Triangles	Other shapes	Vases	Mace heads	Spools-Pestles
Panaghia, Paros	EC I						1 Spondylus		
Kastri, Thasos	EH II						1 Charonia	1 Spondylus	
Zygouries	EH II								1 Spondylus

57

TABLE 3. Ornaments

SITE	DATE	BEADS	BRACELETS	PENDANTS	RINGS	NECKLACES	KALYPTRA
Apidima Mani	Palaeolithic						34 Nassa Neritea
N.Nikomedeia Macedonia	AN	Nassa neritea	3 Glycimeris	27 Cardium		14 Cardium	
Knossos, Crete	AN	1 Conus 18 Dentalium		25 Glycimeris 150 Cardium 130 Cerastoderma			
Franchthi, Argolid	MN-NN	3 Nassa s.p. Dentalium		Monodonta 2 Luria 1 Columbella	4 Monodonta	Dentalium	
Salonica, Macedonia	MN			1 Spondylus			
Cyclop's Cave	Acer.-LN	2 Spondylus	2 Spondylus				
Kitsos Cave Attica	MN-NN	5 Cerithium 1 Columbella 5 Conus 3 Arcularia 2 Nassa	2 Glycimeris	5 Conus 2 Spondylus	1 Murex 10 Luria 8 Columbella 7 Cardium		
Tsangli Thessaly	NN		1 Spondylus				
Poliochni Lemnos	NN			1 Luria			
Sitagroi Kavala	NN-L.Br.	8 Spondylus					
Paradeisos, Kavala	NN-L.Br.	68 Glycimeris 9 Columbella 5 Dentalium	2 Spondylus				
Vasilika Macedonia	MN-NN	1 Dentalium	9 Glycimeris 8 Spondylus	1 Conus 1 Mactra 8 Murex		Glycimeris Columbella Murex	
Achilleion Thessaly	MN	Tubular		Bivalves		6 Dentalium	
Kastro Rhodes	NN			Zonnaria Pirum			
Tharrounia Euboea	NNIaII	4 Spondylus discs 1 Asteroid Spondylus		1 Glycimeris 1 Venus 1 Cardium 1 Luria			
Agh. Gala Chios	Neolithic			2 Glycimeris			
Phaistot, Crete	NN			1 Conus			
Servia Macedonia	MN-NN		1 Spondylus	Cardium			
Dimitra Macedonia	MN-NN	34 Glycimeris 18 Cardium 1 Dentalium 1 Unio 7 Conus 3 Euthria 4 Nassa 74 Spondylus	30 Spondylus	2 Spondylus			
Saliagos Cyclades	MN-NN	8 Spondylus	32 Spondylus	1 Glycimeris			
Dikili-Tash Macedonia	NN	42 Spondylus	6 Spondylus	2 Glycimeris 35 Cardium 1 Spondylus			

TABLE 3 continued (Ornaments).

ME-LH Period

SITE	DATE	BEADS	PENDANTS	RINGS	NECKLACES
Kirra Phokis	MH				Necklace from shell
Agh. Stephano S. Laconia	MH-LN		1 Luria 2 Conus	1 Monodonta	
Kommos, Crete	MM-LMIIIA1		92 Clycimeris	1 Monodonta	
Symi Viannoy Crete	MMIII-LMIII	15 Conus	24 Glycimeris 21 Columbella 1 Acanthocardia		
Phylakopi Melos	LC		4 Spondylus		1 Patella
Nichoria Messenia	LH	496 Dentalius 1 Conus	1 Cardium		
Prosymna Peloponnese	LH		4 Natica 1 Fasciolaria 6 Cerithium		25 Cardium 21 Glycimeris
Perati, Attica	LH		30 Couns		
Koukounaries Paros	LC		1 Cyclope	2 Monodonta	Necklace from 33 Conus 1 from Pisania
Palace of Nestor, Pylos	LH		1 Conus		
Lindos, Rhodes	RH		1 Glycimeris		
Vroulia, Rhodes	LH		1 Murex 3 Luria Glycimeris Cerithium		
Mucaene, Argolid	LH	75 Dentalium 38 Monodonta	8 Murex	2 Monodonta	
Chania, Crete	LM			2 Monodonta	
Royal Road Knosson	LM	15 Conus	1 Columbella 1 Glycimeris	1 Monodonta	
Unexploerd mansion, Knossos					

TABLE 4. Representations of shells in other materials

SITE	DATE	OBJECT / MATERIALS
Malia	MM II	Clay Rhyton
Knossos	MM IIB	3 Painted tritons 1 Alabaster triton
Phylakopi, Melos	LCI-III	Clay Cardium
Cemetery Phaistos	LM	Alabaster triton
Gournia	LM I	2 Clay tritons
Pyrgos	LM IB	Red faience triton
Rhodes Lardes Staphylia	LM III	Marble triton
Mycenae	LH III	Faience triton

TABLE 5. Seals

CMS	No.	Motif	Date	Provenance	Material	Shape	Dimensions (cm)
II5	301	Octopus	MM IB-IIa	Phaistos, room 25	Clay	Lentoid	1.3
VII	219	Octopus	MM IIB	Cretan	Steatite, yellow	Lentoid	1.0, 1.4
VII	79	Octopus	MM IIB	Cretan	Jasper, ochre-green	Amygdaloid	1.6, 1.2
VII	80	Octopus	MM IIIB	Cretan	Jasper, green	Amygdaloid	1.8, 1.4
IV	235	Octopus	LM IB	Malia	Jasper, green	Amygdaloid	2.0, 1.4
IX	10D	Octopus	LH?	Mycenaean	Serpentine, green-black	Acorn-shaped	2.9,.2.6
VII	117	Octopus	EH IIIA	Mycenean	Agate, blue	Lentoid	2.1
II5	303	Octopus	MM IB-IIA	Phaistos, room 25	Clay	Lentoid	1.3
II5	302	Octopus	MM IB-IIA	Phaistos, room 25	Clay	Lentoid	1.2
XIII	62	Carcinus	MM	Cretan	Marble, black	Disk-shaped, curved sides	1.5
VII	30	Carcinus	MM IIA	Cretan	Steatite, green-brown, cream	Trihedral prism	1.5, 1.2
IV	59	Bivalve (Glycimeris)	MM I	Siteia	Clay, yellow	Conical	1.58
IX	24	Nassa	MM IB-IIA	Cretan	Steatite, yellow	Trihedral prism	1.2, 1.1
VIII	51	Echinus	MR IA	Cretan	Jasper, green	Trihedral prism	1.5, 1.9
VII	73	Echinus	MM IIIB	Cretan	Steatite, green	Amygdaloid	1.6, 1.3
II5	306	Triton	MM IB-IIA	Phaistos (room Sottoscala)	Clay	Amygdaloid	2.2, 1.0
II5	305	Triton	MM IB-IIA	Phaistos, room LI	Clay	Amygdaloid	1.7, 1.0
II5	304	Triton	MM IB-IIA	Phaistos, room II	Clay	Amygdaloid	2.2, 1.0
?	?	Triton	?	Idaean Cave	Crystal	Lentoid	?
VII	75	Crustacean (Lobster)	MM IIIB	Cretan	Cornelian	Glandular	2.0, 1.5
VII	76	Crustacean (Lobster)	MM IIIB	Cretan	Cornelian	Lentoid	1.6
VII	234	Crustacean (Lobster)	MM IIA	Cretan	Agate	Lentoid	1.55
VII	30	Crab	MM IIA	Cretan	Steatite, green-Brown, cream	Trihedral prism	1.5, 1.2
IV	190	Sepia	LM IA	Messara	Jasper, greenish	Amygdaloid	1.4, 1.8
I	7	Sepia	LH I	Mycenaean	Sardonite	Amygdaloid	1.5, 1.1
IX	68	Sepia	LM IA	Cretan	Sardonite	Cylindrical, compressed	1.4, 1.0
IV	195	Sepia	LM IA	Lastros, Cretan	Obsidian	Lentoid	1.2, 0.6
IV	196	Sepia	LM IA	Siteia	Jasper, black	Amygdaloid	1.9, 1.1
IV	214	Sepia	LM IA	Phaistos	Jasper, green-blue	Amygdaloid	1.7, 1.2
IV	46D	Sepia	LM	Messara	Sardonite, Brown-yellow	Lentoid	1.6, 0.7
IV	47D	Sepia	LM	Loutraki, Chania	Jasper, red-brown	Amygdaloid	1.85, 1.52
IV	6	Sepia	EH	Aegina	Crystal	Amygdaloid	1.9, 1.5
XIII	42	Sepia	LM	Cretan	marble, black	Amygdaloid	1.8, 1.2
VIII	45	Sepia	MM II	Cretan	Basalt grey	Amygdaloid	1.2, 1.6
VIII	43	Sepia	MM II	Cretan	Agate, white	Lentoid	2.0, 0.3
I	453	Sepia	LM IA	Cretan	Stone, red	Lentoid	1.5
I	455	Sepia	LM IA	Cretan	Sardonite	Rectangle	0.9, 1.0
I	454	Sepia	LM IA	Cretan	Jasper	Amygdaloid	1.9, 1.4
I	450	Sepia	LM IA	Cretan	Jasper	Amygdaloid	1.6, 2.1
I	451	Sepia	LM IA	Cretan	Cornelian	Amygdaloid	1.3, 1.1
I	452	Sepia	LM IA	Cretan	Cornelian	Amygdaloid	1.2, 1.8
VII	61	Sepia	MM IIIB	Cretan	Jasper, green	Amygdaloid	1.9., 1.4
VI	205	Sepia	EH/EL	Melos	Jasper	Amygdaloid	1.3, 1.8
VIII	51	Sepia	LM IA	Cretan	Jasper, greenish	Amygdaloid	1.9, 1.5
VII	50	Sepia	MM IIIB	Cretan	Cornelian	Amygdaloid	1.1, 1.4
VII	51	Sepia	MM IIIB	Siteia	Cornelian	Glandlar	1.7, 1.2

Table 5 continued.

CMS	No.	Motif	Date	Provenance	Material	Shape	Dimensions (cm)
VII	78	Sepia	MM IIIB	Cretan	Jasper, green	Amygdaloid	1.8, 1.2
VIII	54	Sepia	LM IA	Cretan	Jasper, greenish	Glandular	1.5, 1.7
VII	224	Sepia	LM IA-B	Cretan	Cornelian	Cylindrical, compressed	1.2, 0.9
VI	212	Sepia	LM IA-B	Cretan	Cornelian	Amygdaloid	2.0, 1.5
VIII	70	Sepia	LM IB	Cretan	Cornelian	Trihedral prism	1.6, 0.8
VI	300	Sepia	LM IIIA-B	Aptera, Chania, Cretan	Crystal	Amygdaloid	1.9, 1.3
VI	273	Sepia	LM IIIA-B	Armenoi, Cretan	Jasper, green	Amygdaloid	2.1, 1.3
IX	75	Sepia	LM IA	Cretan	Jasper, green	Amygdaloid	2.0, 1.6
IX	184	Sepia	LH	Cretan	Serpentine, Green-black	Lentoid	1.95
IX	76	Sepia	MM IIIB	Cretan	Cornelian	Lentoid	1.6
IX	77	Sepia	MM IIIB	Cretan	Sardonite	Amydaloid	2.0, 1.5
IX	78	Sepia	MM IIIB	Cretan	Jasper, green	Amygdaloid	1.8, 1.3
IX	79	Sepia	MM IIIB	Cretan	Jasper, green	Amygdaloid	1.6, 1.2
IX	80	Sepia	MM IIIB	Cretan	Jasper, green	Amygdaloid	1.8, 1.4
IX	81	Sepia	MM IIIB	Cretan	Agate, Veined, yellowish	Amygdaloid	2.0, 155
IX	90	Sepia	MM IIIB	Cretan	Sardonite	Trihedral prism	1.7, 1.1

TABLE 6. Copus sp - Toys

Game pieces of Conus sp.

Site	Date	No.	
Agh. Stephanos	MH II-LH I	2	
Prosymna		5	
Koukounaries, Paros	LH	2	
Agh. Triada Mesara	LH	8	
Dimini (tholos tomb)	LH	2	
Vromousa, Chalkida	LH I-IIIC	20	
Knossos	LM II-IIIC	19	
Prof. Ilias, Tiryns	LH II-IIIC	2	
Agora, Athens	LH IIIA		1
Argos	LH IIIA-IIIC	8	
Lefkandi	LH IIIC	28	
Perati	LH IIIB-IIIC	338	

Conus sp.

Site	Date	No.
Kitsos Cave, Attica		5
Paradeisos, Thrace	LN-Chalcolithic	1
Saliagos, Antiparos	LN	2
Agora, Athens (grave XXI)	LH IIIA	1 (together with gold and glass paste beads)
Thebes, room B, Oedipus St.	LH	3
Chalkida, Vromousa tomb	LH I-IIIC	20
Lefkandi, Euboea	LH IIIC	25
Askos, Thessaly	LH	2
Agh. Stephanos, Laconia	LH	2
Lerna, Argolid, settlement and graves	EH-LH	15
Unexplored Mansion, Knossos	LM II	16
Mycenae, Kalkani cemetery	LH	3
Mycenae, citadel	LH	33
Perati, Attica	LH II-IIIC	30
Tiryns, Prof. Ilias	LH II-III	2

Cone shells are found in excavations from the Neolithic to the Late Bronze Age. During the latter period in particular they had a variety of uses (ornaments, weights, game-pieces). Tables published so far do not refer to the uses of these objects, even though these can be determined. The uses of cone shells differ in each eriod and the superficial use of such tables leads to erroneous conclusions.

BIBLIOGRAPHY

The bibliography is divided into general and specialized topics (jewellery, representations, purple dye) and is completed by studies focused on geographical regions.

GENERAL TOPICS

SPECIALIST TOPICS
JEWELLERY
SYMBOLISM AND REPRESENTATIONS
PURPLE DYE

MACEDONIA - THRACE
THESSALY
PHOCIS - AETOLOACARNANIA
BOEOTIA
ATTICA
PELOPONNESE
AEGEAN ISLANDS (excepting the Cyclades)
CYCLADES
CRETE
 DODECANESE
IONIAN ISLANDS

Bibliography of sites not mentioned in the text
EASTERN MEDITERRANEAN
EGYPT
BALKANS
TROY AND ANATOLIA
ITALY - SPAIN - FRANCE
CYPRUS

GENERAL ITEMS

AGER D.V.
Palaeoecology. An introduction to the study of how and where animals and plants lived in the past, (London 1963) JAS.

AMANDRY P., TABORIN Y.
Coquilles. Partie II, Os et Coquilles, Chapitre IX, L'Antre Corycien II, Paris, BCH Supplement IX, (1984), 378-380.

ANDEL T.H. van, SHACKLETON J.C.
Late Paleolithic and Mesolithic coastlines of Greece and the Aegean, J.F.A., 19, (1982), 445-454.

ANGEL J.L.
Ecology and population in the Eastern Mediterranean, WA 4, (1972-3), 88-105.

BAIKIE J.
The Sea-kings of Crete, (London, 1913).

BALLEY G.N.
The role of molluscs in coastal economies. The results of midden-analysis in Australia, J.A.S. 2, (1975), 45-62.

BANCROFT E.
Experimental Researches Concerning the Philosophy of Permanent Colors, vol.1, (London 1974).

BASCH L.
Le musée imaginaire de la marine antique, Institut hellenique pour la preservation de la tradition nautique, (Athènes, 1987).

BERGER R. PROTSCH R.
The domestication of plants and animals in Europe and the Near East, Orientalia 42, (1973), 214-27.

BLUMMER H.
Technologie und Terminologie der Gewerbe und Kunste bei Griechen und Roemern, (Leipzig und Berlin, 1912).

BRADLEY R.
Trade completion and artefact distribution, W.A. 2 (1970-71), 347-52.

BRECHT G.A.
Testing of Materials as used for bone points of the upper Paleolithic. In Méthodologie appliquée l'industrie de l'os préhistorique Colloques Internationaux NRS no. 968, (Paris, 1977), 119-123

BRODRICK A.H. ed)
Animals in Archaeology, (London, 1972).

BROTHWELL D. and P.
Food in Antiquity. A survey of the diet of early people, (London, 1969).

BROTHWELL D., HIGGS E. ed)
Science in Archaeology, (London, 1969).

BUCHOLZ H.G., KARAGEORGHIS V.
Altagais und Altkypros, (Tübingen, 1971).

BUCHOLZ H.G., JOHRENS, G., MAULE, I.
"Jagd und Fischfang", Archaeologia Homerica, (Göttingen, 1973).

BURNEY C.B.M.
The Haua Fteah (Cyrenaica) and the Stone Age of the South - East Mediterranean, Cambridge University Press, (Cambridge, 1967).

BUTTLER W.
"Beiträge zur Frage des Jungsteinzeitlichen Handels", Sprockhoff ed, Marburger Studien (Darmstadt, L.C. Wittlich Verlag, 1938), 26-33.

BUTZER K.
Archaeology as Human Ecology: Method and Theory for a Contextual Approach, Cambridge University Press, (Cambridge 1983).

CALLEN E.
Diet as revealed by coprolites. In "Science in Archaeology", D. Brothwell and E. Higgs eds, (London, 1969), 235-44.

CAMPBELL A.C.
The Hamlyn Guide to the Seashore and Shallow Seas of Britain and Europe, (London, 1976).

CHILDE V.G.
The Danube in Prehistory, (London 1929).

CHILDE V.G.
The Dawn of European Civilization, (London, 1957).

CHILDE V.G.
What happened in History, (London, 1964).

CLARK J.C.D.
Prehistoric Europe, the Economic Basis, (London, 1952).

CLARK J.C.D.
The Stone Age Hunters, (London, 1969).

CLARK G.
Symbols of excellence. Precious materials as expressions of status, (Cambridge, 1986).

COMCA E.
Parures néolithiques en coquillages marins découvertes en territoire roumain, Dacia 17, (1973), 61-76.

CORNWALL J.W.
The world of Ancient Man, (London, 1964).

CORNWELL J.W.
Anthropology for Archaeologists, Cornell Univ. Press, (1981).

DALTON G.
Aboriginal Economies in Stateless Societies, Exchange Systems in Prehistory, T.K. Earle and Ericson eds., Academic Press, 1977, 191.

DARQUES P., POURSAT CL. (ed.)
L'iconographie minoenne, Actes de la Table ronde d'Athènes, (Paris, 1981).

DAVIDSON A.
Mediterranean Seafood, (London, 1972).

DAVIDSON D.A., SHACKLEY M.,
Geoarchaeology: Earth Science and the Past, (London, 1976).

DEITH M.R.
Seasonality from Shells: An Evaluation of Two Techniques for Seasonal Dating of Marine Molluscs, in Fieller N.R.J., Gillbertson D.D. and Ralph N.G.A. (eds.), Paleobiological Investigations: Research Design, Methods and Data Analysis, British Archaeological Reports International Series 266, (Oxford 1985), 119-130.

DEITH M.R., SHACKLETON J.C.
The contribution of shells to site interpetation: approaches to shell material from Franchthi Cave, in BINTLIFF J.L., DAVIDSON D.D., et al., Conceptual Issues in Environmental Archaeology, Edinburgh Univ. Press, (1988).

DELVOYE C.
Remarques sur la seconde civilisation néolithique du continent grec et des îles avoisinantes, BCH 73, (1949), 29.

DESHAYES J.
Dikili Tash et les problèmes du Néolithique et du Bronze Ancien en Macedoine, RA (1970), p. 161-192.

DOLLFUS M.A.
Les mollusques terrestres, Bull. Soc. Ant de France, (1978), 30-39.

DOUMAS C.
Thera: Pompeii of Ancient Aegean, (London, 1983).

EBERT M.
Reallexicon der Vorgeschichte vol.10, (Berlin, 1927-28).

EHRICH R.W. (ed.)
Chronologies in Old World Archaeology, (Chicago, 1965).

EVANS J.G.
Land Snails in Archaeology, (New York, 1973).

ΦΑΛΑΡΑ Π..
Ψάρια και ψαρέματα, (Piraeus, 1990).

FISCHER P.
Rôle des coquillages dans les premières civilisations humaines, Journal de Conchyologie 89, (1949), 82-157.

FLAMAND G.B.M.
Sur l'utilisation comme instruments néolithiques des coquillages fossils a taille intentionelle, XIXL Congres A.F.A.S.), (Ajaccio, 1901-1902).

FORBES E.
Reports on the Molusca and Radiata of the Aegean Sea and their distribution considered as bearing on Geology, British Association for the Advancement of Science, Report 13, (1843), 130-193.

FORBES M.H.C.
Farming and foraging in prehistoric Greece: a cultural ecological perspective, in DIMEN, Muriel & FRIEDL, Ernestine (eds), Regional Variations in Modern Greece and Cyprus: toward a perspective on the ethnography of Greece, Annals of the New York Academy of Science, (New York 1976), 268.

FURNESS A.
Some early pottery of Samos, Kalimnos, and Chios PPS 22, (1956), 173-212.

FORSYTH W.S.
Inshore Sea Fishing, (London, 1949).

GIMBUTAS M.
Bronze Age Cultures in Central and Eastern Europe, (Hague, 1965).

GLOTZ G.
"The Aegean civilisation" in the History of civilisation, (New York 1925).

HANSEN H.
Early civilisation in Thessaly, The Johns Hopkins Univ. Studies in Archaeology, no.15, (Baltimore, 1971).

HEURTLEY W.A.
Prehistoric Macedonia: An archaeological reconnaissance of Greek Macedonia west of the Struma) in the Neolithic, Bronze and Early Iron Age, (Cambridge, 1939).

HIGGS E.S., VITA-FINZI C.
The Climate, environment and industries of Stone Age Greece: Part II, PPS 32, (1966), 1-29.

HIGGS E.S., VITA-FINZI C., HARRIS D.R. and FAGG A.E.
The Climate, environment and industries of Stone Age Greece: Part III, P.P.S. 33, (1967), 1-29.

HIGGS E.S. (ed.)
Papers in Economic Prehistory. Studies by members and associates of the British Academy. Major research project in the Early History of Agriculture, (Cambridge University Press, 1972).

HIGGS E.S. et WEBLEY D.
Further information concerning the Environment of Palaeolithic Man in Epirus, P.P.S. 37, 2, (1971), 367-380.

HIGGS E. (ed.)
Palaeoeconomy, (Cambridge, 1975).

HUTCHINSON R.W.
Prehistoric Greece , (London, 1962).

KARALI L.
L'utilisation des mollusques dans la Protohistoire de l'Égée, doctoral thesis, (1979).

ΚΑΡΑΛΗ Λ.
Η αρχαιολογία και η μελέτη των θαλασσινών οστρέων, Αρχαιολογία 19, 1986), 57-59.

KARALI L.
Εισαγωγή στην Περιβαλλοντική Αρχαιολογία, Πανεπιστημιακές Σημειώσεις, (Αθήνα, 1990).

KARALI L.
Sources of Ivory in the Aegean Bronze Age: An environmental Approach, in L. Fitton (ed.), Ivory in Greece and the Eastern Mediterranean from the Bronze Age to the Hellenistic Period, British Museum Occasional Paper 85, British Museum, (London, 1992), 57-60.

ΚΑΡΑΛΗ Λ.
Αγγλο-Ελληνικό Λεξικό Αρχαιολογικών-Περιβαλλοντικών όρων, (Αθήνα, 1993).

KARALI L.
La contribution de la recherche environmentale à la reconstitution des premiers centres urbains en Europe Sud - Est, VII Semaines philippopolitaines (forthcoming).

KARALI L.
Uses of sea-shells in Mycenaean Greece, Anthropologika Analekta (forthcoming).

KENNA V.E.G.
Cretan Seals. With a catalogue of the Minoan Gems in the Ashmolean Museum, (Oxford, 1960).

KENNA V.E.G.
C.M.S. Band VIII, Die englischen Privatsammlungen, (Berlin, 1966).

KENNA V.E.G.
C.M.S., Band VII, Die Englischen Museen II, (Berlin, 1967).

KENNA V.E.G.
Corpus der Minoischen und Mykenischen Siegel, XII, Nordamerika I, New York, The Metropolitan Museum of Art, (Berlin, 972).

KENNA V.E.G. et THOMAS E.
C.M.S., Band XIII: Nordamerica II, (Berlin, 1974).

KOIKE H.
Seasonal dating and valve-pairing technique in shell-midden analysis. J.A.S., (1979), 63-74.

KOSMOPOULOS-WALKER L.
The Prehistoric Inhabitation of Corinth I, (Munich, 1948).

KOURTESSI-PHILIPPAKIS G.
Le Paleolithique de la Grèce continentale, (Paris, 1986).

KRZYSZKOWSKA O.
Ivory, and related materials, Bull. Suppl. 59, (London, 1990).

KUTZBACH J.E.
Climate of the Early Holocene: climate experiment with the Earth's orbital parameters from 9000 years ago, Science 214, (1981), 59-61.

LAMBERT N.
Perles en coquille d'Arca senilis dans le Neolithique de Mauritanie occidentale, Bulletin de l'I.F.A.N. 30, 1968), 1322-1328.

LEROI-GOUHRAN A.
L'homme et la matiere, (Paris, 1943).

LEVI D.
Abitazioni prehistoriche sulle pendici meridionali dell'Acropoli, A.S.A.A. 13-14, (1930-31), 411-498.

LABADOR F.
Sur l'utilisation et la valeur des Cawris: "Pustularia Monetaria Moneta" (Linée 1758), dans les transactions commerciales africaines, Journal de Conchyliologie, CIX, (no.1) (1971), 5-14.

LOZEK V.
Beiträge des Molluskenforschung zur prähistorischen Archäologie Mitteleuropas, Zeitschrift für Archäologie 1, (1967), 88-138.

NANDRIS J.
The development and relationships of the earlier Greek Neolithic, Journal of the Royal Anthropological Institute 5, (1970), 192-213.

ΜΑΡΑΓΚΟΥ Λ.
Κυκλαδικός Πολιτισμός, Η Νάξος στην τρίτη χιλιετία π.Χ., (Athens, 1990).

MARIANI L.
Antichità Cretesi, Mon. Ant., 6, (1895), 154-347.

MATZ Fr.
Der Kretisch-Mykenische Bild Komposition, Jabruch des D.A.I.T., 38-39, 2e v., (1923-29), 294.

MEEHAN B.
Shell bed to shell midden, Australian Institute of Aboriginal studies, (Canberra, 1982).

MEIGHAN W.A. et al.
Ecological interpretation in Archaeology, Part I., Amer. Antiq., 24, (1958), 1-23.

MELVILL J.C.
A survey of the Genus Cypraea, Man. Mem., I, (1887-1888), 184-252.

MICHAEL H.N., RALPH K.E.
Dating Techniques for the Archaeologist, The Massachusetts Institute of Technology, (1971).

MILOJCIC V.
Chronologie der Jüngeren Steinzeit Mittel- und Südosteuropas, Verlag Gebr. Mann., (Berlin, 1949).

MILOJCIC V.
Präkeramishces Neolithicum auf der Balkanhalbinsel, Germania 38, (1960), 320-25.

ΜΥΛΩΝΑΣ Γ..
Η Νεολιθική Εποχή εν Ελλάδι, Βιβλιοθήκη της εν Αθήναις Αρχαιολογικής Εταιρείας, No. 24, (Athens, 1928).

MONTELIUS O.
La Crèce preclassique, (Stockholm, 1924 and 1928).

MOSSO A.
The dawn of Mediterranean civilization, T.Fischer Unwin, (London, 1910).

MOUNTJOY P.A.
The marine style pottery of LMIB/LHIIA, B.S.A., 79, (1984).

NANDRIS J.
The development and relationships of the Earlier Greek Neolithic, Journal of the Royal Anthropological Institute 5, (1970), 192-213.

NARR K. (ed.)
Handbuch der Urgeschichte I, Ältere und Mittlere Steinzeit, Jäger und Sammlerkulturen, (Bern und München, 1966).

NATIONAL BANK OF GREECE (ed.)
Neolithic Greece, (Athens, 1973).

NILSSON M.
Minoan Mycenean Religion, Zweite Auflage, (Lund, 1950).

ONTPIA XP.
Γενική Ζωολογία, Εκδόσεις Συμμετρία, τ. 2, (Athens, 1987).

OULIE M.
Les animaux dans la peinture de la Crète préhellenique, (Paris, 1925).

ΠΑΝΤΕΛΙΔΟΥ Μ.
Αι Προϊστορικαί Αθήναι, (Athens, 1975).

ΠΑΝΤΕΛΙΔΟΥ Μ.
Η Νεολιθική Νέα Μάκρη, Τα Οικοδομικά, (Αθήνα, 1991), 16, 179.

PAPATHANASSOPOULOS G. (ed)
Neolithic Culture in Greece, Museum of Cycladic Art, N. P. Goulandris ed, (Athens, 1996).

PAULY G.- WISSOVA A.F.
Real Encyclopaedie des Klassischen Altertums, 2nd series Part 3, (Stuttgart, 1921).

PERKINGS A., WEINBERG S.S.
Connections of the Greek Neolithic and the Near East, AJA 62, (1958), 225.

PENDLEBURY J.D.S.
The Archaeology of Crete. An Introduction. Methuen, (London, 1939).

PERSSON AXEL W.
The Royal Tombs at Dendra near Midea, (Lund, 1931).

PHILIPPSON A.
Das Mittelmeergebiet; seine geographische und Kulturelle Eigenart, (Leipzig, 1904).

PIETTE E.
Études d'ethnographie préhistorique, (Paris, 1948).

PINI I.
Beiträge zur Minoischen Gräberkunde, Steiner, (Wiesbaben, 1968).

PINI I.
Iraklion. Archaeologisches Museum, Teil. 5, Die Siegelabdrücke von Phastos, (Berlin, C.M.S., II 5, 1970).

PINI I., CASKEY J.L., CASKEY M., PELON O., HEATH WIENCKE M., YOUNGER J.G.
Kleinere Griechische Sammlungen, C.M.S., Band V., Teil 1., (Berlin, 1975).

PINI I., CASKEY J.L., CASKEY M., PELON O., HEATH WIENCKE M., YOUNGER J.G.
Kleinere Griechische Sammlungen, C.M.S., Band V., Teil 2., (Berlin, 1975).

PHILIPPSON A.
Das Mittelmeergebiet; Seine geographische und Kulturelle Eigenart, (Leipzig, 1904).

POPLIN F.
À propos du nombre de restes et du nombre d'individus dans les echantillons d'ossements, Cahiers du Centre de Recherches Préhistoriques, Univ. Paris I, U.E.R. Art et Archéologie, 5, (1976), 61-74.

POWELL J.
Fishing in the Prehistoric Aegean, Studies in Mediterranean Archaeology and Literature, Pocket-Book 137, (Jonsered, 1996).

PRITCHARD J.B.
Recovering Sarepta, A Phoenician City, Princeton University Press, (1978), 126-127.

REESE D.S.
Finfish and Shellfish in Mediterranean Archaeology, in Old World Archaeology Newsletter 5/2, (Middletown, Conn., 1981), 8-10.

REESE D.S.
Marine Shells in the Levant: Upper Paleolithic, Epipaleolithic and Neolithic, in O. Bar-Yosef and F. R. Valla, eds., The Natufian Culture in the Levant, Archaeological Series 1. Ann Arbor: International Monographs in Prehistory, (1991), 613-628.

REESE D.S.
The Trade of Indo-Pacific Shells into the Mediterranean Basin and Europe, in Oxford Journal of Archaeology, 10/2, (1991), 159-196.

RENFREW C.
The Art of the First Farmers, (Sheffield, 1969a).

RENFREW C.
The Emergence of Civilisation. The Cyclades and the Aegean in the Third Millenium B.C. Methuen, (London, 1972).

RENFREW C.
"Trade and Craft Specialization" In D.R. Theocharis, Neolithic Greece, (1973), 179-91.

RENFREW C.
The Tree-Ring Calibration of Radiocarbon: An Archaeological Evaluation, in Problems in European Prehistory, Edinburgh Univ. Press, (1979), 338-66.

RENFREW C.
Archaeology: Theories, Methods and Practice, Thames and Hudson, (London, 1991).

REY L.
Observations sur les premiers habitats de la Macedoine, (Paris, 1921).

SAUL M.
Shells. Country Life, (London, 1974).

SCHACHERMEYER F.
Die Abfolge der neolitischen Kulturen in Griechenland, (Athens, 1953), 89-104.

SCHACHERMEYER F.
Prähistorische Kulturen Griechenlands, Real-Encyclopadie 22, 2, vol. 1351, (1954).

SCHACHERMEYER F.
Die altesten Kulturen Griechenlands, (Stuttgart, 1955).

SCHACHERMEYER F.
Das aegäische Neolithikum, Studies in Mediterranean Archaeology, 6, (Lund, 1964).

SCHACHERMEYER F., BUCHOLZ H., ALEXIOU S. and HAUPTMANN H.
Forschungsbericht über die Ausgrabungen und Neufunde zur aegäischen Frühzeit, AA 1971, (1961-65), 81.

SCHACHERMEYER F.
Die Agaische Fruhzeit. Wien, Verlag der Osterreichischen Academie der Wissenschaffen, (Wien, 1976).

SCHACKLETON N. and RENFREW C.
Neolithic Trade Routes re-aligned by Oxygen Isotope Analyses, Nature vol. 228, no. 5276, 12.12. (1970), 1062-1065.

SCHUETZENBERGER M.P.
Die Farbstoffe. 2 vols., (Berlin, 1869-70).

SCHWARTZ J.H.
The palaeozoology of Cyprus: a preliminary report on recently analysed sites, WA 5, (1973-74), 215-220.

SHACKLEY M.
Using Environmental Archaeology, (London, 1985).

STAMPFUSS R.
Die ersten altsteinzeitlichen Hohlenfunde in Griechenland, Mannus 34, (1942), 132.

STANLEY D.J. (ed.)
The Mediterranean Sea: A natural sedimentation laboratory, Dowden, Hutchinson and Ross, Inc. Stroudsburg, Pensylvania, (1972).

ΣΥΡΙΟΠΟΥΛΟΣ Κ.
Η προϊστορία της Πελοποννήσου, Βιβλιοθηκη σης εν Αθηναις Αρχαιολ εσσιριας νο 51 (Αθήνα, 1964).

ΣΥΡΙΟΠΟΥΛΟΣ Κ.
Η προϊστορία της Στερεάς Ελλάδας, Βιβλιοθηκη σης εν Αθηναις Αρχαιολ εσσιριας νο 61 (Αθήνα, 1968).

THIMME J.
Art and Culture of the Cyclades, (Chicago, 1977).

THOMAS K.P.
Prehistoric Coastal Ecologies. A view from outside Franchthi Cave, Greece, Geoarchaeology, vol.2, no. 3, (1987).

TREUIL R.
Le Néolithique et le Bronze Ancien Égéen, (Paris, 1983).

TRINGHAM R.
Hunters, Fishers and Farmers of Eastern Europe, 6000-3000 BC., Hutchinson Univ. Library, (London, 1971).

UCKO P.J. et DIMBLEY G.W. (ed.)
The Domestication and Exploitation of Plants and Animals, (London, 1969).

VAN EFFENTERRE H. und N.
Corpus der Minoischen und Mykenischen Siegel IX, Paris, Cabinet des Medailles, (Berlin, 1972).

VERMEUELE E.
Greece in the Bronze Age, (Chicago, 1964).

VICHERY K.F.
Food in Early Greece. Illinois Studies in the Social Sciences XX, no. 3, (1936), 89.

WARREN P.
Minoan Stone Vases, Univ. Press, (Cambridge, 1969).

WAUGH G.D.
(Simposium on): Edible Molluscs. The ecology and mode of life of the edible molluscs, Proc. Malacol. Soc., 34, (1960), 113-156.

WEINBERG S.S.
Aegean Chronology: Neolithic Period and Early Bronze Age, AJA 55, (1965), 121.

WEINBERG S.S.
The relative chronology of the Aegean in the Stone and Early Bronze Age, Dans Ehrich, (1965).

WEINBERG S.S.
The Stone Age in the Aegean, (Cambridge Ancient History I, 1 Chap. X) 3e ed., (1970), 557.

WRIGHT H.G.
Palaeocology, Climatic Change and Aegean Prehistory, N.C. Wilkie and W.D.E. Coulson (ed.), contributions on Aegean Archaeology, Center for Ancient Studies, University of Minnesota, 1985, 183.

ZERVOS Chr.
L'art de la Crète néolithique et minoenne, (Paris, 1959).

ZERVOS C.
L'art des Cyclades, (Paris, 1957).

ZERVOS Chr.
Naissance de la civilisation en Grèce, Vol. I-II, (Paris, 1962/1963).

ZOIS A.
Κρήτη εποχή του Λίθου. Athens center of Ekistiky, Ancient Greek cities 18, 1973).

SPECIAL ITEMS

Ornaments

ANSELL A.D.
Observations on predation of Venus striatula (da Costa) by Natica Alderi Forbes), Proc. Malac. Soc., 34, (1960), 157-64.

COMCA E.
Parures néolithiques en coquillages marins découvertes en territoire roumain, Dacia 17, (1973), 61-76.

FLINDERS PETRIE W.M.
Amulets. Illustrated by the Egyptian collection in University College, (London, 1914).

JACKSON J.
The use of cowry-shells for the purposes of currency, amulets and charms, Manchester, vol. 60, part III, no. 13, (1915-16), 72.

KARALI L.
Parure en coquillage du Site de Dimitra en Macedoine protohistorique, in R. Laffineur and L. Basch (ed.), Thalassa, L'Égée Préhistorique et la Mer (Aegaeum 7), Université de Liège, (Liège, 1991a), 315-322.

ΚΑΡΑΛΗ Λ.
Βραχιόλια από Σπόνδυλο, Ανθρωπολογικά Ανάλεκτα 50/2, Β' Ανθρωπολογικό Συμπόσιο, Αθήνα, Δεκέμβριος 1987, 1992α), 57-61.

KARALI L.
La Parure en coquillage en région méditerranéenne, Αρχαιογνωσία 7, (Αθήνα, 1993), 41-64.

ΚΑΡΑΛΗ Λ.
Κοσμήματα της Νεολιθικής εποχής από οστό, όστρεο και λίθο, Neolithic Culture in Greece, Museum of Cycladic Art, N.P. Goulandris Foundation, Greek and English ed., (Athens, 1996), 165-166, 335-338.

LAMBERT N.
Perles en coquille d'Arca senilis dans le néolithique de Mauritanie occidentale, Bulletin de l'I.F.A.N. 30, (1968), 1322-1328.

ΠΑΠΠΑ, Μ, Νεολιθική εγκατάσταση στο χώρο της Αιεθνοίο εηθεσης Θεσσαλονικης, ΑΕΜΘ 7, (1993), 304-305.

PAVUK J.
Discussion of the diffusion of Spondylus shells in neolithic Europe: Vencl., Sl., Arch. Rozh, 11: 6, (1959), 699-742.

RADUNTSCHEVA A.
Sur certaines espèces d'amulettes de l'enéolithique; (Archaeologia Sofia) 13, 3, (1971), 52-57.

REESE D.S.
The use of Cone shells in Neolithic and Bronze Age Greece BSA 78, (1983), 353-7.

REESE D.S.
Topshell Rings in the Aegean Bronze Age BSA 79, (1984), 237-8.

REESE D.S.
On Cassid Lips and Helmet Shells, Bulletin of the American School of Oriental Research 275, (1989), 33-39.

REESE D.S.
The Archaeological Usage of Nassariid Shells in the Mediterranean Basin, The Journal of Mediterranean Anthropology and Archaeology, (forthcoming).

RODDEN R.J.
The spondylus-shell trade and the beginnings of the Vinča culture J. Filip, ed. Actes du VIII Congres International des

Sciences Préhistoriques et Protohistoriques I, Institut d'Archéologie, (Prague, 1970), 411-413.

SARGNON O.
Les bijoux Préhelleniques, Bibliothèque archéologique et historique Vol. CVIII, (Paris, 1987).

SHACKLETON N.J.
"Spondylus Artifacts in Neolithic Europe: An Overview" AJA 88, (1984), 259.

TSUNEKI A.
A reconsideration of spondylus shell rings from Agia Sofia, Magoula, Greece, Bull of Ancient Orient Museum IX, (1987), 1-15.

TSUNEKI A.
The manufacture of Spondylus shell objects at Neolithic Dimini, Greece, Orient XXV, (1989), 1-21.

VIALOU D.
La parure, in Lambert N. (ed.), La grotte Préhistorique de Kitsos (Attique), Recherches sur les grandes civilizations 7, vol. 1, (1981), 391-419.

WILLMS Ch.
Neolithisches Spondylusschmuck, Hundert Jahre Forschung, Germania 63, (1985), 331.

Symbolism and representations

DARQUE P.
Les coquillages en Pierre en terre et en faience dans le Monde Égéen, Appendix dans C. Baurain and P. Darcque, Un triton en pierre a Malia, BCH CVII (1983), 132-138.

DETOURNAY B.
Figurines (Chapitre IVA) in B. Detournay J.C. Poursat and F. Vandenabeele, Le Quartier Mu II, Études Crètoises XXVI, (Paris, 1980).

KARALI L.
Marine Invertebrates and Minoan Art, in D. Reese ed., Pleistocene and Holocene Fauna of Crete and its First Settlers, Prehistory Press, (1996), 413-419.

FURUMARK A.
The Mycenaean Pottery: Analysis and Classification, (Stockholm, 1940-41).

GABLE E.
Formation processes and the animal bones from the Sanctuary of Phylakopi in C. Renfrew (ed.), The Archaeology of Cult, The Sanctuary at Phylakopi, BSA Suppl. vol. 18, 479-482.

GOBERT E.
Le Pudendum magique et le problème des Cawris, Revue-Africaine, 15, (1951), 5-62.

HAGG R.-MARINATOS N.
Sanctuaries and cults in the Aegean Bronze Age Athens, Swedish Institute, (Athens, 1980-1981).

HALSTEAD P.H. and JONES G.
Animal bones and burial customs in Early Iron Age Thassos, The Faunal remains from the cemeteries of Kastri settlement, Appendix II, in Koukouli-Chrysanthaki, Prehistoric Thasos, (Theologos, 1992), 753-756.

JOLEAUD L.
Rôle magique et monetaire des coquilles de dentales fossiles et actuelles dans les temps préhistoriques et modernes, Revue Scientifique 74, (1935), 495-500.

MATZ Fr.
Der Kretische Mykenische Bild Komposition, Jahrbuch des D.A.I.T., 2e, (1923-29), 38-39.

MOUNTJOY P.A.
Late Minoan IB pottery: the Marine style, PhD, (London, 1973).

MUHLY P.
Fauna from the Poros Tomb, (Athens, 1992).

NILISON M.
Minoan Mycenean Religion, (Lund, 1950).

PICARD CH.
Les religions préhelleniques, Crète et Mycènes, (Paris, 1948).

REESE D.S.
Faunal remains from the Altar of Aphrodite Ourania, in Hesperia 58 (1), (1990), 63-70.

REESE D.S.
Strange and Wonderful: Exotic Fauna Remains from Sanctuary Sites, Newsletter of the American School of Classical Studies at Athens, fall, 13, (1984).

REESE D.S. ASTROM P.
"Triton Shells from East Mediterranean Sanctuaries and Graves", in Astrom P. and Reese D.S., "Triton Shells in East Mediterranean Cults", Journal of Prehistoric Religion III, IV, (1990), 7-14.

RENFREW C.
Approaches to Social Archaeology, (London, 1984).

RUTKOWSKI B.
The Cult Places of the Aegean, (New Haven, 1986).

SAKELLARAKIS I.A.
Le thème du pecheur dans l'art préhistorique de l'Égée, AAA, (1974), 370-390.

SAKELLARIOU A.
Die Minoischen und Mykenischen Siegel des National Museums in Athen, C.M.S. I, (Berlin, 1964).

UCKO P.J.
Anthropomorphic Figurines of Predynastic Egypt and Neolithic Crete with comparative material from the Prehistoric Near East and Mainland Greece. London Royal

Anthropological Institute, Occasional paper no. 24, (London, 1968).

WACE A.J.B. and BLEGEN C.W.
The Pre-Mycenean Pottery of the Mainland, BSA, 22, (1916-1918), 175-189.

Purple

ALOUPI E., MANIATIS Y., PAPADELIS T. and KARALI L.
Analysis of Purple Material Found in Akrotiri, In Hardy D.A., Doumas C.G., Sakellarakis S.A., Warren P.M. (eds.), (1990), 488-490.

BARKER J.T.
Tyrinian purple: "an ancient dye, a modern problem", Endeavor, vol. 33 no. 118, (1974), 11-17.

BERTHOLLET C.L., A.B.
Elements of the Art of Dyeing, (London, 1824).

BISCHOFF J.N.
Versuch einer Geschichte der Färbekunst, (Stendal, 1780).

BONNET A., JULLIEN A.
Toxicité comparée des extraits de la glande a pourpre chez Murex trunculus et Murex brandaris, Compt. Rend. Soc. Biol. Lyon, vol. 135, (1941), 958-60.

BOUCHILLOUX S., ROCHE J.
Sur la pourpre des Murex trunculus et ses precurseurs, compt. rend. soc. biol. Lyon, vol. 148, (1954a), 1583-87.

BOUCHILLOUX S., ROCHE J.
Sur les prochromogenes et les pigments purpuriques de Murex trunculus Linne, compt. rend. soc. biol. Lyon, vol. 148, (1954), 1732-34.

BOUCHILLOUX S., ROCHE J.
Contribution a l'étude biochimique de la Pourpre des Murex, Bull. Inst. Oceanogr. Monaco, no. 1054, (1955), 1-23.

BRUEHL L.
Die Rohstoffe des Tierreichs, vol. 2, Lief. 2, (Berlin, 1929), 358-79.

BRUIN F.
Royal purple and the dye industry of the Mycenaeans and Phoenicians. Societés et Compagnies de commerce en Orient dans l'ocean Indien, in Mollat M. (ed.), Actes du 8e colloque international d'histoire maritime, Bibliothèque Generale de l'École Pratique des Hautes Etudes, VI Section, Beyrouth, Septembre, (1966), 73-90.

BRUNEAU Ph.
Documents sur l'industrie delienne de la pourpre, BCH, (1969), p. 759-91, (1978) vol. 102, p. 110, (1979), vol. 103, p. 83.

BRUNELLO F.
The art of dyeing in the history of mankind, Neri Pozza, (Vincenza, 1973).

BUCHLER A.
Dyeing among primitive people, Ciba Review, vol. 68, (1948).

CARDOT H. and JULLIEN A.
Action de la pourpre sur l'excitabilité du nerf et du muscle, compt., rend., soc. biol. Lyon, vol. 129, (1940), 521-23.

COLE W.
Purpura Anglicana, being a discovery of a fish found on the shores of the Severn, which gives a curious purple, Phil. Trans., London, vol. 15, (1685), 1278.

COLDSTREAM J.N. and HUXLEY G.L.
Kythera, Faber and Faber Limited, (London, 1972).

COLONNA F.
De Purpura Rome, Kiel, 1616).

DEDEKIND A.
Ein Beitrag zur Purpurkunde, (Berlin, 1898-1911).

De NEGRI A. and De NEGRI G.
Della Materia colorante dei Muricia della porpora degli antichi, Gazz. Chim. Ital., (1875), 437.

DERRIEN E.
L'odeur de la pourpre, Bull. Acad. Sc. et Lettres, Montpellier, (1911), 168-190.

DRIESSEN L.A.
Über eine charackteristische Reaktion des antiken Purpurs auf der Faser, Melliand Textilber, vol. 25, (1944), 66.

EDEY, MAITLAND A. et al
The Sea Traders, The Royal Purple and how it was manufactured, (New York, 1974), 61.

ETTINGER L., FRIEDLAENDER P.
Über 6.6-Dibromindirubin, Ber. Deutsch Chem. Ges., vol. 45, (1912), 2081.

FAYMONVILLE K.
Die Purpurfärberei der verschiedenen Kulturvölker des klassischen Altertums, (Heidelberg, 1900).

FISCHER P.H.
Sur le rôle de la glande purputigens des Murex et des Pourpres, Compt. Rend. Acad. Sci., vol. 180, (Paris, 1925), 1369-71.

FORBES E.
Zur Kenntnis des Farbstoffs des antiken Purpures aus Murex brandaris, Monatsch. für Chemie, vol. 29, (1907), 991-96.

FORBES E.
Über den Farbstoff des antiken Purpures aus Murex brandaris, Ber. Otsch. Chem. Ges., vol. 42, (1909), 765-770.

FORBES E., BRUCHNER S., DEUTSCH G.
Über die Farbstoffe aus Purpura aperta und Purpura lapillus, Ber. Otsch. Chem. Ges., vol. 55, (1956).

FORBES R.J.
Studies in Ancient Technology, vol. 4, (1964), 114-122.

FRIEDLANDER P.
Über Schwefelhaltige Analoga der Indigogruppe, Ber. Otsch. Chem. Ges., vol. 39, (1906), 1060-1066.

GATTEFOSSE J.
La pourpre getule, Hesperis, vol. 44, (1957), 329-34.

HEINISCH H.E.
Ancient Purple, a historical survey, Fibre. Engin. Chem., vol. 18, no. 6, (1957), 203-6.

JACKSON J.W.
The geographical distribution of the shell-purple industry, Memoirs Manchester Phil. Soc. vol. LX, part. 2, no.7, (1916).

JACKSON J.W.
Shells as Evidence of the Migrations of Early Culture, Longmans, Green and Co., Manchester and (New York, 1917).

JENSEN, LLOYD B.
"Royal purple of Tyre" Journal of Near Eastern Studies, Vol. 22, (Chicago, 1963), 104-118.

JIDEJIAN N.
Tyre through the ages, Dar el-Mashrea Publ., (Beirut, 1969).

JULLIEN A.
Variations dans le temps de la teneur des extraits de glande a pourpre en substance active sur le muscle de sangsue, compt. rend. soc. biol. Lyon, vol. 129, (1940), 524-527.

JULLIEN A., BONNET D.
Toxicité de la pourpre en rapport avec la presence des substances à action stimulante sur le muscle de sangsue, compt. rend. Acad. Sc., Paris, vol. 212, (1941), 932-34.

JULLIEN A., GARABEDIAN M.D., GIBAULT R.
Observations relatives aux proprietés pharmacologiques des constituants de la pourpre chez Murex trunculus, compt. rend. soc. biol. Lyon, vol. 227, (1941),1636-1639.

JULLIEN A., RIPPLINGER J.
L'extrait dessèche de glande a pourpre de Murex trunculus et son action biologique, Bull. Soc. Hist. Nat. Doubs., No 52, (1949), 29-30.

JULLIEN A.
Recherches sur les constituants et les proprietés de la pourpre. Ann. Sc. de Franche-Compte., vol.1, (1964).

ΚΑΡΑΛΗ Λ.
Πορφύρα: Μια πολύτιμη Χρωστική της Αρχαιότητας, Ανθρωπολογικά Ανάλεκτα 49, (1988), 41-43.

ΚΑΡΑΛΗ Λ.
Η Ιστορική και Αρχαιολογική μαρτυρία για την Πορφύρα, (forthcoming).

ΚΑΡΔΑΡΑ Χρ.
Βαφή, βαφεία και βαφαί κατά την αρχαιότητα, Hesperia 43, (1974), 447-453.

KIRKSTEAD S.P.
Natural Dyes, (Boston, 1950).

KNECHT E., RAWSON C. and LOWENTHAL R.
A Manual of Dyeing, (London, 1893).

LEDERER E.
Biochemistry of natural pigments, Ann. Rev. Biochem., vol. 17, (1948), 495.

LEGGETT W.F.
Ancient and Medieval Dyes, Chemical Publishing Company, Brooklyn, (1944), 56-60, 64-69.

LETELLIER A.
Recherches sur la pourpre produite par le Purpura lapillus, Compt. Rend. Acad. Sc., vol. 109, (Paris, 1889), 82-85.

LISON L.
Études histochimiques sur la glande a pourpre des Murex, Journ. de Physiol. et pathol. gener., vol. 31, (1933), 82-99.

LUCAGE-DUTHIERS H.
Mémoire sur la Pourpre, Annales des Sciences Naturelles (Zool.), (Paris, 1859), 5-84.

ΜΟΑΤΣΟΥ Π.Γ.
Πορφύρα, (Αλεξάνδρεια, 1932).

MOORE H.B.
The biology of Purpura lapillus, Journal of the Marine Biological Association, vol. XXI, (1936), 61-89, vol. XXIII, (1939), 57-74.

MUHLY J.
Homer and the Phoenicians, Berytus, vol. 19, (1970), 19-64.

PRATT I.
The Chemistry and Physics of Organic Pigments, (New York, 1947).

PRITCHARD J.B.
Recovering Sarepta. A Phoenician City, Princeton University Press, (Princeton, 1978), 126-127.

RAWLINSON G.
History of Phoenicia, (London, 1889).

REESE D.S.
Industrial Exploitation of Murex shells: Purple-dye and Lime Production at Sidi Khrebish, Benghazi Berenice), Libyan Studies, (London, 1980), 79-93.

REESE D.S.
Faunal Remains from the Kommos Temples, Crete, AJA 88/2, (1984), 257.

REESE D.S.
The Mediterranean Shell Purple-dye Industry, in American Journal of Archaeology 90/2, (1986), 183.

REESE D.S.
Palaikastro Shells and Bronze Age Purple-dye Production in the Mediterranean Basin, BSA 82, (1987), 201-206.

REINHOLD M.
History of Purple as a status symbol in Antiquity, Latomus, (1970), 1-16.

SALTZMAN M., KEAY A.M., CHRISTENSEN J.
The identification of Colorants in Ancient Textiles, Dyestuffs, vol.4, (1963), 241-250.

STIEGLITZ R.R.
The Minoan Origin of Tyrian Purple, Biblical Archaeologist 57/1, (1994), 46-54.

Attika

CHEVALLIER H.
Les Mollusques Part IV, La Grotte de Kitsos Lauvrion, BCH XCVII, (1973), 443-59.

CHEVALLIER H.
Les Mollusques du gisement Préhistorique de Kitsos (Attique), Lambert N. (ed.), La grotte Préhistorique de Kitsos (Attique) II, Recherche sur les grandes civilizations 7, (Paris, 1981), 611-32.

HAUSSOULLIER B.
Spata, BCH II, (1878), 185-221.

ΙΑΚΩΒΙΔΗΣ Σ.Ε.
Περατή το νεκροταφείον, Βιβλιοθήκη της εν Αθήναις Αρχαιολογικής Εταιρείας, (Αθήνα, 1970).

KARALI L.
Sea shells from a Mycenean Well in the Athenian Agora, (forthcoming).

MYLONAS G.E.
Aghios Kosmas, An Early Bronze Age Settlement and Cemetery in Attica, Princeton University Press, (Princeton, 1959), 121-137, 191.

PAPADIMITRIOU T.
La grotte de Pan, BCH, 83, (1959), 587-89.

RALLI-TZELEPI Z.N.
Contribution a l'étude conchyliologique du littoral de l'Attique, (Athènes, 1946).

THEOCHARIS D.R.
Nea Makri eine grosse neolithische Siedlung in der Nahe von Marathon, AM 71, (1956).

WELTER G.
Aigina, (Berlin, 1938).

Boeotia

REESE D.S.
Molluscs from Early Bronze Age Lithares, Appendix 4 in Tzavella-Evjen H, Lithares, Deltion Sup. 32, (Athens 1984), 197-201 (Greek), 219-220 (English summary).

SPYROPOULOS T.G.
Drosia, BCH 96, (1972).

ΣΠΥΡΟΠΟΥΛΟΣ Τ.Γ.
Δροσιά, AA 25, (1972), 222-224.

VIALOU D.
La Parure, in Lambert N. (ed.), La grotte Préhistorique de Kitsos (Attique) I, Paris: Recherche sur les grandes civilizations 7, (1981), 391-419.

Dodekanisa

BLINKENBERG C.
Lindos, Fouilles de l'Acropole 1902-1914, I Les Petits Objets 175-82 Walter de Gruyter, (Berlin, 1931).

LEVI D.
La grotta di Aspripetra a Cos, ASAA 8-9, (1925-26), 235-312.

MAIURI A., JACOPICH G.
Clara Rhodos, Studi e Materiali publicati a cura dell'Istituto Storico Archaeologico de Rodi, vol. I, Rodos, (1928).

ΣΑΜΨΩΝ Α.
Η Νεολιθική περίοδος στα Δωδεκάνησα, (Αθήνα, 1987).

ΣΑΜΨΩΝ Α.
Η Νεολιθική κατοίκηση στο Γυαλί της Νισύρου, (Αθήνα, 1988).

Eptanisa

DORPFELD W.
Alt-Ithaka, Verlag Richard Unde, (Munich, 1927).

SORDINAS A.
Investigations of the Prehistory of Corfu, Balkan Studies 10.2, (1969), (1964-66), 383-414.

Thessaly

ΓΑΛΛΗΣ Ι.Κ.
Άτλας Προϊστορικών οικισμών της Ανατολικής Θεσσαλικής Πεδιάδας, (Λάρισα, 1992).

ΘΕΟΧΑΡΗΣ Δ.Ρ.
Εκ της Προκεραμεικής Θεσσαλίας, Θεσσαλικά 1, (1958), 70.

ΘΕΟΧΑΡΗΣ Δ.Ρ.
Εκ της Προκεραμεικής Θεσσαλίας, Πύρασος, Θεσσαλικά 2, (1959), 29.

ΘΕΟΧΑΡΗΣ Δ.Ρ.
Η αυγή της Θεσσαλικής Προϊστορίας, (Βόλος, 1967).

FALKNER G.
Systematische Übersicht über die Molluskenfunde von Magula Pevkakia, in Jordan B., Tierknochenfunde aus der Magula Pevkakia in Thessalien, (München, 1975), 189-190.

GIMBUTAS M. et al
Achilleion: A Neolithic settlement in Thessaly, Greece (6.400-5.600), (Los Angeles, 1989).

GRUNDMANN K.
Magula Hadzimissiotiki, Eine Steinzeitliche Sieldung im Karla See, A.M., (1937).

HALSTEAD P. and JONES G.
Early Neolithic Economy in Thessaly - Some evidence from Excavations at Prodromos. Anthropologika 1, (1980), 93-117.

HANSCHMANN E.
Die Mittlere Bronzezeit II (Argissa Magula IV). Rudolf Habelt Verlag, (Bonn, 1981).

MILOJCIC V.,
Vorbericht über die Ausgrabungen auf den Magulen von Otzaki Arapi und Gremnos bei Larisa, AA, (1955), 182.

MILOJCIC V.
Hauptergebnisse der deutschen Ausgrabungen in Thessalien, (Bonn, 1960), 1953-58.

MILOJCIC V., BOESSNECK J., HOPF M.
Die Deutschen Ausgrabungen auf der Agrissa-Magula in Thessalien I: Das Präkeramiche Neolithicum sowie die Tier und Pflanzenreste. Beiträge zur ur-und frühgeschichtlichen Archaeologie des Mittelmeerkulturraumes, vol. 2, (Bonn, 1962).

MILOJCIC V., BOESSNECK J., JUNG D., SCHNEIDER H.
Paläolithicum um Larissa in Thessalien, Beitrage zur Ur und frühgeschichtlichen Archäologie des Mittelmeerkulturraumes Band I, Hebelt, (Bonn, 1965).

MILOJCIC V.
Bericht über die Ausgrabungen auf der Gremnos Magula bei Larisa, AA, (1965), 141.

MILOJCIC V., HAUPTMANN T.
Die Funde der frühen Dimini Zeit aus der Arapi-Magula, Thessalien, Rudolf Habelt, (Bonn, 1969).

MILOJCIC V., MILOJCIC J.
Die Deutschen Ausgrabungen auf fer Otzaki Magula in Thessalien, Rudolf Habelt, (Bonn, 1971).

MILOJCIC V.
Die Grabung auf der Agia Sofia Magula, Magula um Larisa in Thessalien 1966, Rudolf Habelt Verlag GMBH, (Bonn, 1976), 4-14.

ΠΑΠΑΔΟΠΟΥΛΟΥ Μ.
Μαγουλίτσα, Νεολιθικός οικισμός κοντά στην Καρδίτσα, Θεσσαλικά 1, (1958), 39-49.

ΤΣΟΥΝΤΑΣ ΧΡ.
Αι Προϊστορικαί Ακροπόλεις Διμηνίου και Σέσκλου, Βιβλιοθήκη της εν Αθήναις Αρχαιολογικής Εταιρείας, (Αθήνα, 1908).

ΧΟΥΡΜΟΥΖΙΑΔΗΣ Γ.
Το νεολιθικό Διμήνι, Εταιρεία Θεσσαλικών Ερευνών, (Βόλος, 1979).

WACE A.J.B., THOMPSON M.S.
Prehistoric Thessaly, (Cambridge, 1912).

Cyclades

CASKEY J.L.
The Early Bronze Age at Ayia Irini in Keos, Archaeology 23/2, (1970), 339-342.

COY J.
Shells in Animal Remains, Appendix 4 in Coleman J.E., Kephala, A late Neolithic Settlement and Cemetery, American School of Classical Studies, (Princeton 1977), 132-3.

HONEA K.
Prehistoric Remains on the Island of Kythnos, AJA, (1975), 277-279.

KARALI L.
Sea shells, landsnails and other marine remains from Akrotiri, in Thera and the Aegean III/2, Hardy D.A. et al. (ed.), (London, 1990a), 37-41.

KARALI L.
Analysis of a purple material found at Akrotiri (Karali L., Aloupi E., Maniatis Y., Paradellis T.), in Thera Foundation, vol.1, (1990b), 488-491.

ΚΑΡΑΛΗ Λ.
Σημασία και χρήσεις των οστρέων στο Προϊστορικό Αιγαίο, Τρίμμερο Αιγαίου: 21-23 Δεκεμβρίου 1989, Ανάτυπο, Παρνασσός, (Αθήνα, 1990c), 123-128.

KARALI L.
Το μαλακολογικό υλικό του Ακρωτηρίου, Ημερίδα 19/12/87, (Athens, 1992), 163-170.

KARALI L.
The sea shells of "The West Building" at Santorini, (forthcoming).

KARALI L.
Shells from Early Bronze Age Markiani in Amorgos, (forthcoming).

ΝΤΟΥΜΑΣ ΧΡ.
Κορυφή του Αρωνιού, Α.Δ. 20, (1965), 41-64.

RENFREW C.
The Archaeology of Cult, The Sanctuary at Phylakopi, BSA Supp. 18, (London, 1985).

SHACKLETON N.J.
The Mollusca, the Crustacea, the Echinodermata, Appendix IX in Evans J.D. and Renfrew A.C., Exvacations at Saliagos near Antiparos, Thames and Hudson, (London, 1968), 68-9, 122-38.

ΤΣΟΥΝΤΑΣ ΧΡ.
Κυκλαδικά, A.E., vol. 137-212, (1898).

ΤΣΟΥΝΤΑΣ ΧΡ.
Κυκλαδικά, A.E., vol. 73-134, (1899).

Crete

BOEKSCHOTEN G.J.
Note on Roman purple winning at Chersonisos, Crete, Basteria 26, (1962), 3-4, 59-60.

BOSANQUET R.C.
On heaps of Murex at Kouphonisi and Palaiokastro, Crete, Vol. 24, J.H.S., (1904), 321.

BOYD-HAWES H., WILLIAMS B.E., SEAGER R.B., HALL E.H.
Gournia, Vasiliki and other prehistoric sites on the Isthmus of Hierapetra (Crete), (Philadelphia, 1908).

CHAPOYTHIER F., DEMARGNE P.
Fouilles executées à Malia, 3e rapport Exploration du palais, Bordure orientale et septentrionale (1927-32), Études crètoises, 6, (1942).

CHAPOUTHIER F., DEMARGNE D., DESSENE A.
Fouilles executées à Malia, 4e rapport, Exploration du palais, Bordure meridionale et recherches complémentaires, 1929-35, 1948-1960, Études crètoises, 12, (1962).

CHEVALLIER H., DETOURNAY B., DUPRE S., JULLIEN R., OLIVIER J.P., SEDERIADES M. et TREUIL R.
Fouilles executées à Malia, Sondages au Sud-Ouest du Palais 1968), Études crètoises, 20, (Paris, 1975).

CHEVALLIER H.
Coquilles Marines, Chapter IX in Études Crètoises XX Fouilles Executées à Malia, Sondages du Sud-Ouest du Palais, (1968), (1975), 157-9.

DAWKINS R.M.
Neolithic Settlement at Magasa, Palaikastro IV, BSA 11, (1904-1905), 260-68.

EVANS A.J.
The tomb of the Double Axes and Associated Group and Pillar Rooms and Ritual Vessels of the Little Palace at Knossos, (London, 1914).

EVANS A.J.
The palace of Minos at Knossos, Vol. I: The Neolithic, Early and Middle Minoan Ages, (London, 1921).

EVANS J.D.
Excavations in the Neolithic Mound of Knossos, 1958-60, Bulletin of the Institute of Archaeology 4, (1964), 34-60.

EVELY D.
Shells, in The Other Finds of Stone, Clay, Ivory, Faience, Lead etc., Section 8, in Popham M.R. et al., The Minoan Unexplored Mansion at Knossos, Thames and Hudson, (London, 1984), 246-7, 255-6, 296-7.

HALL E.H.
Excavations in Eastern Crete Sphoungaras, University of Menn. Mus. Anthr. Publ., III, 2, (Philadelphia, 1912).

ΧΑΤΖΗΔΑΚΙΣ I.
Τύλισος Μινωϊκή A.E., (1912), 197-2331.

HATZIDAKIS J.
Tylissos à l'Époque Minoenne, Paris: Librairie Paul Geuthner, (1921), 78-9.

KARALI L.
Les coquillages du Quartier Mu a Malia, In Études crètoises, (forthcoming in Études crètoises).

KARALI L.
La Representation des Mollusques sur les Sceaux Minoens, in L'Iconographie Minoenne, Darcque P. and Poursat J.C. eds.), BCH Suppl. vol. XI, École française d'Athènes, (Paris, 1985), summary.

PELON O.
Fouilles executées à Malia, Exploration des maisons et quartiers d'habitation (1963-66), Études crètoises 16, (Paris, 1970).

PELON O.
Maison d'Hagia Varvara et architecture domestique a Malia, BCH 90, (1966), 552-585.

PENDLEBURY H.W., PENDLEBURY J.D.S. and MONEY-COUTTS
Shells, in Excavations in the Plain of Lasithi I The Cave of Trapeza, BSA 36, (1935-6), 126-7.

PERNIER L.
Il palazzo minoico di Festos, Scavi e Studi della missione archaeologica italiana a Creta dal 1900 al 1934, I, Gli strati piu antichi e il primo palazzo, Roma, (1935).

ΠΛΑΤΩΝ N.
Ζάκρος το νέον Μινωϊκόν Ανάκτορον, Αρχαιολογική Εταιρεία, (Αθήνα, 1974).

REESE D.S.
Recent and Fossil Shells from Tomb XVIII, Gypsades Cemetery, Knossos, Crete, BSA 77, (1982), 149-50.

REESE D.S.
Recent and Fossil Shells from the Sanctuary of Hermes and Aphrodite, in Lebessi A., Syme Viannou, Crete. A.E., (1986), 183-188.

REESE D.S.
The EM IIA shells from Knossos, with comments on Neolithic to EM III shell utilization, BSA, 82, (1987), 207-211.

REESE D.S.
Fauna from the Poros Tomb, Appendix G, in Metaxa-Muhly P., Μινωϊκός λαξεντός τάφος στον Πόρο Ηρακλείου ανασκαφής (1967), Βιβλιοθήκη της Αρχαιολογικής Εταιρείας 129, (Αθήνα, 1992), 180-181.

REESE D.S.
The Minoan Fauna, Chapter 5 in Shaw J.W. et Shaw M.C. (eds.), Kommos I (1), The Kommos Region, Ecology, and Minoan Industries, Princeton University Press, (Princeton 1995), 163-291.

REESE D.S.
The Faunal Remains, Block AG; the Triton Shell Vessel, Building AB; The Faunal Remains, Building AM; The Faunal Remains, Building AD Center, in Betancourt P.P. and Davaris C. (eds.), Pseira I The Minoan Buildings on the West Side of Area A, University Museum Monograph 90, University of Pennsylvania, (Philadelphia 1995), 11, 42, 45-46, 56-57, 83, 129-130.

REESE D.S.
The Minoan Fauna, in Betancourt P. (ed.), Minoan Pseira I, Philadelphia: The University Museum, University of Pensylvania.

REESE D.S.
Marine Invertebrates from the Unexplored Mansion, Knossos, Crete, in excavation report by Sackett L.H. and Popham M., (forthcoming).

RUSHE C. and HALSTEAD P.
Bone, Shell and Soil Samples, in Manteli K. and Evely D., The Neolithic levels from the Throne Room System, Knossos, BSA 90, (1995), 13-15.

SEAGER R.B.
The cemetery of Pachyammos Crete, University of Pensylvania, The University Museum, Anthropological Publications, vol.7, no.1, (Philadelphia, 1916).

SEAGER R.S.
"Explorations in the island of Mochlos", (New York, 1912).

SHACKLETON N.J.
Knossos marine mollusca, in Evans, J.D., Knossos Neolithic Part II, BSA 63, (1968), 264-6.

SHACKLETON N. J.
The shells, Appendix VI in Warren P., Myrtos, An Early Bronze Age Settlement in Crete, The Alden Press, (Oxford 1972), 321-5.

TARAMELLI A.
Grotte de Miamu, AJA I, (1897), 287-312.

WARREN P.
Myrtos: an Early Bronze Age Settlement in Crete, BSA Suppl., vol. 7, (London, 1972).

WARREN P., JARMAN M.R., JARMAN H.N., SHACKLETON N.J., EVANS J.D.
Knossos Neolithic, Part II, BSA 63, (1968), 239-76.

XANTHOUDIDIS S.
The vaulted tombs of Mesara, An account of some early cemeteries of Southern Crete, (London, 1924).

ΖΩΗΣ Α.
Ανασκαφή Βρυσών Κυδωνίας 1, Ιστορική και Αρχαιολογική Εταιρεία Δυτικής Κρήτης, (Αθήνα, 1976).

Macedonia-Thrace

BINTLIFF J.L.
The Plain of Western Macedonia and the Neolithic Site of Nea Nikomedeia, PPS 42 (1971), 241.

DESHAYES J.
Dikili-Tash and the Origins of the Troadic Culture, Archaeology 25, 3, (1972), 198-205.

DESHAYES J.
Dikili-Tash et les problèmes du Néolithique et du Bronze Ancien en Macedoine, Bulletin de la Societé Française d'Archaeologie classique III, (1968-69), 161-192.

FOTIADIS M.
Natural and Human Ecology in Serres Basin, Diss., (1984).

FOTIADIS M.
Economy, Ecology and Settlement among Subsistence Farmers in the Serres Basin, Northeastern Greece, 5000-1000 B.C., Ph.D. Program in Classical Archaeology, Indiana University, (1985).

GARAŠANIN M., MILUTIN V.
Neolithicum und Bronzezeit in Serbien und Macedonien, Bericht der Römisch-Germanischen Kommission, (1958), 39, 112.

GARAŠANIN M., DEHN W.
Thrakisch-Makedonische Wohnhugelfunde in der Sammlung des vorgeschichtlichen Seminars zu Marburg/Lahn, JbZMusMainz 10, (1963).

HANSEL B.
Ergebnisse der Grabungen bei Kastanas in Zentral Makedonien 1975-78, JbZMusMainz 26, (1979), 167.

HEURTLEY W.A.
Human and Animal Remains, Heurtly W.A. and Radford C.A.R., Two Prehistoric Sites in Chalcidice, BSA XXIX, (1927-28), 175.

ΚΑΡΑΛΗ Λ.
Μαλακολογικό υλικό: Παράρτημα III, στο Γραμμένος Δ., Πεντάπολη Σερρών, Α.Ε., (1981), 115-118.

KARALI L.
Le Rôle des Mollusques à l'ère Préhistorique dans L'île de Thassos, Actes de Symposium International Thracia Pontica IV, 6-12 October 1988, Sozopol, (1988), 309-320.

ΚΑΡΑΛΗ Λ.
Μαλακολογικό υλικό από τα Βασιλικά στην Μακεδονία, στο Γραμμένος Δ., Νεολιθικές έρευνες στην Μακεδονία, (Αθήνα, 1991).

ΚΑΡΑΛΗ Λ.
Μελέτη του μαλακολογικού υλικού από τα Νεκροταφεία Καστρί και Λαρνάκι, Παράρτημα III, στο Κουκούλη-Χρυσανθάκη Χ., Προϊστορική Θάσος, Α.Δ. 45, (1992), 756-759.

KARALI L.
Le material malécologique, dans Treuil R. ed., Dikili Tash, village préhistorique de Macedoine Orientale, vol. I, 1, École Française d'Athènes, (Paris, 1992), 112-3, 153-164.

KARALI L.
Dimitra-Materiel malacologique, in Γραμμένος Δ., Νεολιθική Μακεδονία, Α.Δ. 56, (1997), 200-211.

ΚΑΡΑΛΗ Λ.
Η συμβολή της μαλακολογικής έρευνας στην μελέτη του παλαιοπεριβάλλοντος της Προϊστορικής Μακεδονίας, Δεύτερο Συμπόσιο Αρχαιομετρίας, Αρχαιομετρικές και Αρχαιολογικές έρευνες στην Μακεδονία και Θράκη, 26-28/3/1993, (forthcoming).

ΚΑΡΑΛΗ Λ.
Το μαλακολογικό υλικό από την Δήμητρα, στο Γραμμένος Δ., Δήμητρα, (forthcoming).

ΚΑΡΑΛΗ Λ.
Τα όστρεα από τη Σκάλα Σωτήρος στην Θάσο, στο Κουκούλη-Χρυσανθάκη Χ., (forthcoming).

KARALI L.
La contribution de la recherche environmentale à la Reconstitution des Premières Centres Urbains en Europe Sud-est, VII Semaines philippopolitaines, (forthcoming).

ΚΑΡΑΛΗ Λ.
Τα μαλάκια ως πρώτη ύλη στην Προϊστορική Θάσο, in Congres: Thasos. Matières Premieres et Technologie de la préhistoire à nos jours, 26-29/9/1995, (forthcoming).

MILOJCIC V.
Southeastern Elements in the Neolithic Cultures of Serbia, Proceeding of the BSA, 44, (1949), 258-299.

MYLONAS G.E.
Excavations at Olynthos, Part: I, The Neolithic Settlement, Baltimore, (1929).

REESE D.S.
Marine and Fresh-Water Molluscs from Late Neolithic/Chalcolithic Paradeisos Klisi-Tepe) in Aegean Thrace, Nothern Greece, in excavation report by Hellstrom P. (ed.), Memoir 7, (Stockholm, 1987), 119-134.

RIDLEY C. and WARDLE K.A.
Rescue excavations at Servia, 1971-73, a preliminary report BSA 74, (1979), 185-226.

RODDEN R.J.
Excavations at the Early Neolithic site at Nea Nikomedia Greek Macedonia, PPSXXVIII, (1962), 267-88.

RODDEN R.J.
Recent Discoveries from Prehistoric Macedonia, Balkan Studies 5, (1964), 24, 109.

SHACKLETON N.J.
Stable Isotope Study of the Paleoenvironment of the Neolithic Site of Nea Nicomedeia, Greece, Nature 227/5261, (1970), 943-4.

SHACKLETON N.J.
Sitagroi: Mollusca, (forthcoming).

SHACKLETON J.
Shells from the Neolithic site of Nea Nicomedeia, (forthcoming).

Islands in North and East Aegean

BERNARBO-BREA L.
Poliochni I, Citta Preistorica nell'isola di Lemnos, Rome, (1964).

BOESSNECK J. and von den DRIESCH A.
"Weitere Reste Exotischer Tiere aus dem Heraion auf Samos", A.M. 98, (1983), 21-4.

THEOCHARIS D.R.
Prehistoric researches in Skyro and Evia, A.E., (1945-47), 1-12.

HOOD S.
Excavations in Chios 1938-1955, Prehistoric Emporio and Agio Galas I and II, Supp. Vol. 16, (London, 1982).

KARALI L.
Sea Shells and Land Molluscs from the Cave Skotini, In Sampson, the cave Skotini Tharrounia, Athens, (1993), 370-378.

ΚΑΡΑΛΗ Λ.
Το μαλακολογικό υλικό από την Καλογερόβρυση, στο Καλογερόβρυση, ένας οικισμός της εποχής του Χαλκού στα Φύλλα Ευβοίας, από Σάμψων Α., (Αθήνα, 1993), 169-173.

ΚΑΡΑΛΗ Λ.
Θαλάσσια όστρεα και χερσαία μαλάκια από το σπήλαιο Σκοτεινή, στο Σάμψων Α., Σκοτεινή, Θαρρούνια: το σπήλαιο, ο οικισμός και το νεκροταφείο, (1993), 370-377.

ΚΑΡΑΛΗ Λ.
Η σημασία των οστρέων της Προϊστορικής Πολιόχνης, Η Πολιόχνη και η Πρώιμη εποχή του Χαλκού στο Βόρειο Αιγαίο, 21-25/4/1996, Ιταλική Αρχαιολογική Σχολή, (forthcoming).

LAMB W.
Excavations at Thermi in Lesbos, Cambridge University Press, (Cambridge 1936), 216-7.

SCHWARTZ C.
Agios Petros. The vertebrate and Molluscan Fauna, Appendix II in Efstratiou N., Agios Petros, A Neolithic Site in the Nothern Sporades, (Oxford, 1985), 51-163.

Peloponnese

ANDEL J.H. van, SHACKLETON J.C., JOLLY J.B., CIANOS N.
Late Quaternary history of the coastal zone near Franchthi Cave, Southern, Argolid, Greece. J.F.A. 7, (1980), 389-402.

BLEGEN C.W.
Zygouries, A Prehistoric Settlement in the Valley of Cleonae, (Cambridge, 1928).

BLEGEN C.W.
Prosymna, The Helladic Settlement, preceeding the Argive Heraeum, (Cambridge, 1937).

CASKEY J.L., CASKEY E.G.
The earliest settlement at Eutresis, Supplementary Excavations 1958, Hesperia 29, (1960), 126-167.

COLDSTREAM J.N., HUXLEY G.L. (ed.) HOPESIMPSON R., LAZENBY J.F., TRIK A.S.
Kythera, Excavations and Studies conducted by the University of Pennsylvania Museum and the British School at Athens, (London, 1972).

COLDSTREAM J.N. and G.L. HUXLEY eds.)
Kythera, Faber and Faber Limited, (London, 1972).

FRODIN O et PERSSON A.W.
Asine, Results of the Swedish Excavations 1922-30, (Stockholm, 1938).

GEJVALL N.G.
The Fauna in Lerna, a preclassical site in the Argolid, vol. I, American School of Classical Studies at Athens, (Princeton, 1969), 50.

GEJVALL N.G.
Animal Bones from the Acropolis, Appendix VI in Astrom P., The Cuirass Tomb and other Finds at Dendra 2, SIMA IV, Paul Ästroms Forlag, (Gothenborg, 1983), 51-4.

JACOBSEN T.
Worked shell, in Excavations in the Franchthi Cave, 1969-71, Part II, Hesperia 42, (1973), 257-8.

JACOBSEN T.
Excavations at Porto Cheli and Vicinity, Prelim. Report, II, The Franchthi Cave, 1967-1968, Hesperia 38, (1969), 343-381.

JACOBSEN T.
The Franchthi cave. A Stone Age site in southern Greece, Archaeology 22, (1969), 1, 4-9.

ΚΑΡΑΛΗ Λ.
Μαλακολογικό υλικό του σπηλαίου Αλεπότρυπα Δυρού Λακωνίας, Ελληνική Σπηλαιολογική Εταιρεία, (1983), 229-232.

ΚΑΡΑΛΗ Λ.
Τα όστρεα και οι χρήσεις τους στο σπήλαιο Αλεπότρυπα Μάνης, Πρώτο Πανελλήνιο Σπηλαιολογικό Συνέδριο: Άνθρωπος και Παλαιοπεριβάλλον, 26-29/11/1992, (forthcoming).

LAMBERT N.
Grotte d'Alepotrypa (Magne), BCH 96, (1972), 845-871.

MC DONALD W.A.
Excavations at Nichoria in Messenia: 1969-71, Hesperia 41, (1972), 218-273.

MC DONALD W.A.
Excavations at Nichoria in Messenia: 1972-73, Hesperia 44, (1975), 69-141.

MARINATOS S.
The palace of Eglianos, AAA, (1962).

REESE D.S.
Recent and Fossil Intertebrates, in Mc Donald W.A., Wilkie N.C. eds.), Excavations at Nichoria in SW Greece II, The Bronze Age occupation, (Mineapolis, 1992).

REESE D.S.
The Molluscs from Bronze Age to Post-Geometric Asine in the Argolid, Greece, Appendix 2 in Dietz S. (ed.), Asine II, Results of the Excavations East of the Acropolis 1970-74 1, (Stockholm, 1992), 139-142.

REESE D.S.
The Mammal Bones and Invertebrates from Hagios Stefanos, in Taylour W. and Janko R. (eds.), Ayios Stefanos, Results of excavations in Lakonia, 1973-77, BSA, Supplementary volume, (London, forthcoming).

REESE D.S., GIFFORD A.H., JANSEN J.H.
Analysis of Submarine Sediments of Franchthi Cave, Greece, (forthcoming).

REESE D.S.
Recent and Fossil Invertebrates, Appendix I, in Mc Donald W.A. and Wilkie N.C., Excavations at Nichoria in Southwest Greece II, The Bronze Age Occupation, University of Minnesota Press, (Minneapolis 1992), 770-778.

SHACKLETON J.
Preliminary observations on the Marine Shells, Appendix I, in Jacobsen T.W., Excavations at Porto Cheli and vicinity, preliminary report II: the Franchthi Cave, 1967-68, Hesperia 38, (1969), 379-380.

SHACKLETON J.C., VAN ANDEL T.M.
Prehistoric shell assemblages from Franchthi cave and evolution of the adjacent coastal zone, Nature 288, (1980), 357-359.

SHACKLETON J.C., van ANDEL T.M.
Prehistoric Shore Environments, at Franchthi Cave, Geoarchaeology 1 2), (1986), 127-143.

SHACKLETON N.J.
Reconstructing Past: Shorelines as an Approach to Detect-mining Factors Affecting Shelfish Collecting in the Prehistoric Past, Bailey G. and Parkington, (Cambridge, 1988), 11-21.

SHACKLETON J.C., DEITH M.R., SHACKLETON N.J.
Marine molluscan remains from Franchthi cave with a report on the oxygen isotope analysis of marine mollusc from Franchthi Cave, Indiana University Press, (1989).

SHACKLETON J.C., DEITH M.R., SHACKLETON N.J.
Review of Marine Molluscan Remains from Franchthi cave, with report on the Oxygen Isotope Analysis of Marine Molluscs from Franchthi Cave, American Journal of Archaeology 94, (1990).

SLOAN R.E., DUNCAN M.A.
Zooarchaeology of Nichoria, Chapter 6 in Rapp G. and Aschenbrenner S.E., (ed.), Excavations at Nichoria in Southwest Greece: Site, Environs and Techniques, University of Minnesota Press, (Minneapolis 1978), 70, 72.

SPERLING J.
Explorations in Elis, 1939, AJA 46, (1942), 77-89.

VALMIN M.N.
The Swedish Messenia Expedition, (Lund, 1938), 359-60.

WALDEN H.W.
Mollusca, Appendix III in Åstrom P. (ed.), The Cuirass Tomb and other Finds at Dendra 2, SIMA IV, Paul Åstroms Forlag, (Göteborg , 1983), 56.

WEINBERG S.S.
Excavations at Prehistoric Elateia, 1959, Hesperia 31, (1962), 158.

Fokis-Etoloakarnania

AMANDRY P., DELIBRIAS G., LAMBERT N. et MICHLAND J.P.
Phocide B. Plateau du Parnasse, BCH 96, (1972), 906-13.

DOR L. JANNORAY J., Van EFFENTERRE H. et M.
Kihhra, étude de préhistoire phocidienne, (Paris, 1960).

ΚΑΡΑΛΗ Λ.
Η σημασία της μαλακολογικής έρευνας στις θέσεις της Αιτωλοακαρνανίας, Πρώτο Αρχαιολογικό και Ιστορικό Συνέδριο Αιτωλοακαρνανίας, (Αθήνα, 1992), 228-232.

Sites not mentioned in the text
Asia Minor and Middle-East

ANNIMELECH M.
Sur les mollusques trouvés dans les couches préhistoriques de Palestine, Jour. Palest. Orient. Soc. 17, no. 81-92, (1937).

BIGGS H.J.
Mollusca from Prehistoric Jericho Journal of Conchology 24, (1980), 379-87.

BLEGEN C.W., J.L. CASKEY, M. RAWSON, J. SPERLING
Troy I. General Introduction, the First and Second Settlements, Princeton University Press, (1950).

DURANTE S.
Marine shells from Balakot, Shahr-I Sokhta and Tape Yahya: their significance for Trade and Technology in Ancient Indo-Iran, South Asian Archaeology 1977, Istituto Universitario Orientale, Napoli, (1979), 317-44.

FRENCH D.H.
Excavations at Can Hasan, Second Preliminary Report 1962, AS XIII, (1963), 28-42.

GARROD D.A.E.
Notes on some decorated skeletons from the Mesolithic of Palestine B.S.A. 37, (1936-37), 123-127.

GARSTANG J.
Prehistoric Mersin, Yumuk Tepe in Southern Turkey, (Oxford, 1953).

GEJVALL N.J.
The Fauna of the different settlements of Troy, Bulletin de la Societe Royale des Lettres de Lund, (1937-38), 51-57.

GRIES P.
Shells, in von der Osten H.H., The Alishar Hoyuk Seasons of 1930-32 III, OIP 30, (Chicago, 1937), 324-327.

GRUVEL A.
Les États de Syrie, (Paris, 1931).

HITTI P.K.
History of Syria including Lebanon and Palestine, 95 (New York 1951), Lebanon in History (New York and London, 1957), 109-110.

MELLAART J.
Catal Hoyuk. A neolithic town in Anatolia, (London, 1967).

MELLAART J.
Excavations at Hacilar, British Institute of Archaeology at Ankara, (Edinburgh, 1970).

PRITCHARD J.B.
Recovering Sarepta, a Phoenician City, (Princeton, 1978).

POULAIN T.
Étude de la Faune de quelques restes humaines et de coquillages provenant de Ras Shamra, Sondages 1955 à 1969, Ugaritica 7, (1978), 161-180.

REESE D.S.
The Marine and Freshwater Shells, Chapter XIII, in McGorven P. (ed.), The Late Bronze Age and Early Iron Age of Central Transjordan: the Bag'ah Valley Project,

Monograph 65, Philadelphia University Museum, (1986), 320-332.

REESE D.S.
Shells at Aphrodisias Joukowsky M.S. (ed.), Prehistoric Aphrodisias, an account of the Excavations and Artifact studies Archaeologica Transatlantica III, Louvain, (1986), 491-96.

REESE D.S.
The Natufian shells from Beidha, Appendix D in Byrd B.F., the Natufian Encampment at Beidha: Late Pleistocene Adaptation in the Southern Levant, Moesqard, Arhus Denmark): Jutland Archaeological Society Publications XXIII: 1, (1989), 102-104.

REESE D.S.
Marine Shells in the Levant: Upper Paleolithic, Epipaleolithic, and Neolithic, in Bar-Yosef O. and Valla R., The Natufian Culture in the Levant, Archaeological series 1, International Monographs in Prehistory, (Ann Arbor 1991), 613-628.

RODDEN R.J.
A European Link with Chatal Huyuk: uncovering a 7th millenium settlement in Macedonia (Parts I-II), Illustrated (London News, 11 and 18 April, (1964), 564-67 and 604-607.

SCHLIEMANN H.
Ilios, the city and country of the Trojans, (London, 1880).

SCHMIDT H.
Heinrich Schliemanns Sammlung trojanischer Altertümer, (Berlin, 1902).

SCHMIDT E.F.
The Alishar Huyuk Seasons of 1928-1929 I, (Chicago, 1932).

SPERLING J.
Kum Tepe in the Troad: Trial excavations 1934, Hesperia 45, 1976), 305-364.

Egypt

LUCAS A.
Ancient Egyptian Materials and Industries, (London, 1934).

REESE D.S., MIENIS H.K., and WOODWARD F.R.
On the Trade of Shells and Fish from the Nile River, Bulletin of American Schools of Oriental Research 264, (1986), 79-84.

Balkans

CHAPMAN J.
The Vinca Culture of South-East Europe, BAR 117, (i-ii), (1981).

CANTACUZINO G.
The Prehistoric necropolis of Cernica and its place in the Neolithic cultures of Romania and of Europe in the light of recent discoveries, Dacia 13, (1969), 45-49.

DETEB M.P.
Parures préhistoriques conservées au Musée national archéologique de Plovdiv, Annuaire du Musée Archéologique de Plovdiv, (1963), 5, 41-58.

FEWKES V.J.
Neolithic sites in the Moravo-Danubian Area, Eastern Yugoslavia, (1963).

GIMBUTAS M.
Obre, Yugoslavia: Two Neolithic Sites, Archaeology 23, no.2, (1970), 287-297.

GIMBUTAS M.
Neolithic Macedonia, as Reflected by Excavation at Anza, Southeast Yugoslavia, M. Gimbutas (ed.), Institute of Archaeology, The University of California, (Los Angeles, 1976).

IVANOV I.
Les fouilles archéologiques de la necropole chalkolithique à Varna (1972-1975), Die Nekropole in Varna und die Probleme des Chalkolithikums, Internationales Symposium, Varna 19-23 Apr. 1976, (Sofia, 1978), 13.

Mediterranean Sea
Croatia-Italy-Spain-France, Africa

DEITH M.R.
Seasonality of shell collecting, determined by Oxygen isotope analysis of marine shells from Asturian sites in Calabria, (1983).

MORELLI N.
Resti Organici renvenuti nella Caverna delle Arene Candide, (Geneva, 1901).

NOVAK G.
Prehistoric Hvar, the Cave of Grabak: Prehistorijski Hvar, Grapčeva spilja, Academia Scientiarium et Atrium Jugoslavica, (Zagreb, 1955).

TABORIN Y.
La parure en coquillage de l'epipaleolithique au Bronze Ancien en France, Gallia-Prehistoire 17, (1974).

RADMILLI A.M.
Piccola Guida della Prehistoria Italiana, Florence, (1962).

REESE D.S.
Faunal remains (Osteological and Marine Forms), 1975-76, Excavations at Carthage, 1976, conducted by the University of Michigan III, Humphrey J.H. (ed.), Ann Arbor: Kelsey Museum, The University of Michigan (1977), 131-166.

REESE D.S.
Faunal remains from three cisterns (1977.1, 1977.2, 1977.3) in Excavations at Carthage 1977 conducted by the University

of Michigan VI, Humphrey J.H. (ed.), Kelsey Museum, the University of Michigan, (Ann Arbor 1981), 191-258.

REESE D.S.
Estudio de las Conchas del Corte 3, Appendix IV, in Semmler E.A., et al., La Mesa de Setefilla, Madrid: Excavations Arqueologicas en Espana, Ministerio de Cultura, (1983), 172-173.

REESE D.S.
Marine Molluscs from Nuraghe Ortu Comidu, Appendix VI, in Balmuth M.S. and Phillips P., Preliminary Report of Excavations 1975-78 of the Nuraghe Ortu Comidu, (Sardara Cagliari), Sardinia, in Notizie degli Scavi di Antichita, in Atti della Academia Nazionale dei Lincei XXXVII, (1986), 403-405.

REESE D.S.
Marine and Fresh-water Molluscs from Castellazo di Poggioreale, Belice Valley, Western Sicily, in Sicilia Archaeologica, Palermo, Italy, (forthcoming).

VOIGT E.
The Molluscan Fauna, in Singer R., Wynne J. (eds.), The Middle Stone Age at Klasies River Mouth in South Africa, Chicago University Press, (1982), 155-185.

America

ABBOTT R.
American Sea Shells, Van Nostrand, Reinhold Co., (New York, 1954).

LAVALLEE D.
Contacts et échanges dans les Andes, Grand Atlas de l'archéologie, Encyclopaedia Universalis, (1985), 366-367.

NUTTALL Z.
A curious survival in Mexico of the use of the Purpura shellfish for dying, Putnam Anniversary Volume, (New York, 1909), 368-84.

Cyprus

DIKAIOS P.
Khirokitia final report on the excavations of a Neolithic settlement in Cyprus, (London, 1953).

ΚΑΡΑΛΗ Λ.
Παλαιοπεριβαλλοντικό υλικό από τη Νεολιθική θέση Καντού-Κουφόβουνος, Appendix, in Μαντζουράνη Ε., Έκθεση Αποτελεσμάτων της Ανασκαφής στη θέση Καντού-Κουφόβουνος κατά τις περιόδους 1994-1995, Επιστημονική Επετηρίς του Τμήματος Αρχαιοτήτων για το 1966, (Λευκωσία, 1996), 25-28.

ΚΑΡΑΛΗ Λ.
Προκαταρκτική παρουσίαση του παλαιοπεριβαλλοντικού υλικού από την Νεολιθική θέση Καντού-Κουφόβουνος, (forthcoming).

KARALI L.
The role of sea-shells in prehistoric Aegean and Cyprus, International Archaeological Symposium: Cyprus and the Aegean in Antiquity, from the Prehistoric period to the 7th century A.D., 8-10/12/1995, (forthcoming).

REESE D.S.
Molluscs from Archaeological Sites in Cyprus: Kastros, Cape St. Andreas, Cyprus and other Pre-Bronze Age Mediterranean Sites, in Fisheries Bulletin 5, Nicosia: Department of Fisheries (1978), 3-112.

REESE D.S.
Shells and Fish from Maa-Palaeokastro, Appendix X, in Karageorghis V. and Demas M., Excavations at Maa-Palaeokastro 1979-1986, Nicosia: Department of Antiquities, (1988), 458-466.

REESE D.S.
The Late Bronze Age to Geometric Shells from Kition, (Appendix VIII A), in Karageorghis V., Excavations at Kition V/II, Nicosia: Department of Antiquities, (1985), 340-71.

REESE D.S.
Marine Shells, in the Land of the Paphian Aphrodite, vol. 2, in Sorensen C.W., The Canadian Palaipaphos, Survey Project, Artifacts and Ecofacts Studies, (Goteborg, 1993), 207-209.

VERMEULE E.D.T., WOLSKY F.Z.
Toumba tou Skourou, A Bronze Age, Potters' Quarter on Morphou Bay in Cyprus, Harvard University Press, (Cambridge, 1990), 391-392.

SOURCES

ΑΡΙΣΤΟΤΕΛΗΣ
Περί τα ζώα, Ιστ. Δ4, 528α "...αι πορφύραι".
HERODOTUS
History, book 4, 6 292, 293.

HOMER
Homeri Opera, Iliadis, Tomus I I-XII), Oxford Classical Texts, 19021/196913).

PAUSANIAS
Description of Greece, book II-V, XXI.

PLINY
Natural History, The Loeb Classical Library, Heinemann W. (ed.), Harvard University Press, (London: vol. I books I-II), 1938/1967 vol. II books III-VII), 1942/1969 vol. IV books XII-XVI), 1945/1968 vol. V books XVII-XIX), 1950/1971.

POLYDEFKIS
Pollux Onomasticon 1, 47-49.

STRABON
The Geography, The Loeb Classical Library, Heinemann W. (ed.), Harvard University Press, (London, XVI, 2-23, 575; XVII, 3.18, cap. 835, 1932-1967).

SUETONIUS
Life of the Twelve Caesars. De Vita Caesarum, Liber I,
XLV.32.

TACITUS
Germania XVII

XENOPHON
Hellenica

SUETONIUS
Life of the Twelve Caesars. De Vita Caesarum, Liber I,
XLV.32.

Fig. 1. First publications of Molluscs.

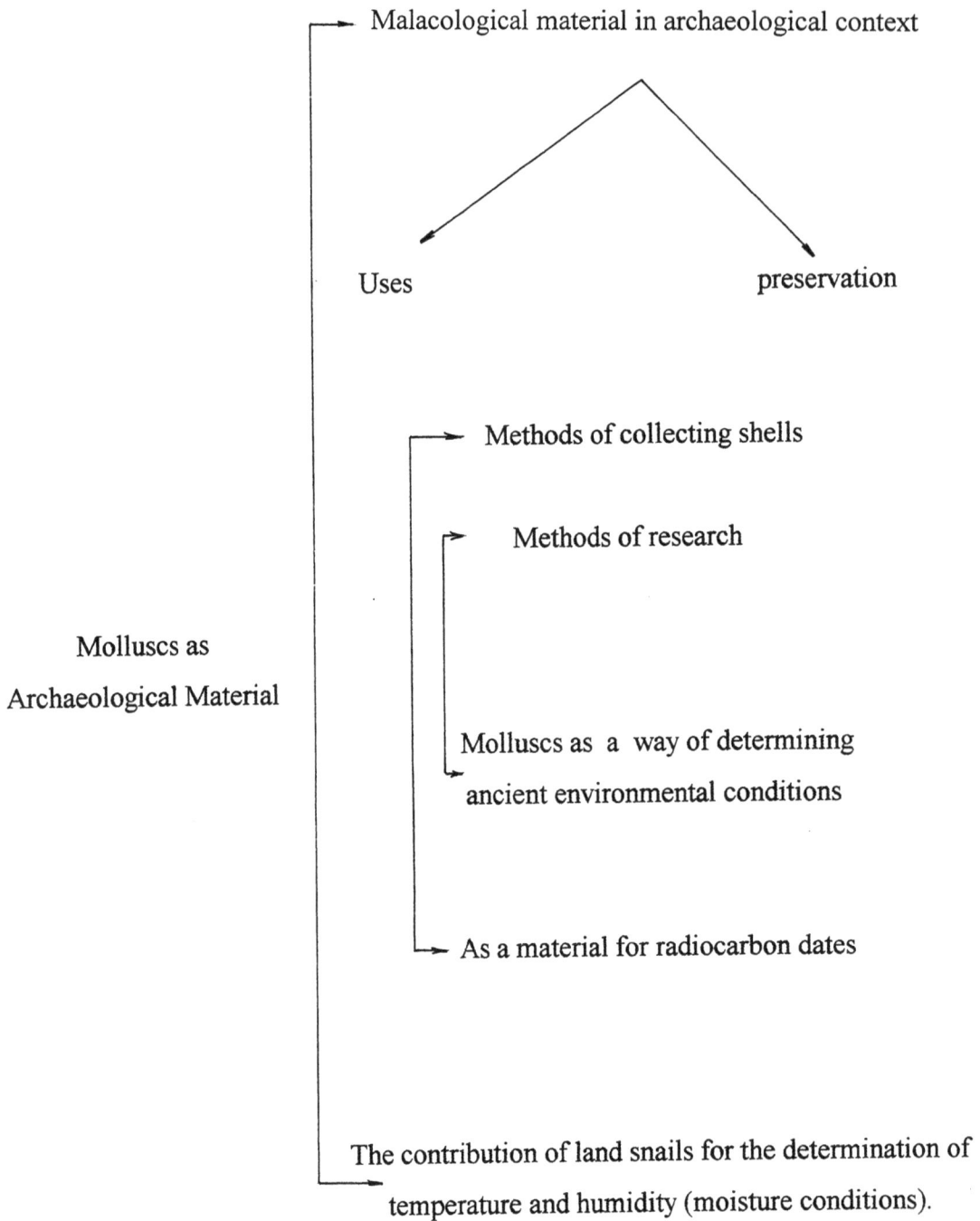

Fig. 2. Malacological material in archaeological context.

Economy and molluscs in prehistoric societies

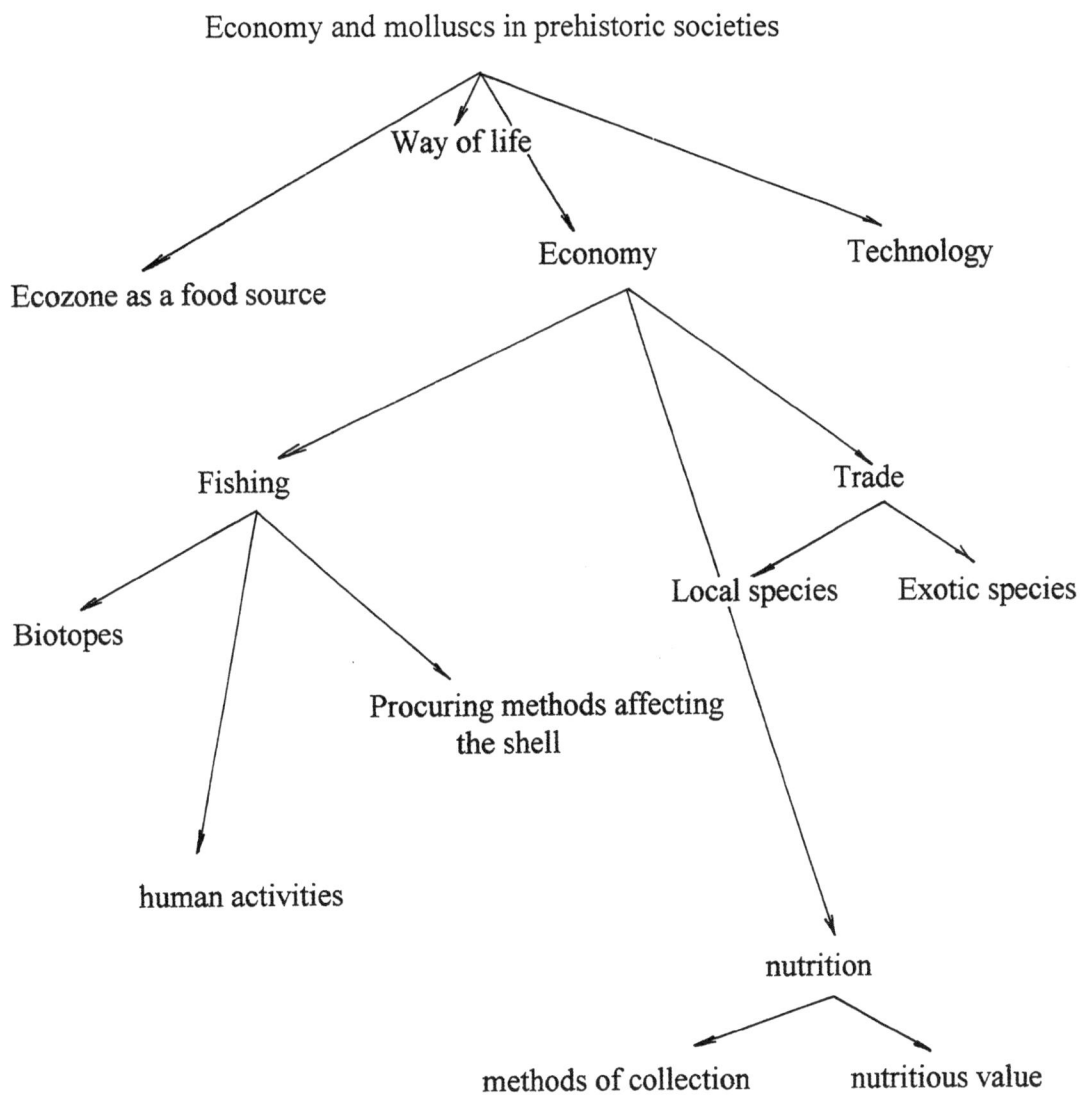

Fig. 3. Economy and molluscs in prehistoric societies.

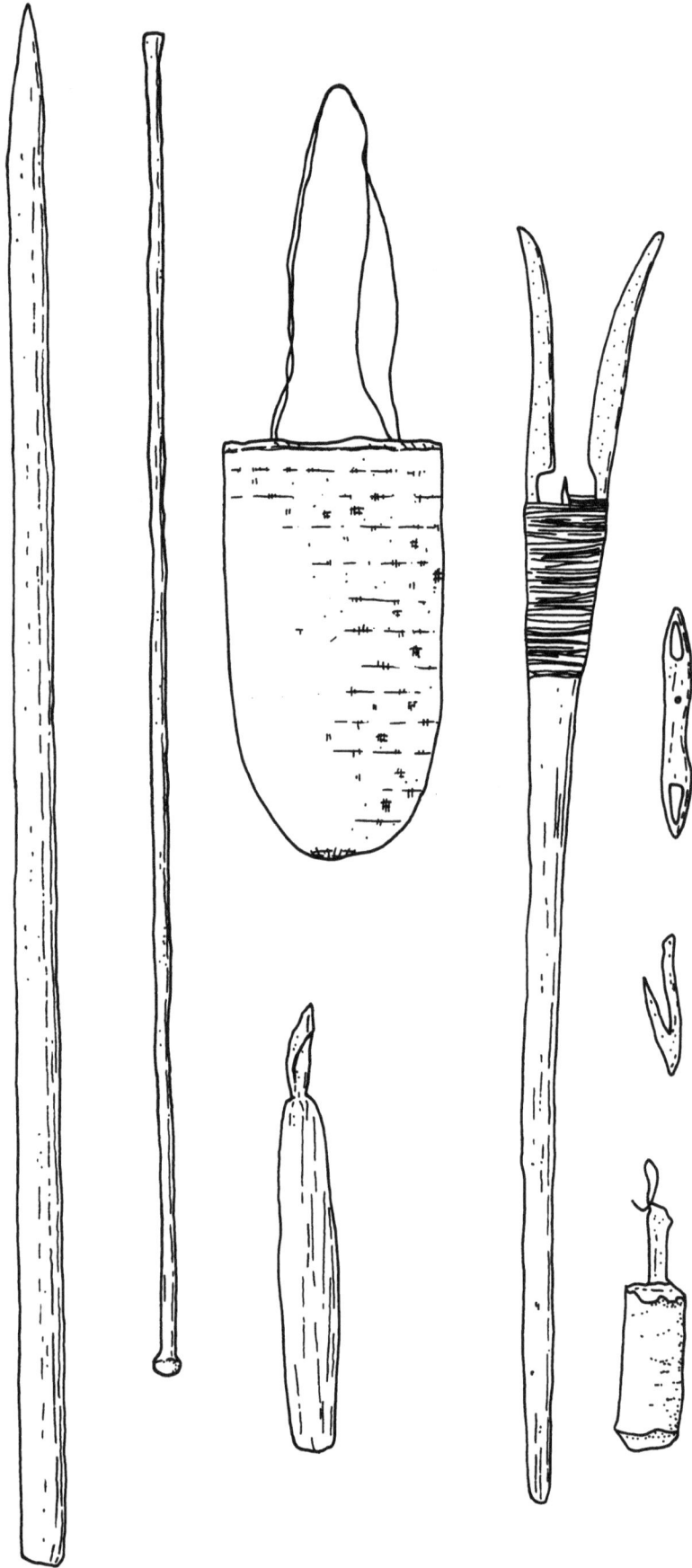

Fig. 4. Reconstruction of fishing tools. These materials are usually not recovered in archaeological context (after Orme, Bryony, *Anthropology for Archaeology*, Cornell Univ. Press, 1981, p.39, 40).

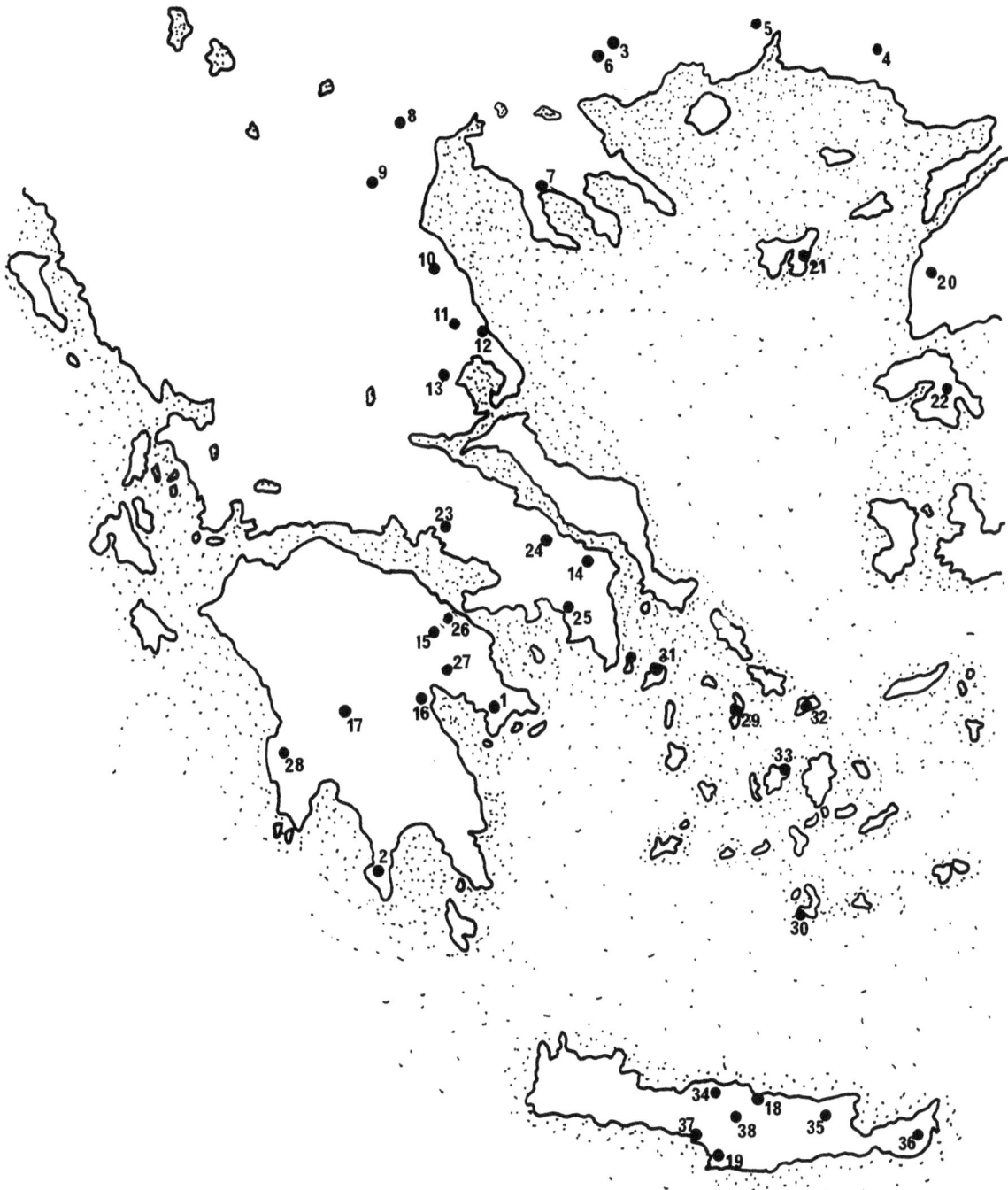

Figure 5. Map of the most important sites mentioned in the text:

1. Franchthi	14. Pan's Cave	26. Mycenae
2. Alepotrypa	15. Prosymna	27. Tiryns
3. Sitagroi	16. Lerna	28. Pylos
4. Paradimi	17. Asea	29. Phylokapi
5. Dikili-Tash	18. Knossos	30. Akrotiri
6. Dimitra	19. Phaistos	31. Kephala/Ay. Irini
7. Olynthos	20. Troy	32. Chalandriani
8. Nea Nikomedeia	21. Poliochni	33. Saliagos
9. Servia	22. Thermi	34. Tylissos
10. Rachmani	23. Kirra	35. Malia
11. Sesklo	24. Eutresis	36. Zakros
12. Dimini	25. Agh.Kosmas	37. Kommos
13. Pyrasos		38. Archanes

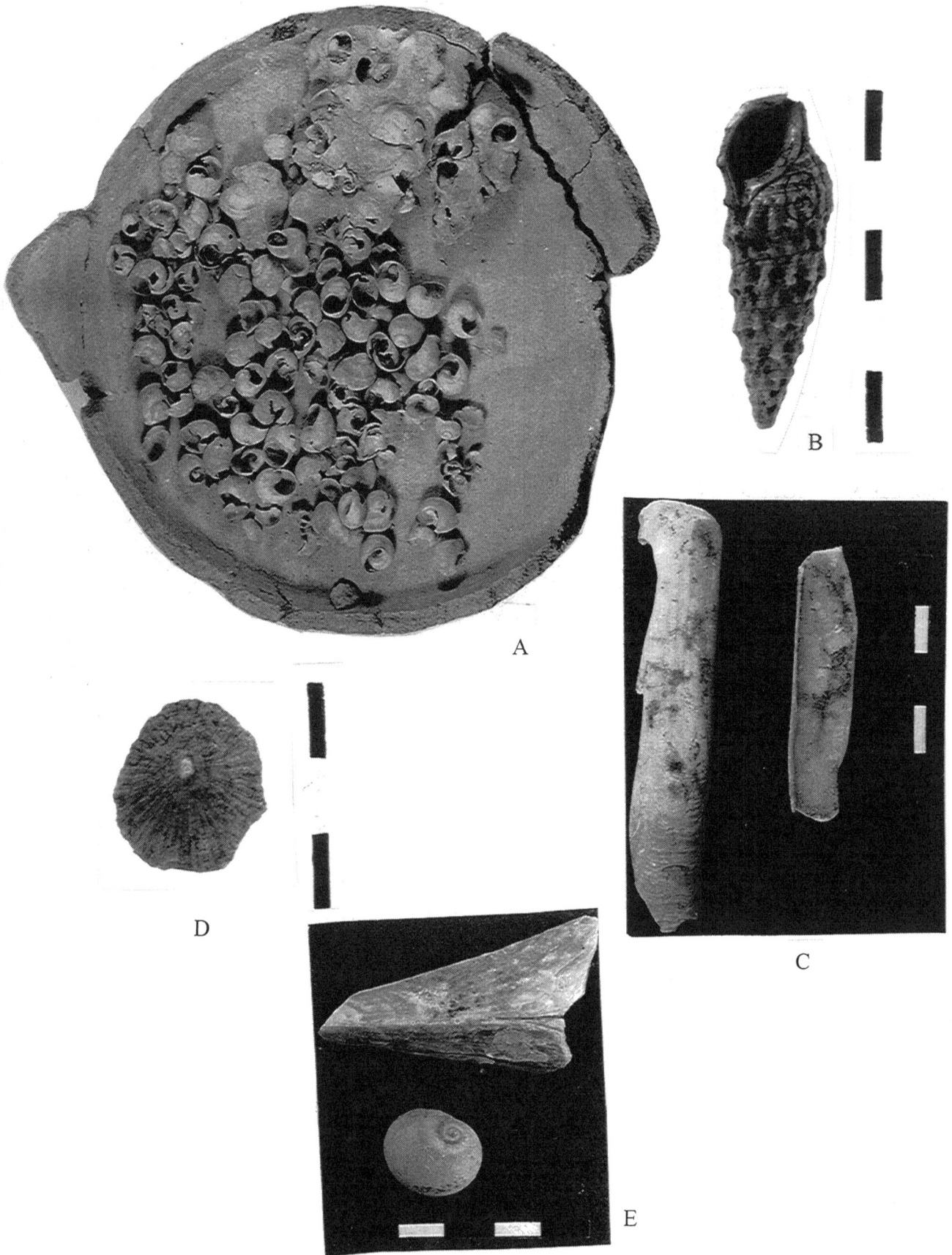

Fig. 6. Shells from Akrotiri. A. Vessel with shells (*Helix sp.*), building D17, pythos B39 (4/9/73, 94/1157). B. *Cerithium vulgatum Brug.* Xeste 3, Sq. 47125, 4975K185, G.44 (11/7/74). C. *Ensis ensis L.*, Dikili Tash, M. Neolithic, X30 level 12. D. *Patella sp.* (3.5cm), Xeste 3, Aug. '94, Sq. 47, 1400MS053, K218, G44. E. *Pinna nobilis L.* Dikili Tash, Late Neolithic, W29 and *Nassa neritea*, Dikili Tash, Late Neolithic, W29.

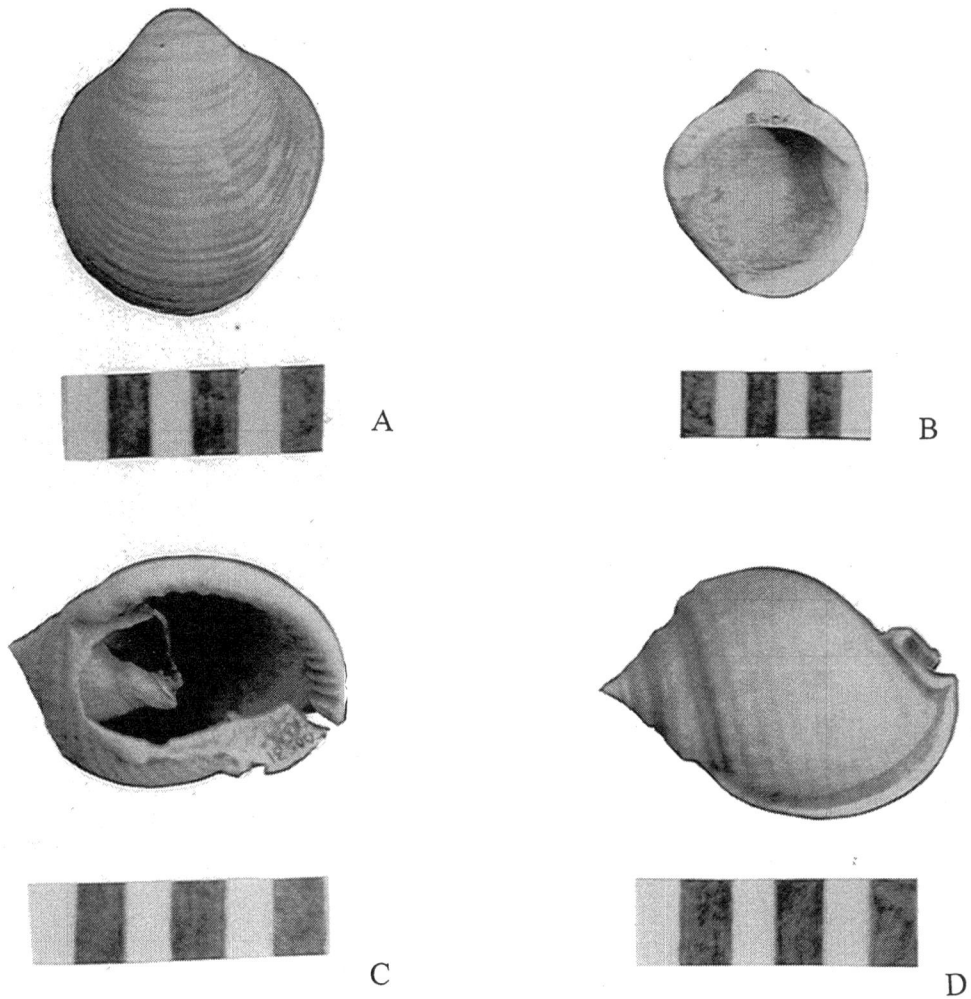

Fig. 7.   A-B. *Glycymeris glycymeris L.*, L.M. IIIc (no.12406, Nat. Arch. Museum of Athens). Phylakopi. C-D. *Cassis sulioa Br.,* Syros, E.C. II, Grave 325 (no. 12500 Nat. Arch. Mus. Of Athens). Chalandriani, Syros

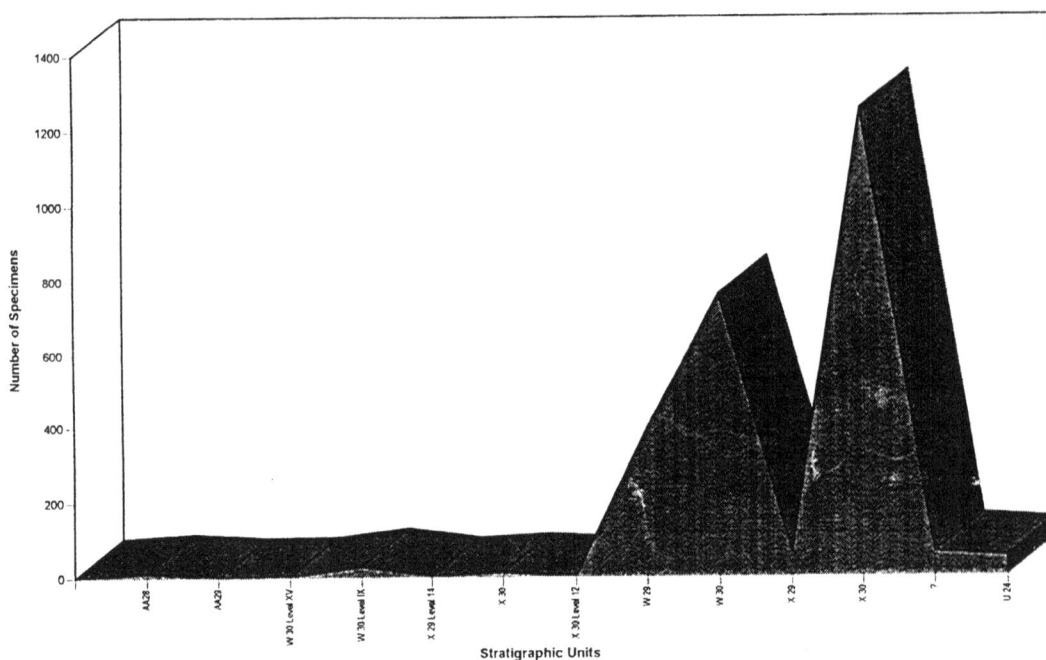

Fig. 8.   Graphic representation of the shell consumption at Dikili-Tash (relative concentration of molluscan finds in the Archaeologicals assamblage from MN to E.B.).

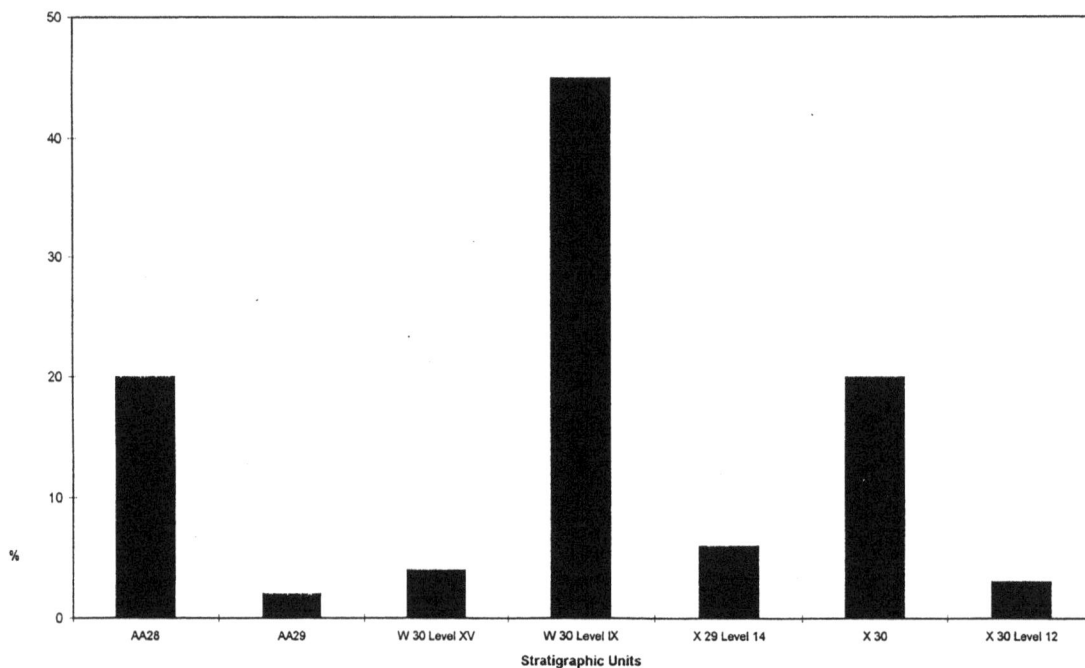

Concentration of Molluscan Finds in the Middle Neolithic Assemblage

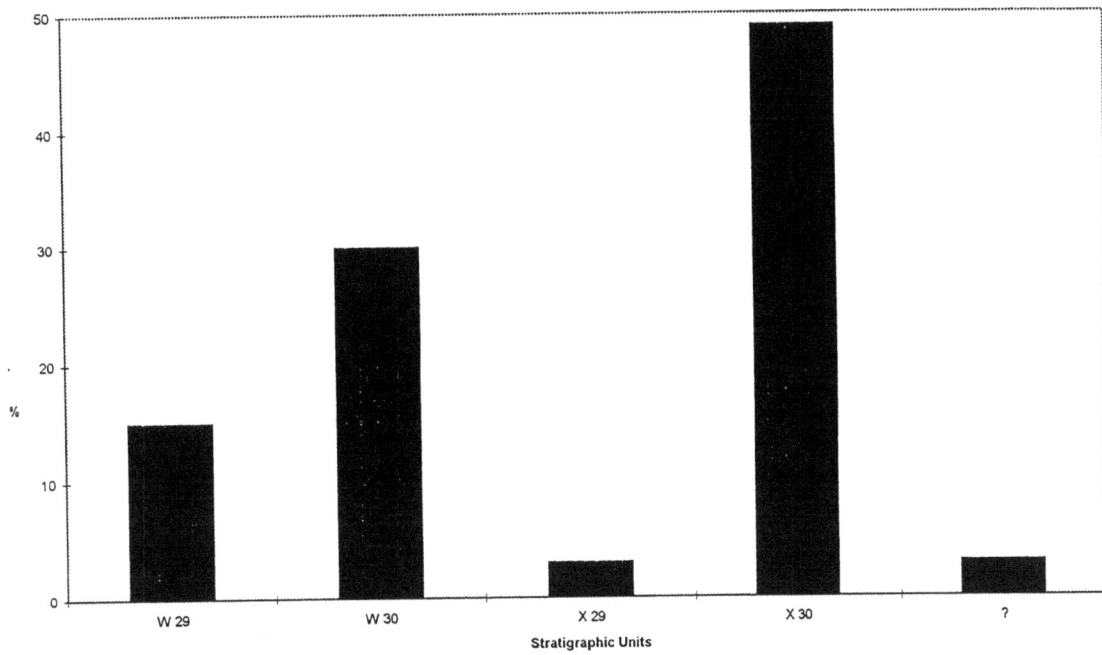

Concentration of Molluscan Finds in the Late Neolithic Assemblage

Molluscs and diet during the Neolithic Period

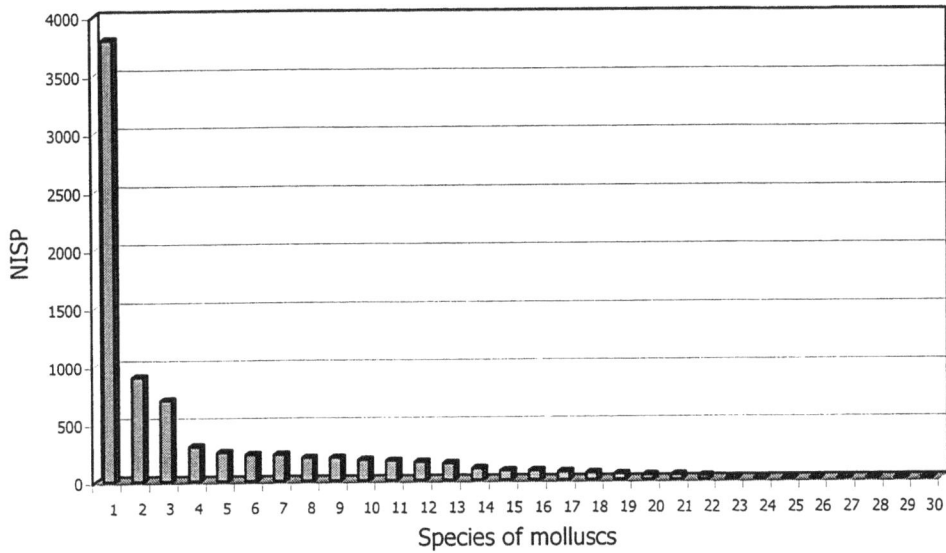

1	Unio
2	Patella
3	Cardium
4	Monodonta
5	Murex
6	Ostrea
7	Helix
8	Venerupis
9	Spondylus
10	Bittium
11	Cerithium
12	Nassa
13	Glycimeris
14	Mytilus
15	Gibbula
16	Area
17	Charonia
18	Conus
19	Pecten
20	Ensis
21	Callista
22	Euthria
23	Columbella
24	Luria
25	Dentalium
26	Chlamys
27	Pinna
28	Cassis
29	Venus
30	Cerastoderma

Fig. 8 (contd). Graphic representation of the shell consumption at Dikili-Tash.

Molluscs and diet during the Early Bronze Age

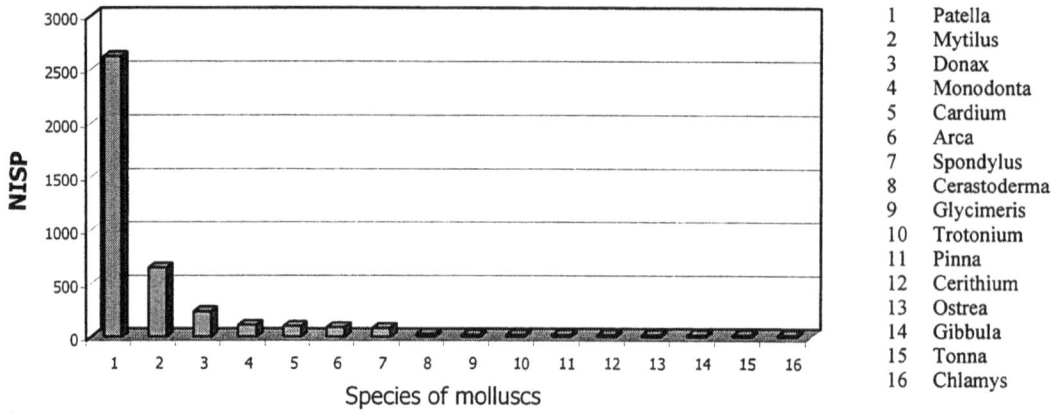

1	Patella
2	Mytilus
3	Donax
4	Monodonta
5	Cardium
6	Arca
7	Spondylus
8	Cerastoderma
9	Glycimeris
10	Trotonium
11	Pinna
12	Cerithium
13	Ostrea
14	Gibbula
15	Tonna
16	Chlamys

Molluscs and diet during the Middle and Late Bronze Age

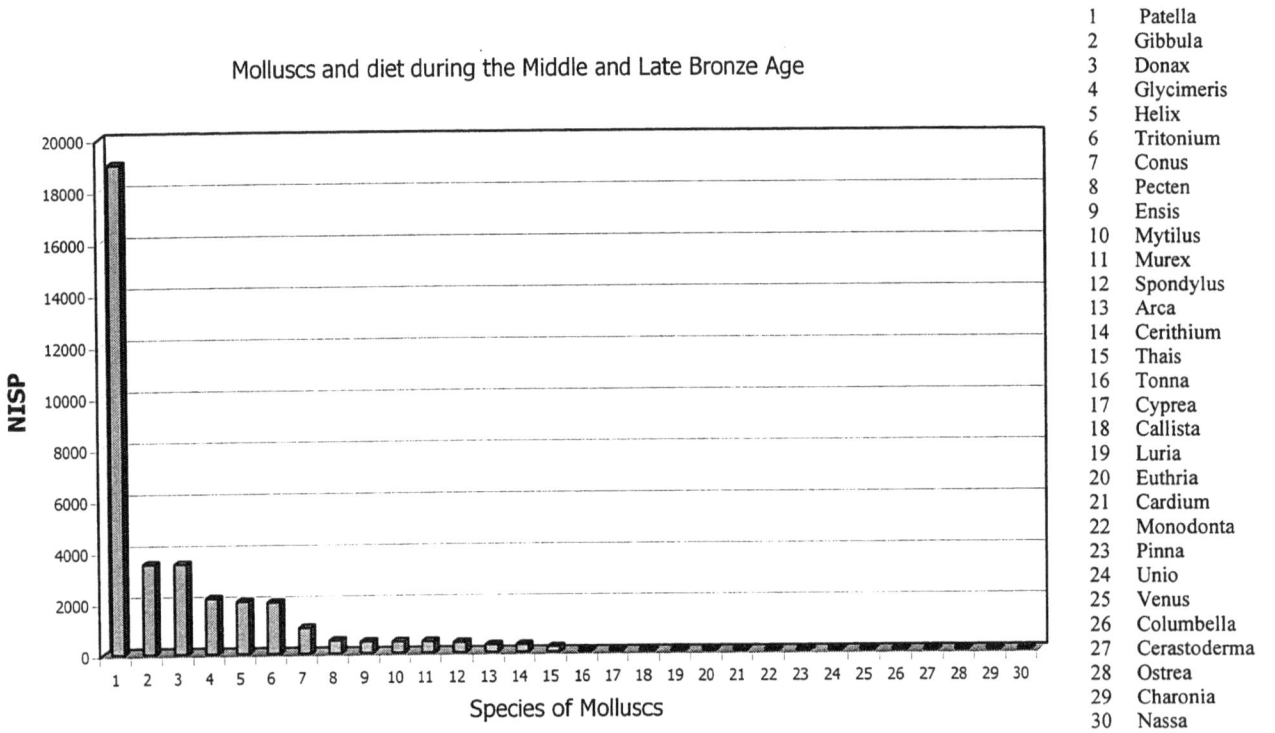

1	Patella
2	Gibbula
3	Donax
4	Glycimeris
5	Helix
6	Tritonium
7	Conus
8	Pecten
9	Ensis
10	Mytilus
11	Murex
12	Spondylus
13	Arca
14	Cerithium
15	Thais
16	Tonna
17	Cyprea
18	Callista
19	Luria
20	Euthria
21	Cardium
22	Monodonta
23	Pinna
24	Unio
25	Venus
26	Columbella
27	Cerastoderma
28	Ostrea
29	Charonia
30	Nassa

Fig. 8 (contd). Graphic representation of the shell consumption at Dikili-Tash.

Molluscs as tools and vessels

Nature   Man

Work processing traces

Specific use of tools   usage trace

Shells without traces of work processing   worked shells

Non identified use

Food remaims

Secondary use

Specific uses

Spoons   Spatula   Polishers   Lamps   maceheads   trumpets   vessels   spools

ovoid-concave   round shaped   ovoid-flattened

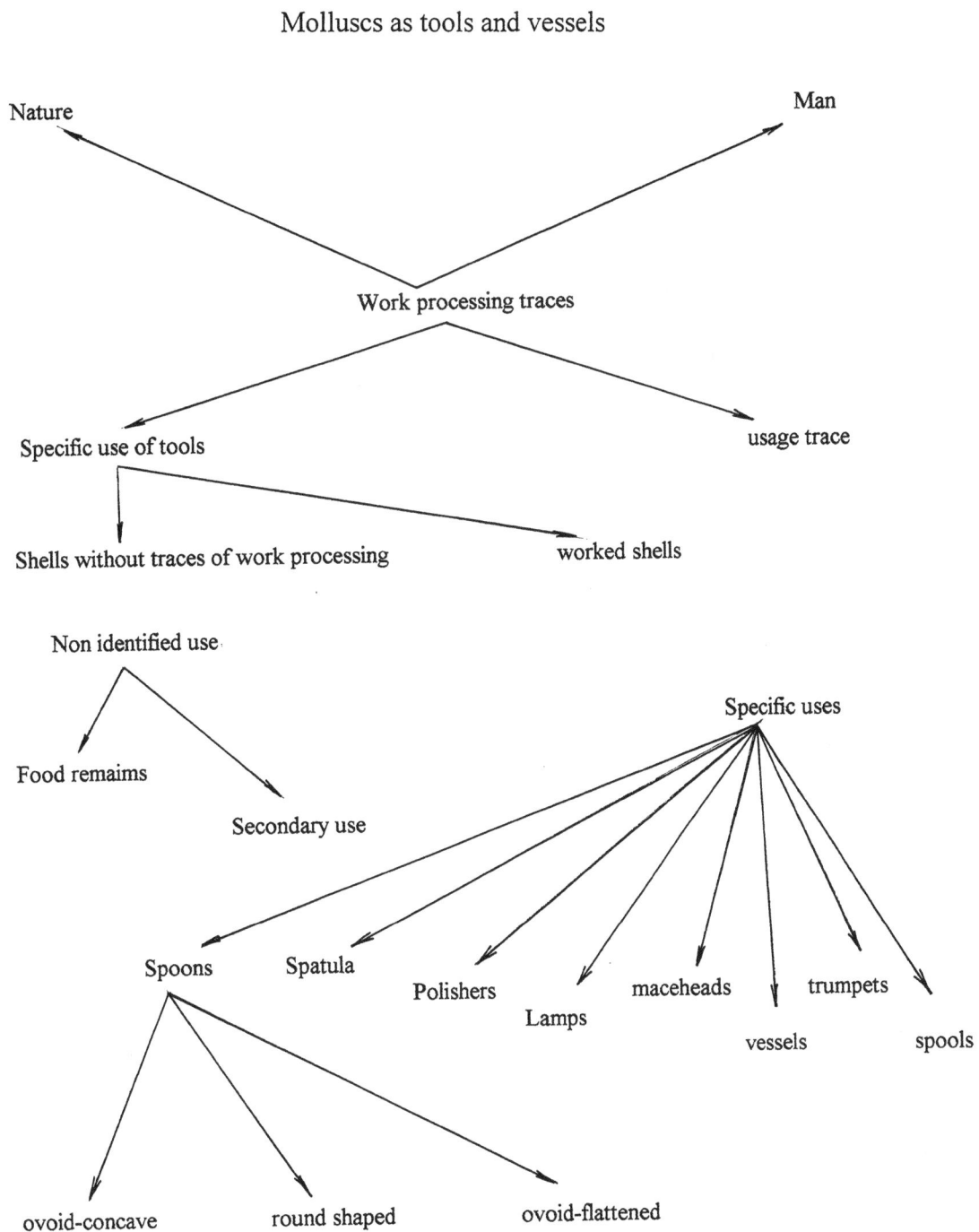

Fig. 9. Molluscs used as tools and vessels from prehistoric sites of the Aegean.

Neolithic tools made out of shells

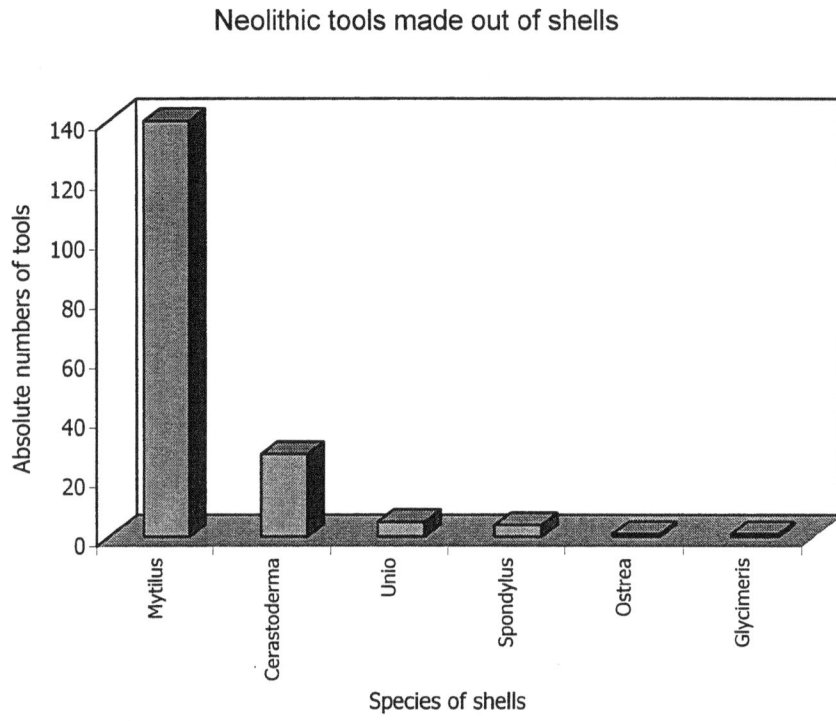

Fig. 9 (contd).   Molluscs used as tools and vessels from prehistoric sites of the Aegean.

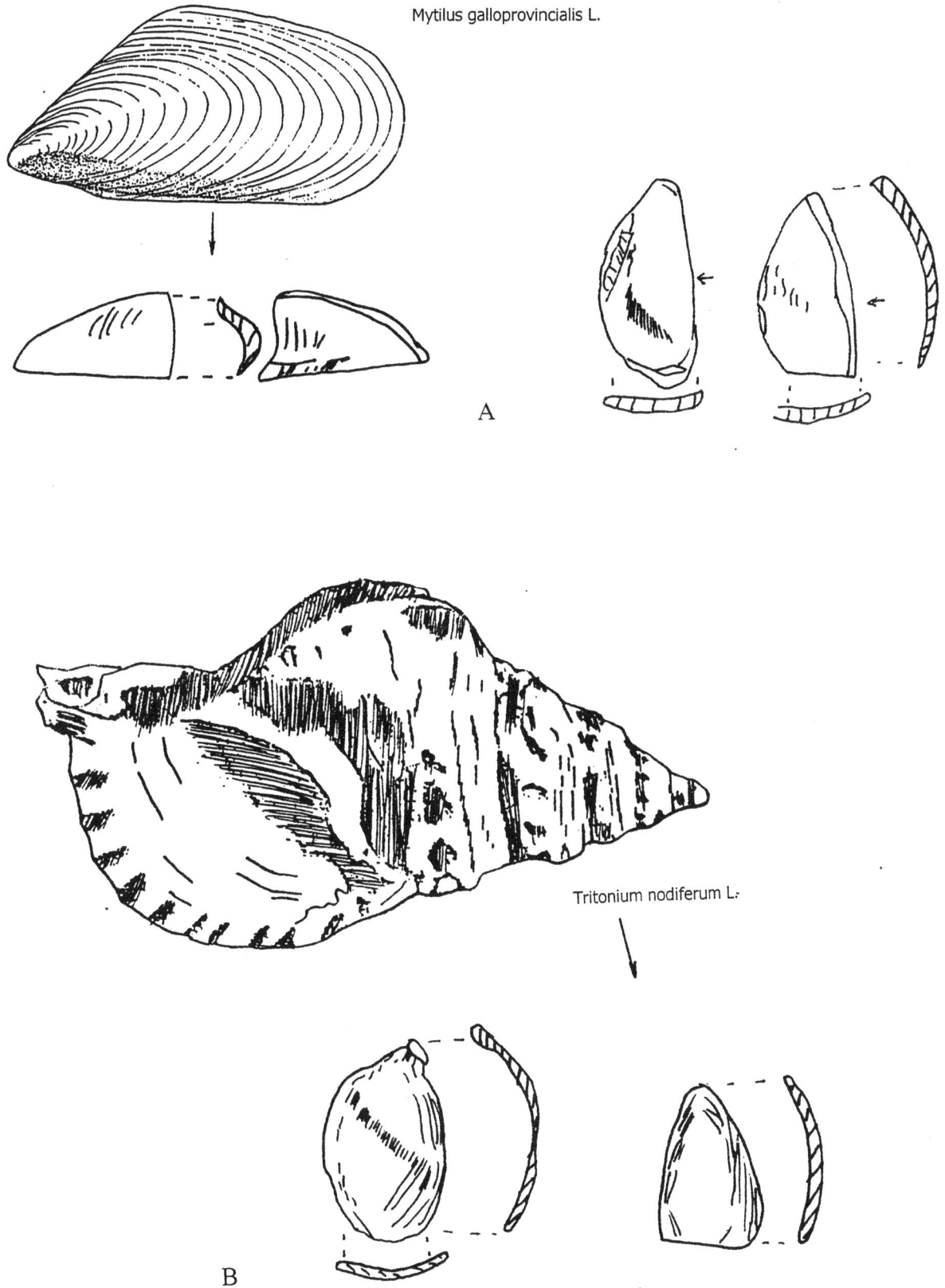

Mytilus galloprovincialis L.

A

Tritonium nodiferum L.

B

Fig. 10. A. Ovoid-concave spoons from Saligos MN-LN (Shackleton 1966, 126, pl. 49) and Dimitra (EN W30) made of Mytilus shell. B. Ovoid-concave spoons from Saliagos (Triton shell) (MN-LN) (Shakleton 1966 126, pl. 49).

Fig. 11. Spoons from Cave of Cyclope made from *Patella sp.* (EN/MN). A. Ga 20 T1 SHG and Ga st 19, t.7, SH 5 (Aceramic). B. 6-7-95 trench Ga, level 15, T12, A/A 2. C 1993, trench G east STA 6-8, A/A 1.

Fig. 12a. Tools and vessels made of shell. A-C Spoons from Saliagos; D Lamp; E Ladle F-G Vessels

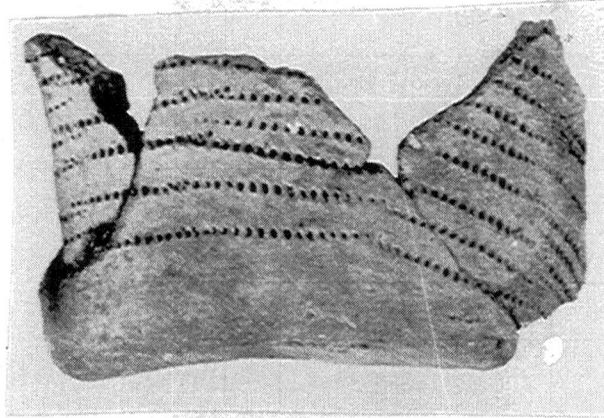

A

B

Fig. 12b. Cardium shell pottery decoration. A. Magoulitsa (schachermeyr 1976, Ft II; Milojcic 1971, TP). B.
Otsaki - Magoulitsa

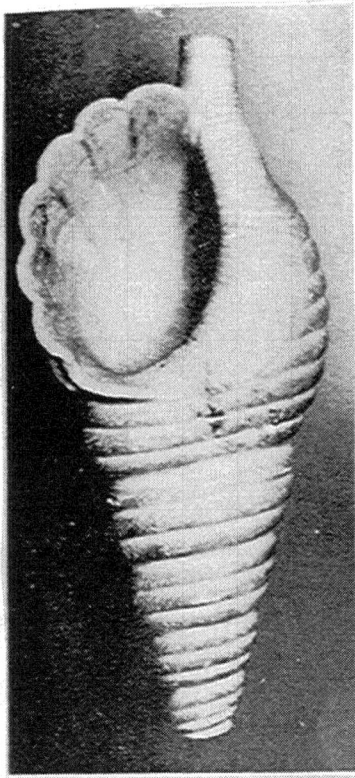

A

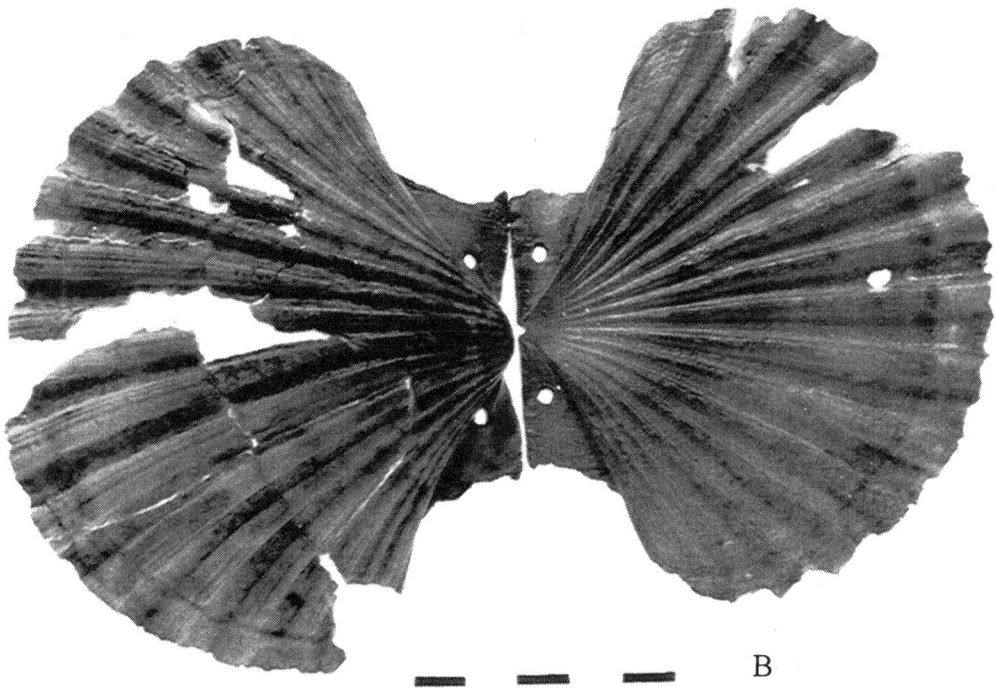

B

Fig. 13. A. Vessels out of Triton: i. Ag. Triada (h:29.6cm) ii. Kalyvia (h:37cm) (Warren 1969, Pl. 35) B. Pecten used as pyxis (L.C. Akrotiri - Thera, House of Women)

99

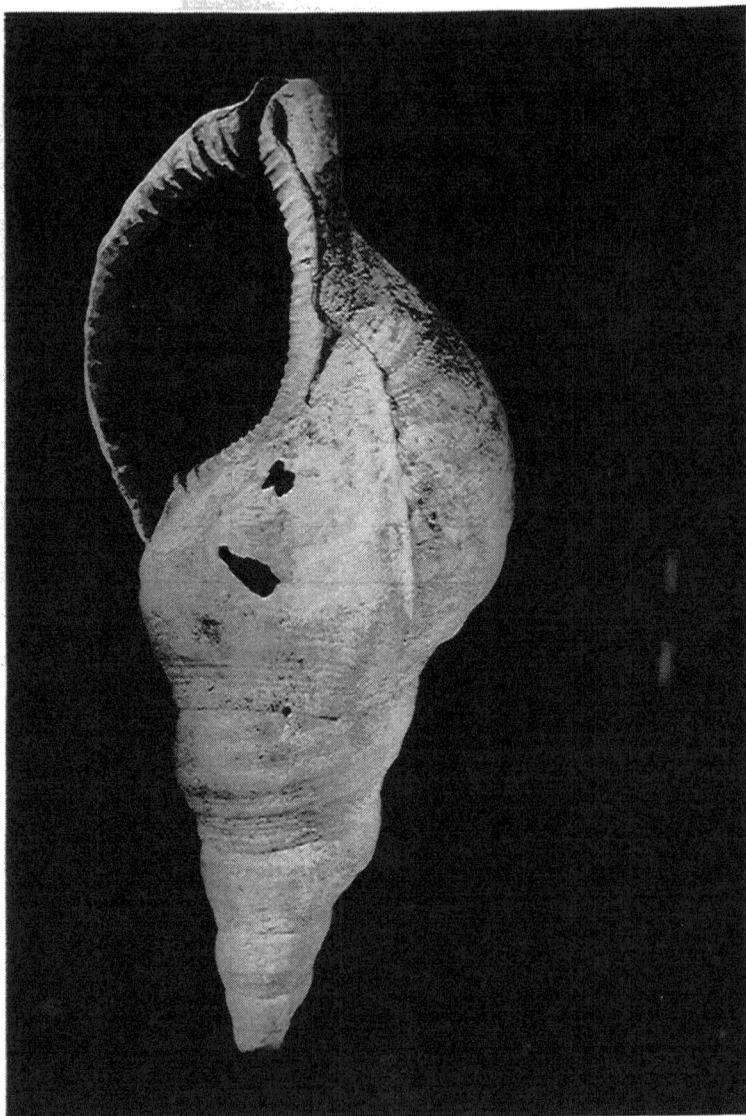

Fig. 14a. *Triton tritonis L.* Akrotiri-Thera, Ladies House.

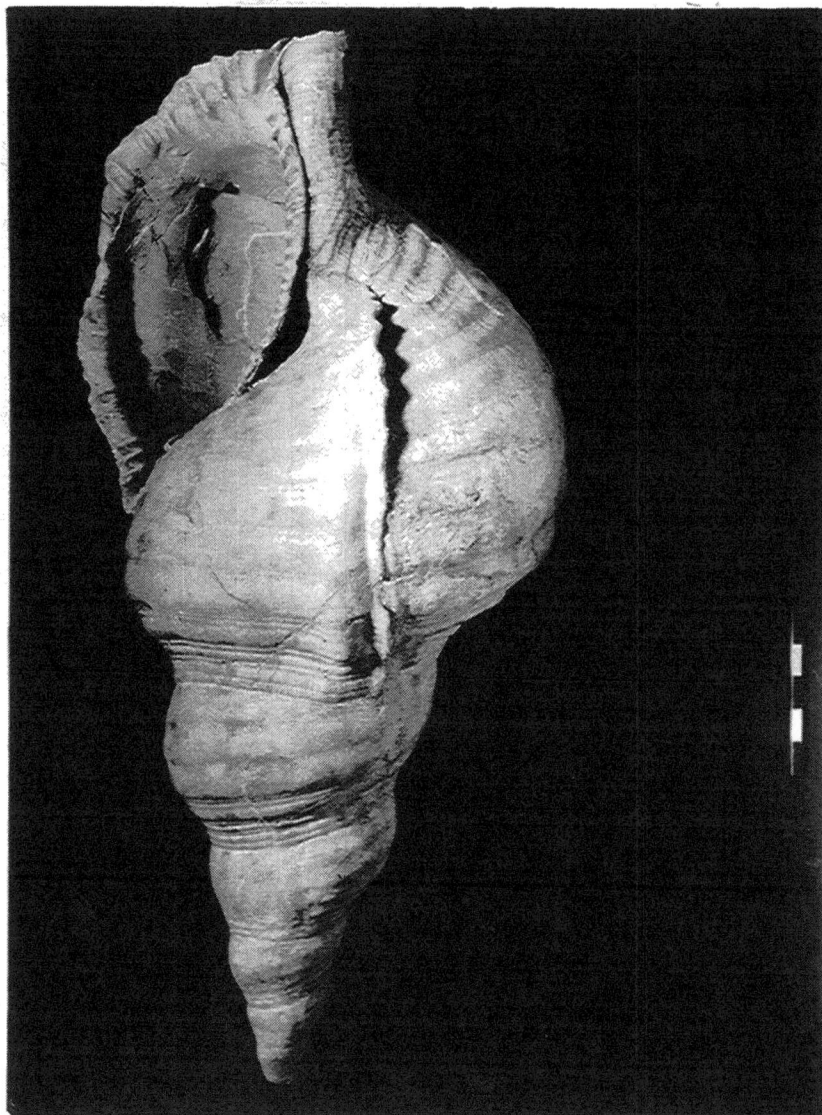

Fig. 14b. *Triton tritonis L.* Akrotiri-Thera, West House.

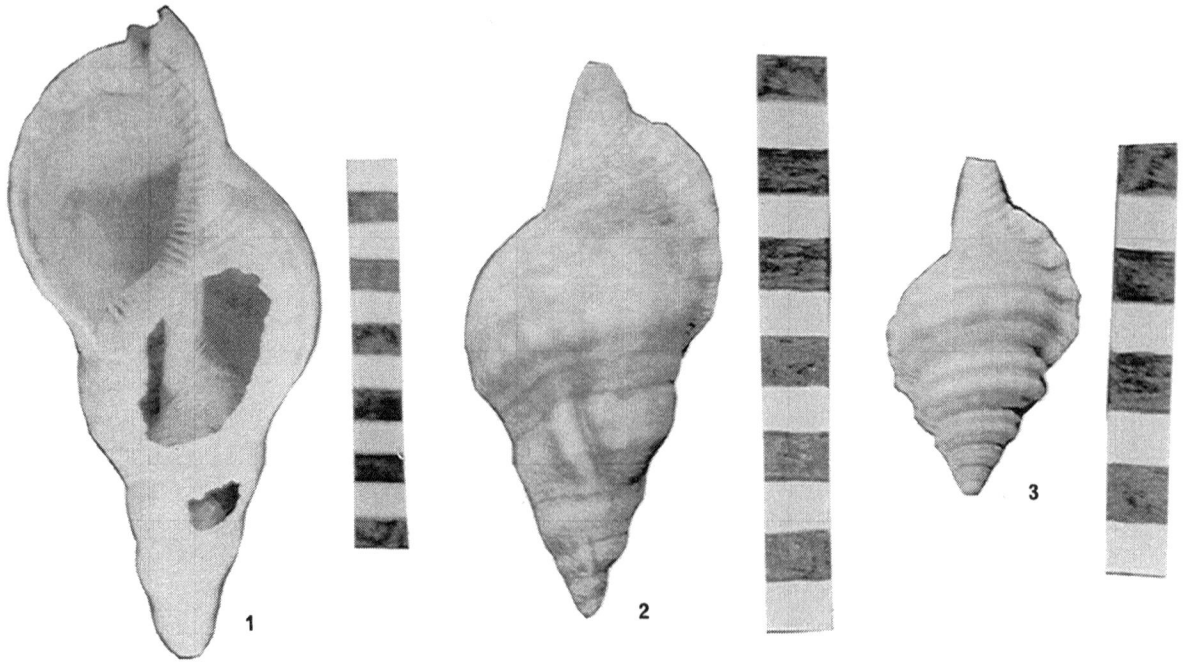

A

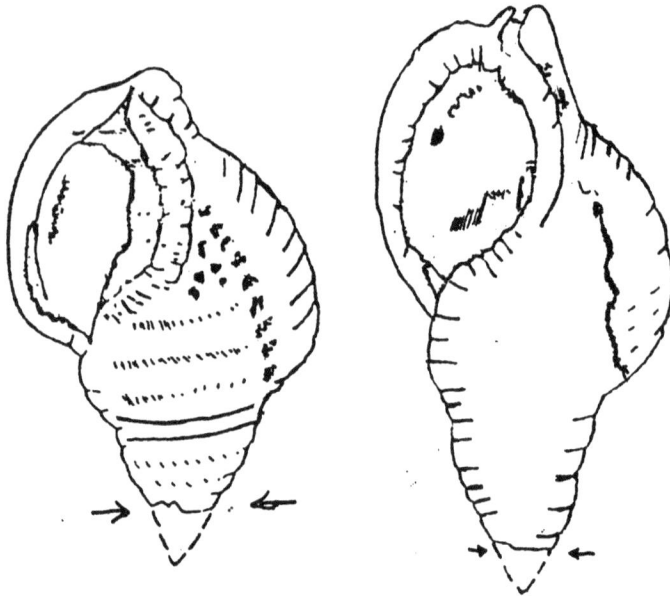

B

C

Fig. 15. A. Cycladic Collection from National Museum in Athens (*Charonia trionis tritonis Linné.* 1-2 from Phylacopy; 3 from Syros). B. Triton shell with lower pointed end cut off, from excavation (Myrtos, Pl. 8AD). C. Use of triton as trumpet as represented on seal (Mariani, Mont.Ant.6, fig. 12).

Ornaments

General elements

- (position-importance)
- (information)
- (criterion of choise)

Provenance material studies

(uses)

Working methods

valve shaping technic

(Perforation)

natural   lithophagus   human

Abration of the curved zone

trepanation

Morphological classification

Bracelets

pendants   rings

Beads   from unworked valve

from worked valve

discs

out of
Cardium sp.

out of mother pearl
Of Unio sp.

out of shell of various species

out of other material

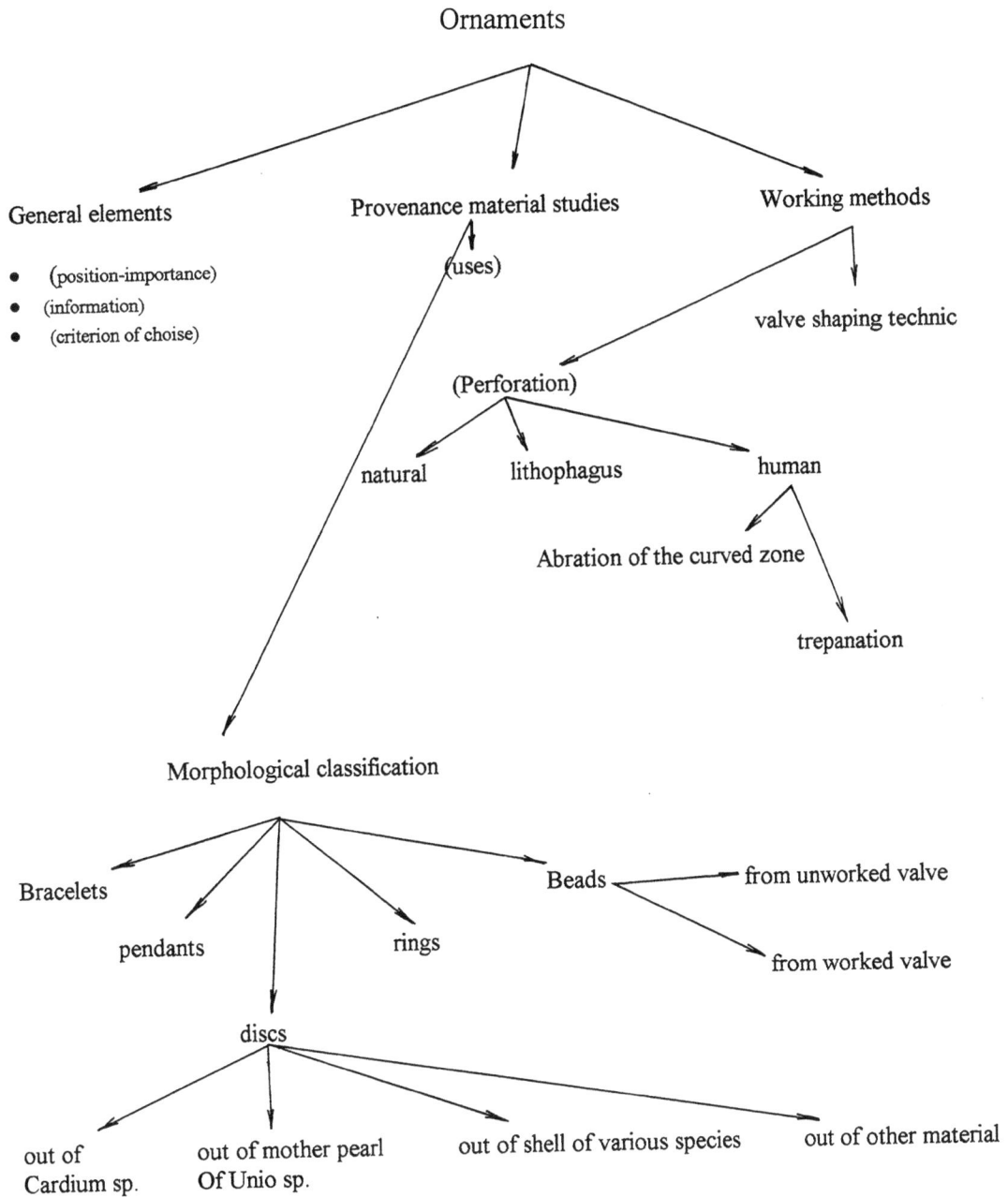

Fig. 16. Ornaments.

Neolithic ornaments made out of shells

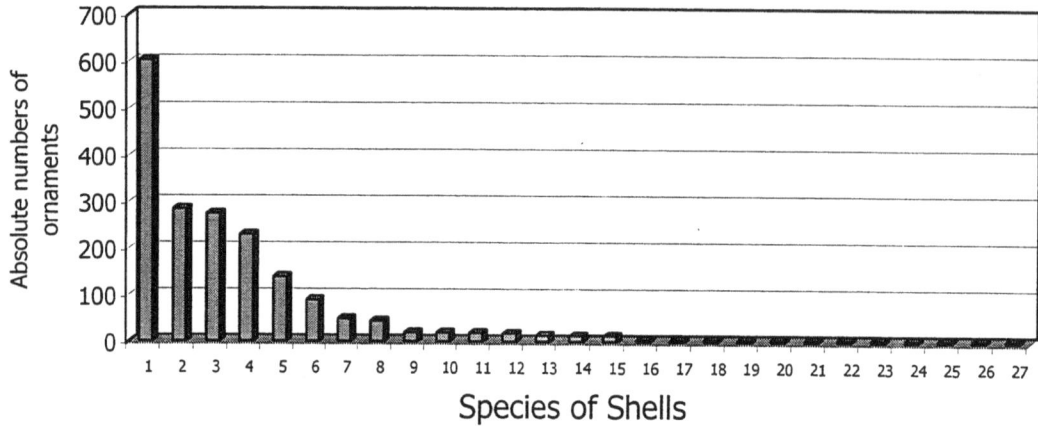

No	Species	No	Species	No	Species
1	Dentalium	10	Luria	19	Mactra
2	Glycimeris	11	Cerithium	20	Zonaria
3	Cardium	12	Nassa	21	Pirum
4	Spondylus	13	Natica	22	Venus
5	Cerastoderma	14	Arcularia	23	Acanthocardia
6	Conus	15	Euthria	24	Pisania
7	Monodonta	16	Tubular	25	Patella
8	Columbella	17	Asteroid	26	Fasciolaria
9	Murex	18	Unio	27	Cyclope

Fig. 16 (contd). Ornaments.

Patella
coerulea

A

Cardium sp.

Columbella rustica

Nassa neritea

B

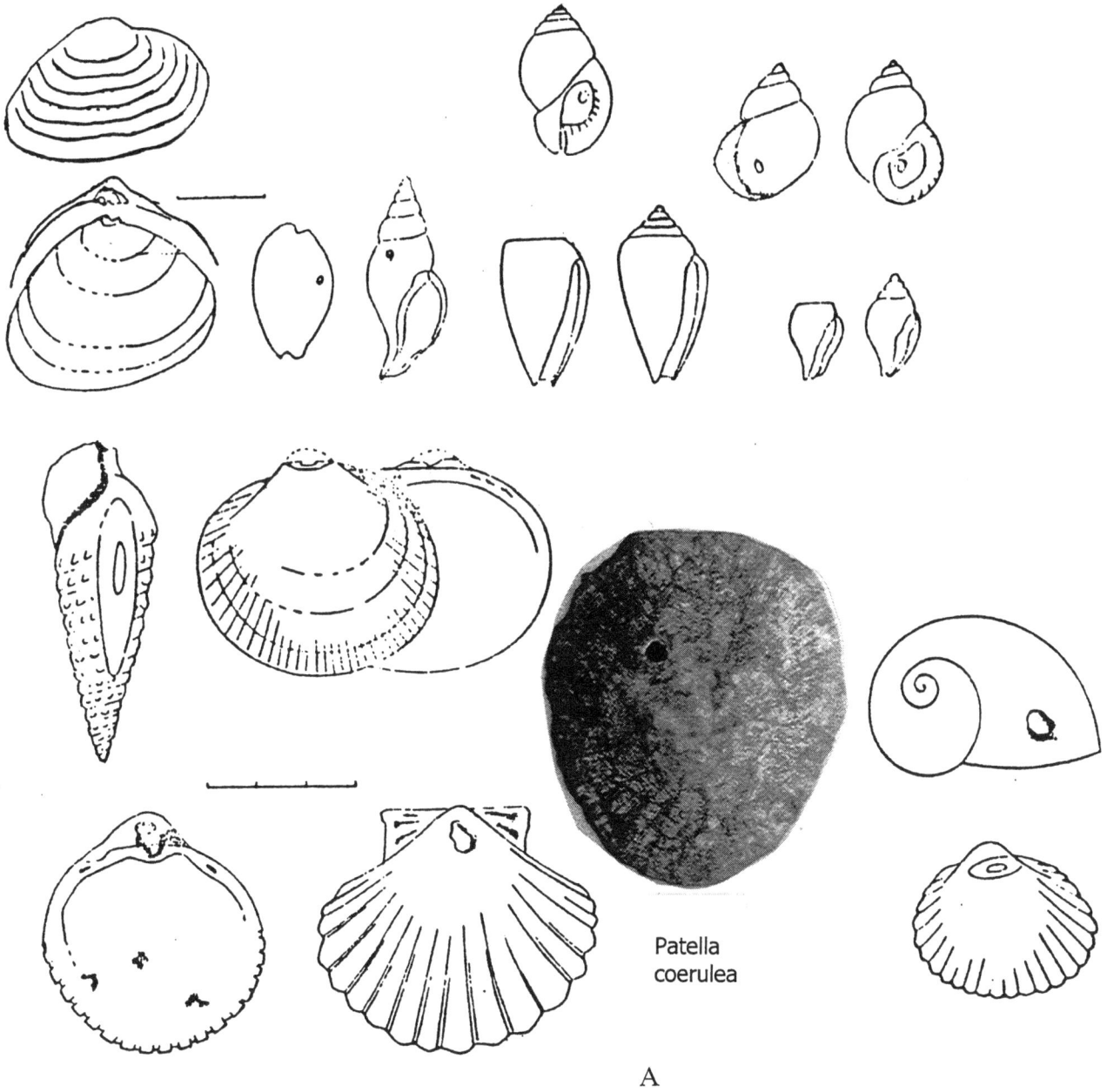

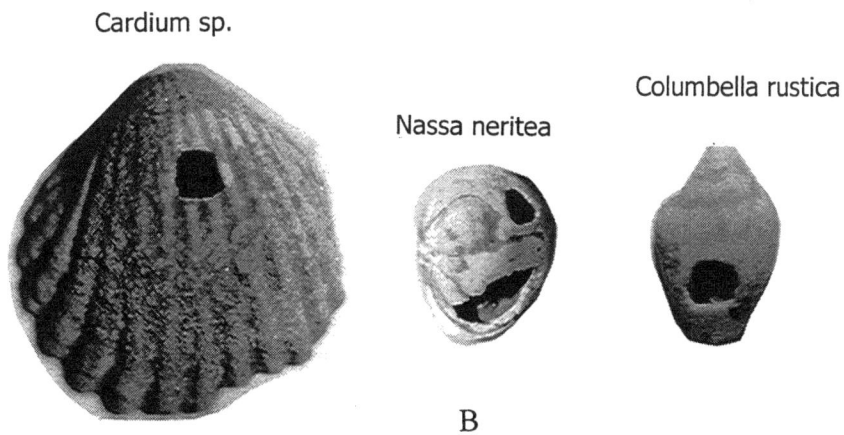

Fig. 17. Perforated shells. A. Holes occurred naturally; B Holes perforated by human activity.
(Photos: Kastri, Thasos, A5A5, N. Neolithic)

A

B

Fig. 18. Perforated shells from: A. E. Neolithic Kalathies, Rhodes (Samson 1987, The Neolithic Period in Dodekannisa); B. *Glycimeris sp.,* MEIII Kaloyerovrisi (Samson 1993, trench B).

Cardium pendant

Patella

Nassa

Cardium

Littorina with holes

Conus

Murex

Cross-shaped pendant,
Middle Neolithic
(Salonika (AEMθ 7, 93)

Discs

Duck-shaped
Pendant, Early
Bronze Age
(Agia Irini
K4282)

Buttons

Animal figurine pendant
L. Neolithic

Beads

Bracelets

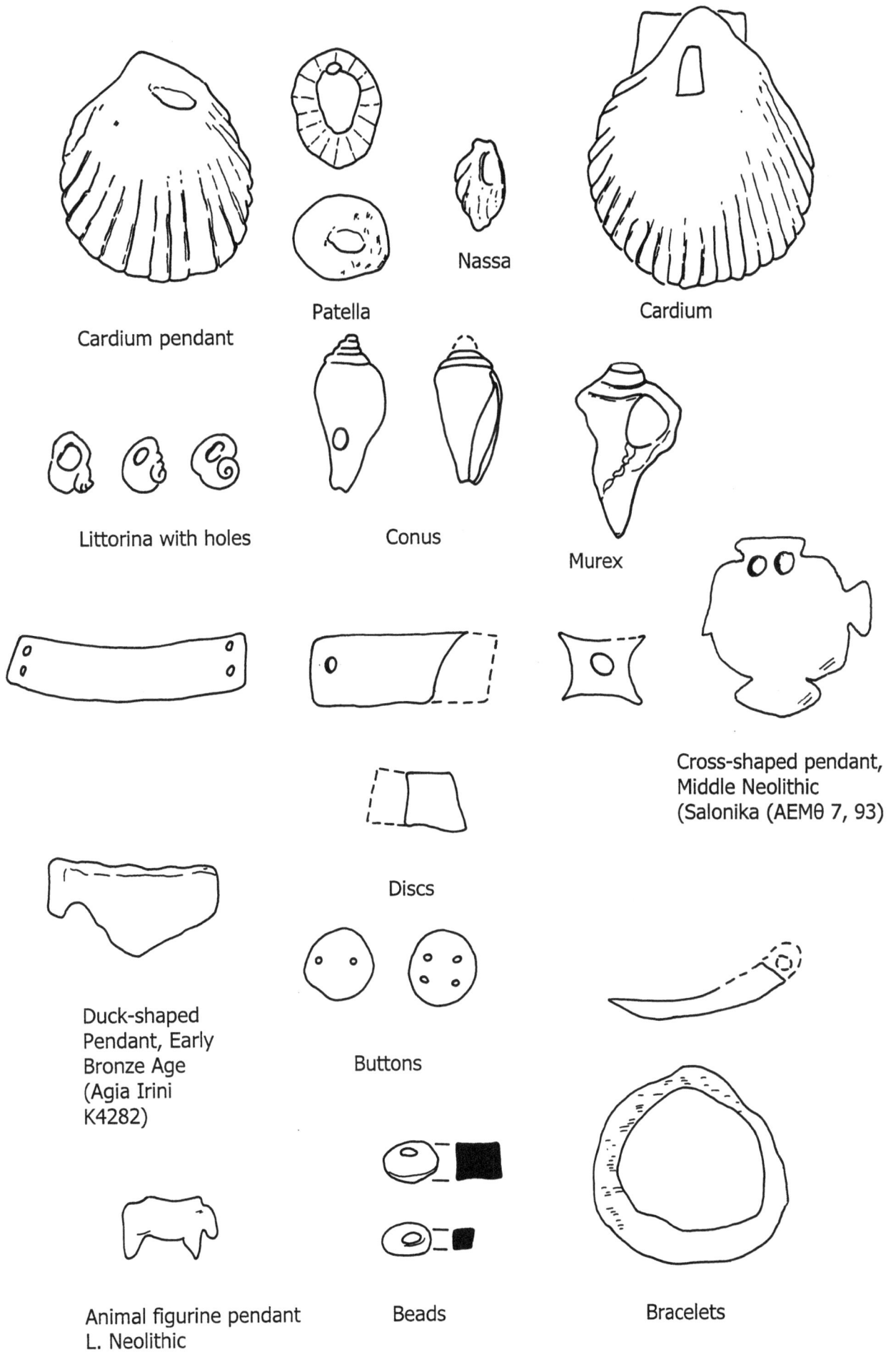

Fig. 19. Shell objects (Kitsos Cave, Laurion, Attica).

front   back   front   back

Dimitra (Late Neolithic)   Rhodocnori

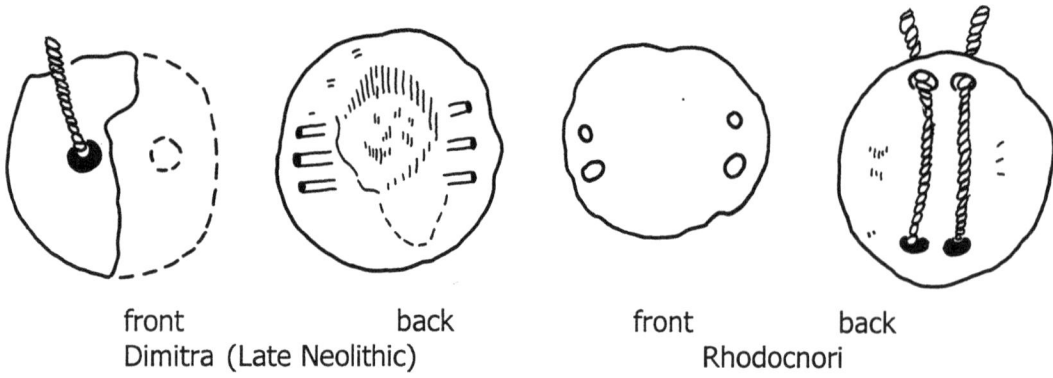

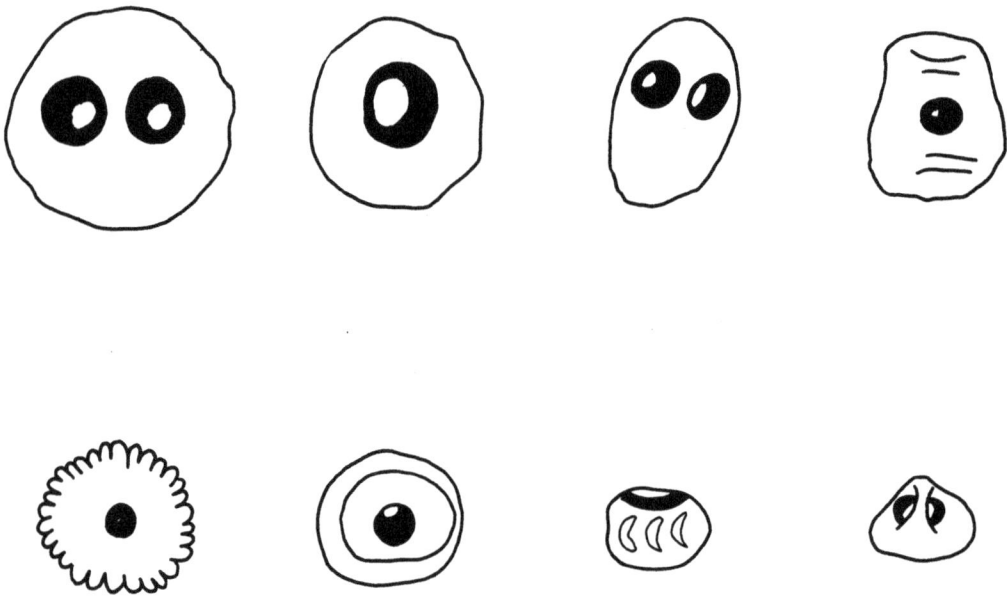

Perforated shells from a private collection (N. Kyparissi-Apostolika, Neolithic Ornemants of Thessa, post-graduate dissertation 1991)

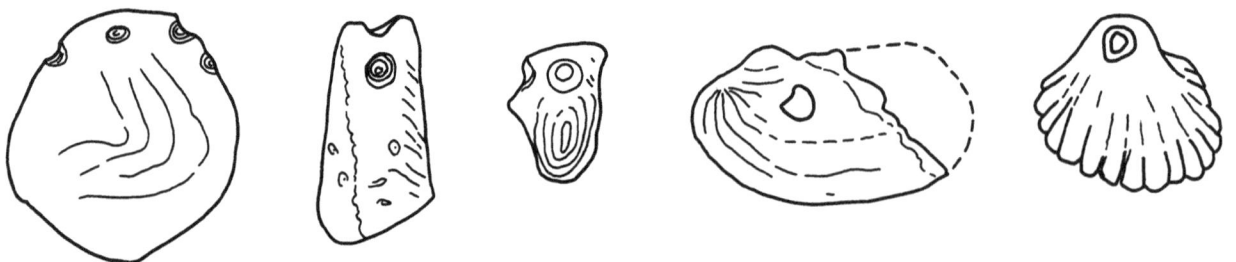

Shells with perforations from Dikili-Tash

Fig. 20. Buttons and pendants made of shell.

Several types of beads

Barrel-shaped bead
Sitagroi, Phase 5,
Muesum Phillipi

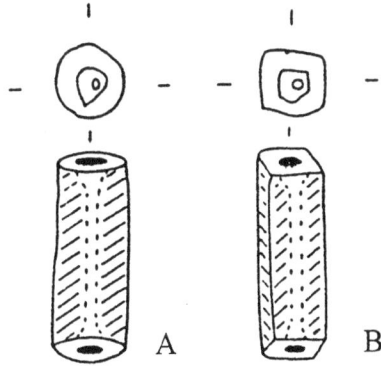

Tube-shaped beads (cylinder / square)
Dikili-Tash a. M446 b. M780

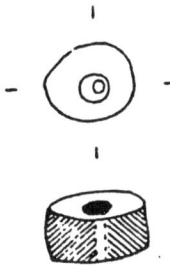

A   B

Round bead

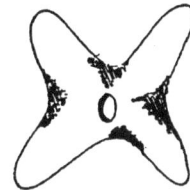

Star-shaped bead (Sitagroi Phase
2, Museum Phillipi)

Trefoil-shaped bead (Dimitra LN)

Fig. 21. Main shapes of beads made of shells.

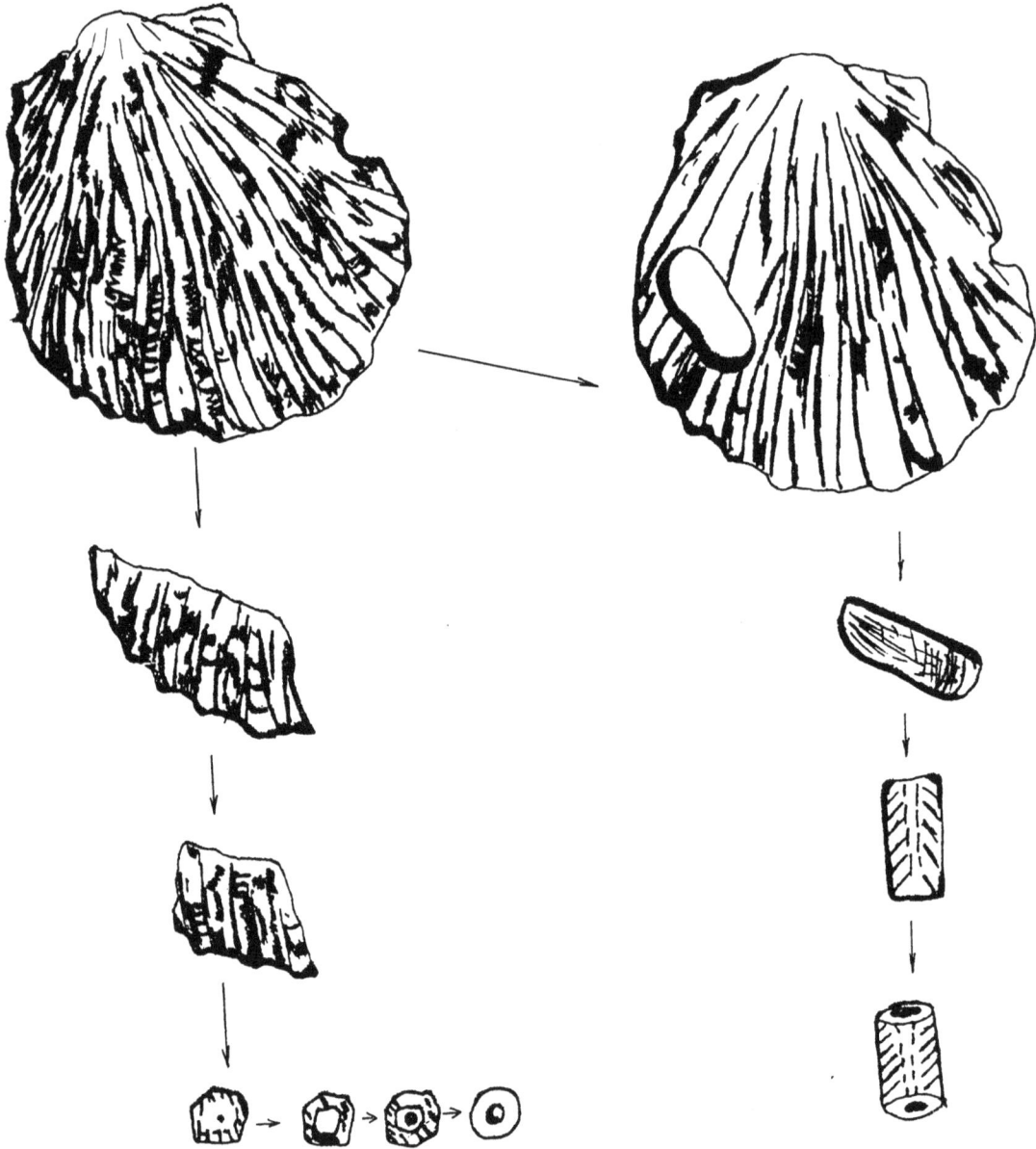

Fig. 22. Working stages for beads from Spondylus shell.

Fig. 23. Beads made of Spondylus sp. and Dentalium sp. / LN, Dikili-Tash. (Top: M752, M780, M729, M1211; Bottom: M260, M405, M424, M436, M446, M500, M501, M729)

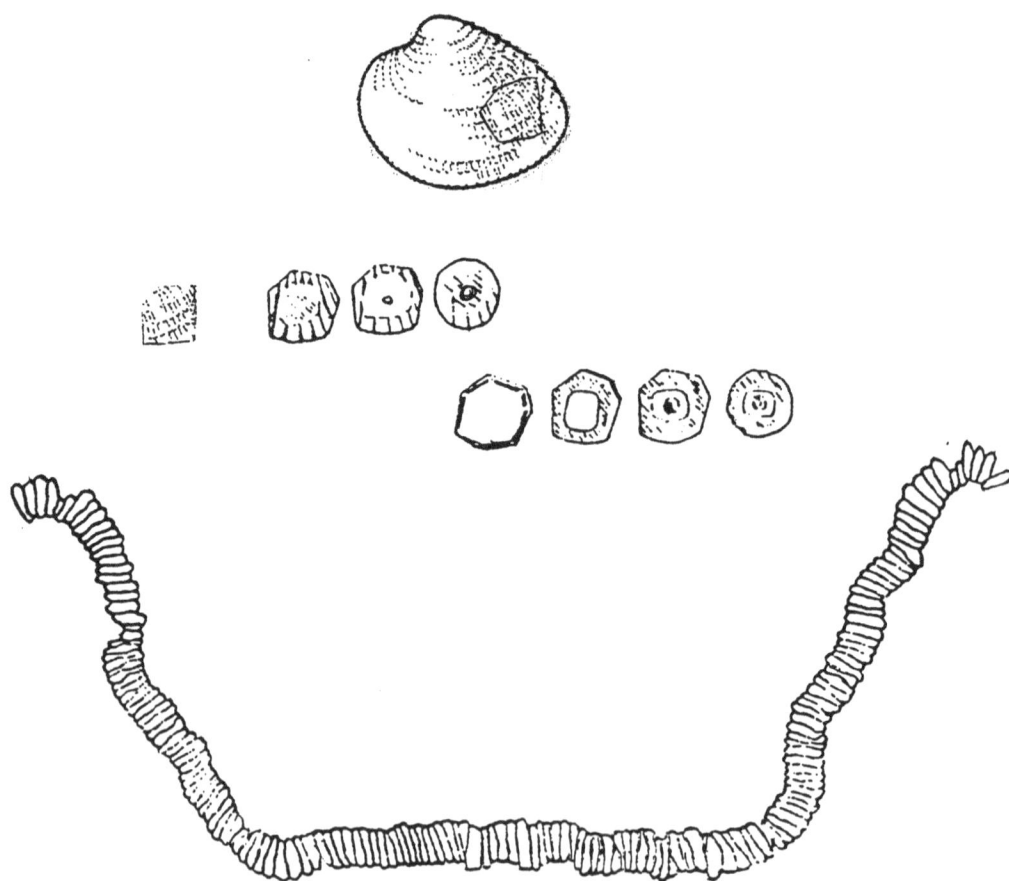

Beads made of Cardium sp. (Taborin, p.141, fig. 16)

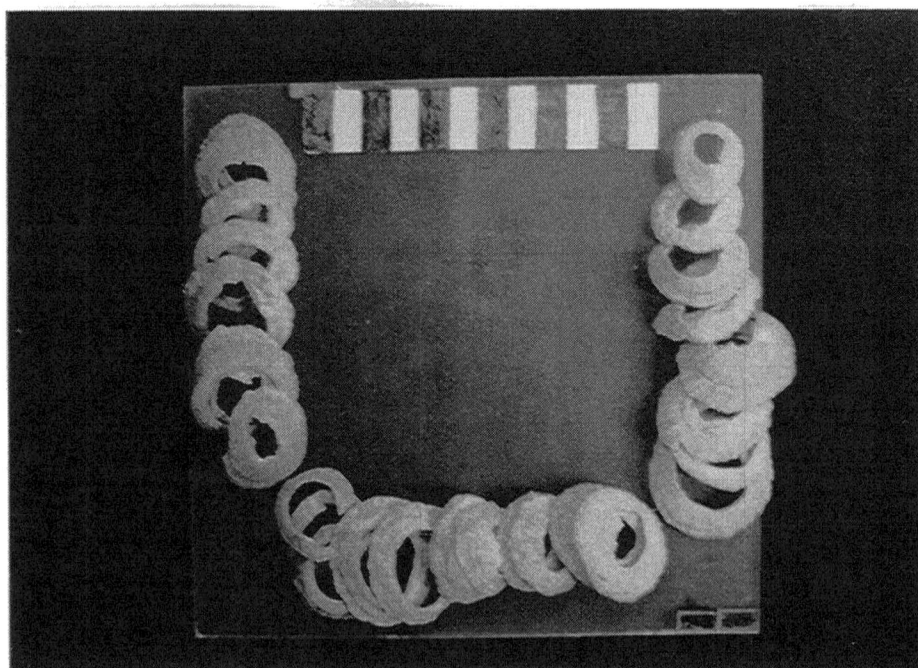

Ring-shaped Patella, recycled food remains from Phylakopi (EC II-III, no 12407, National Archaeological Museum of Athens)

Fig. 24.

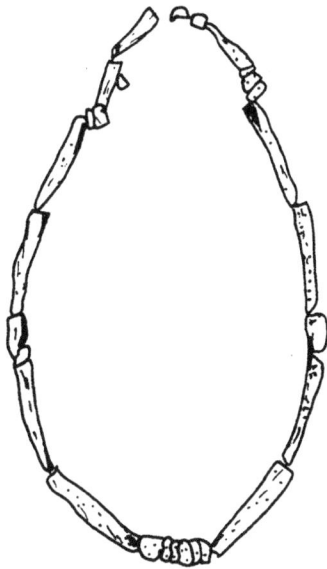

Dikaios 1953, fig. 54
No. 928

Dikaios 1953, pl. XCIX

Dikaios 1953, pl. LXV III A, LN

Fig. 25. Bead-bracelets made of *Dentalium sp.*.

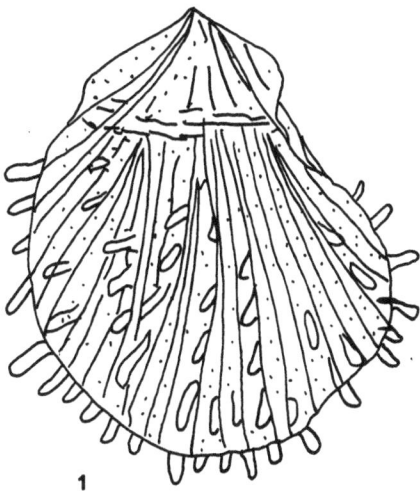

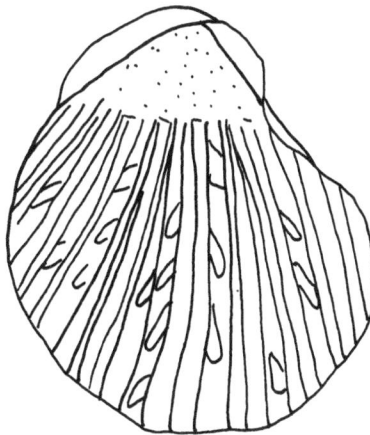

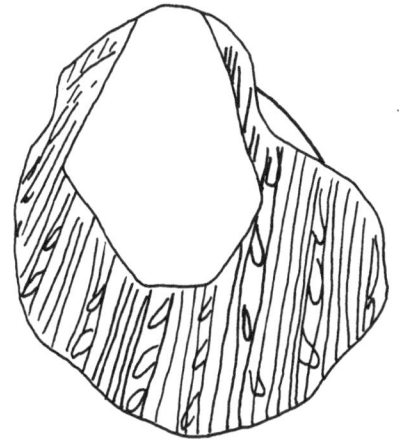

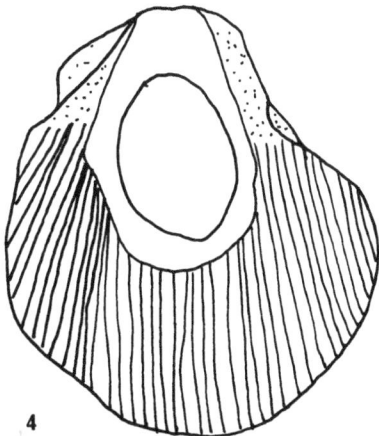

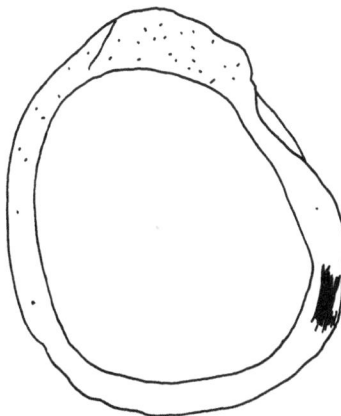

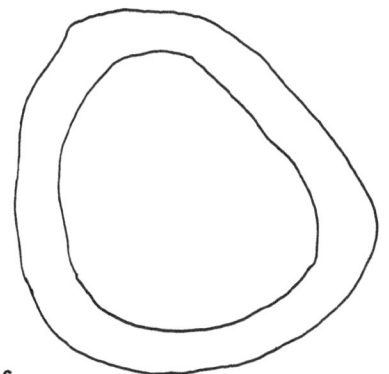

Fig. 26. Working stages for Spondylus bracelets.

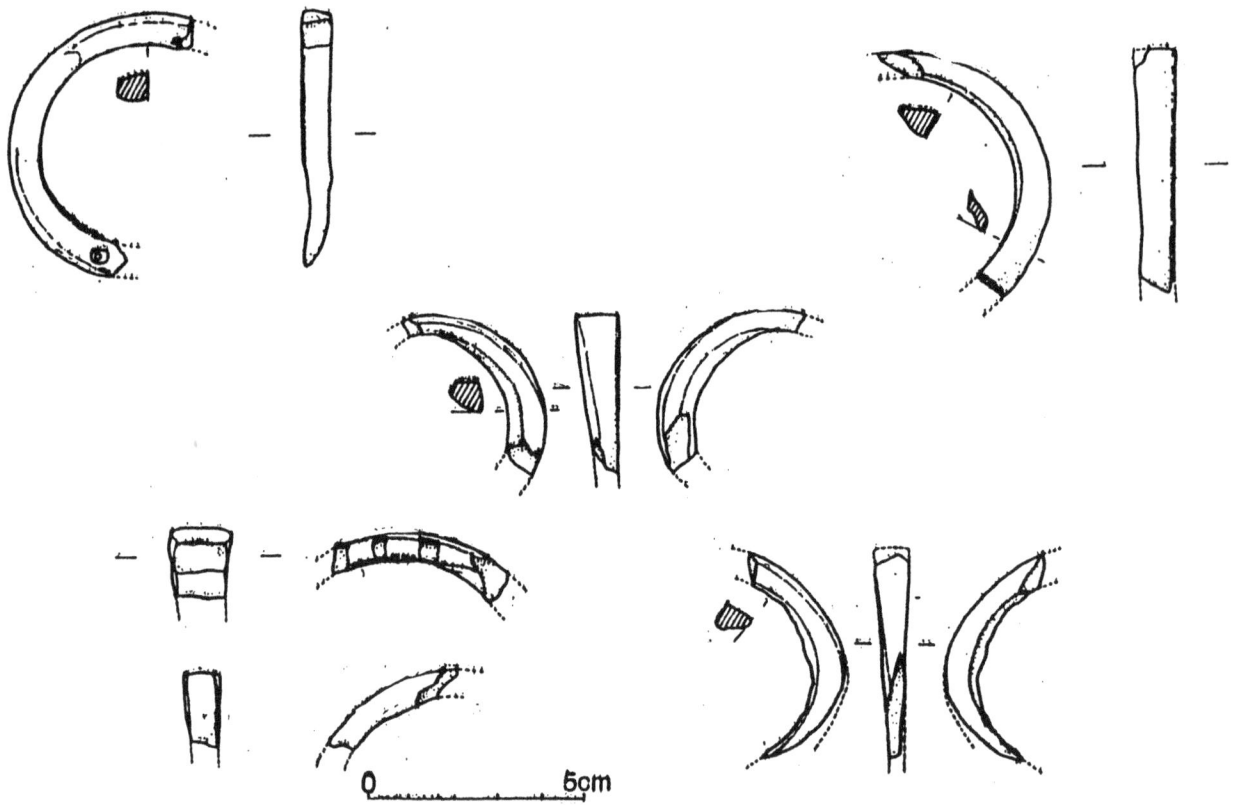

Fig. 27. Various examples of Spondylus bracelets.

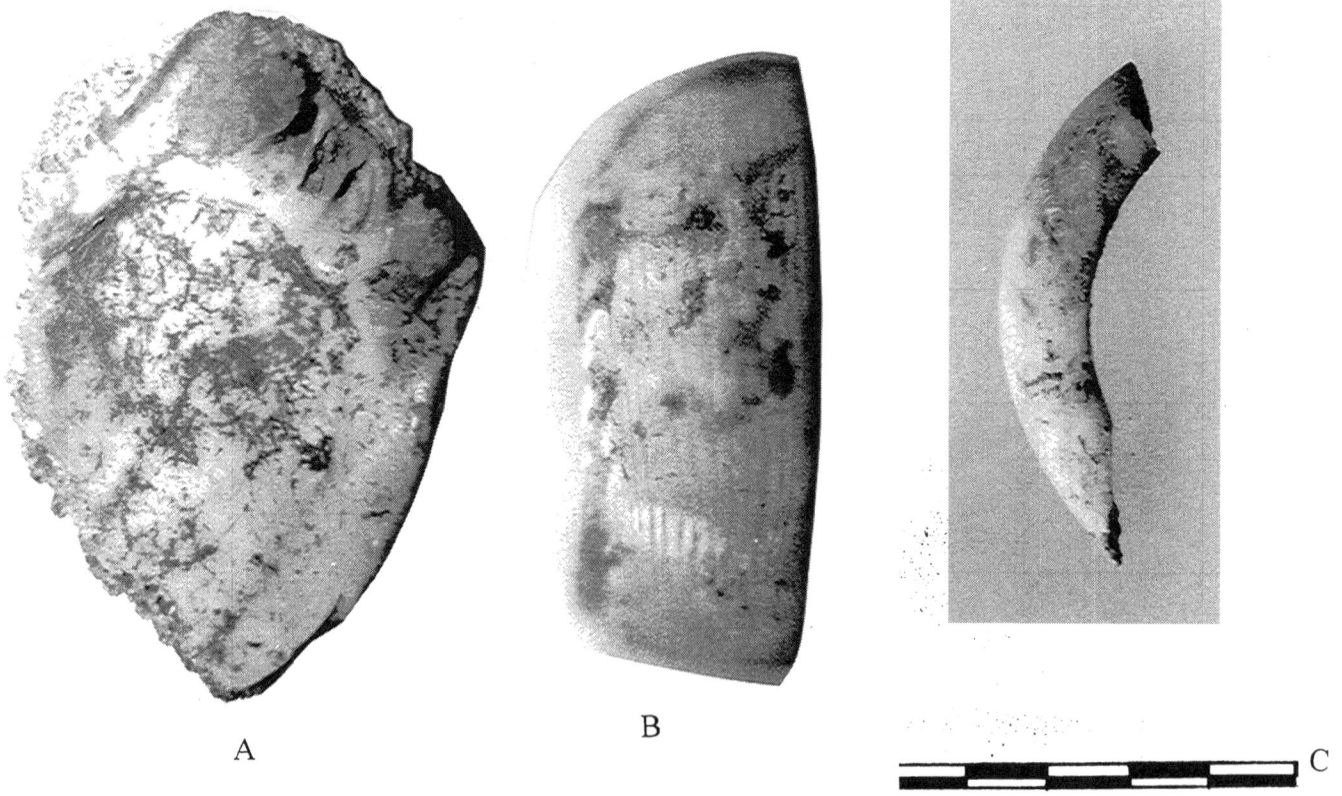

A

B

C

Fig. 28. A. Spondylus, Dimitra NN (Grammenos, D, Neolithic Studies in Central and Eastern Macedonia, 1991, pl. 30,12) B. Spondylus bracelet, Dimitra MN III (Grammenos, op.c.) C. Bracelet from Dikili Tash (M. 1233).

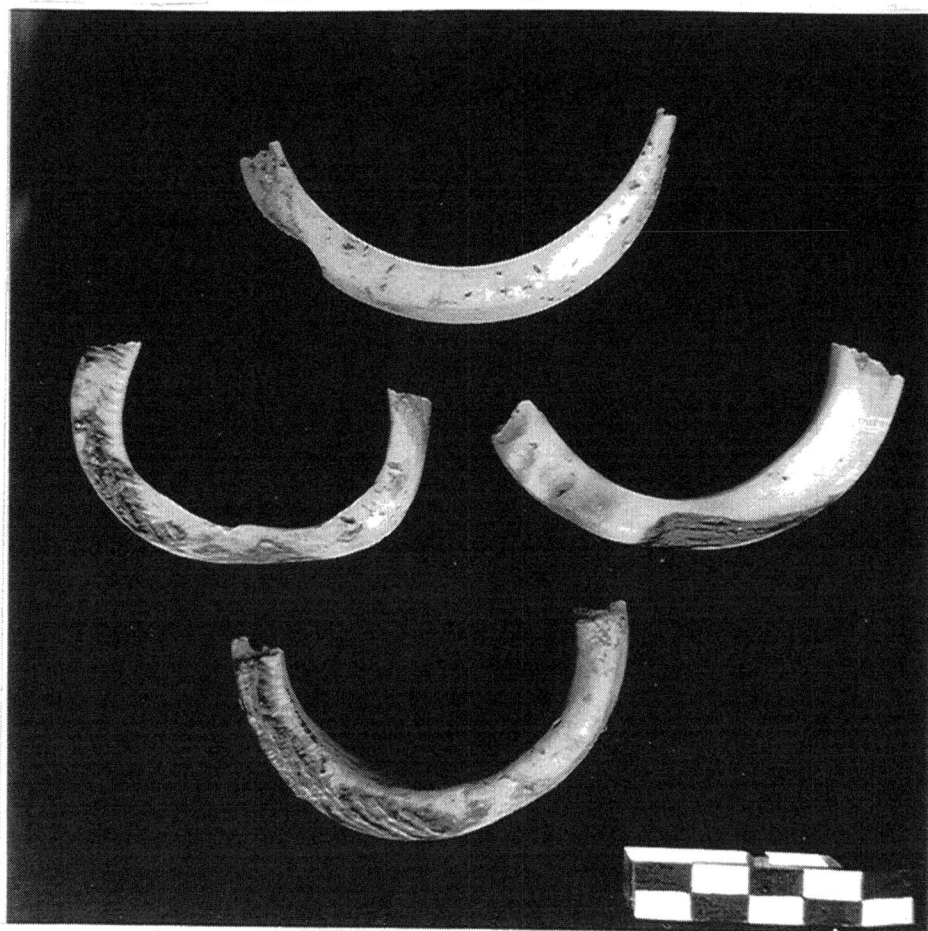

Fig. 29. Bracelets made of Spondylus / LN, Dikili-Tash (Top: M1910, M1915, M1919, M1920; Bottom: M465, M396, M285, M239).

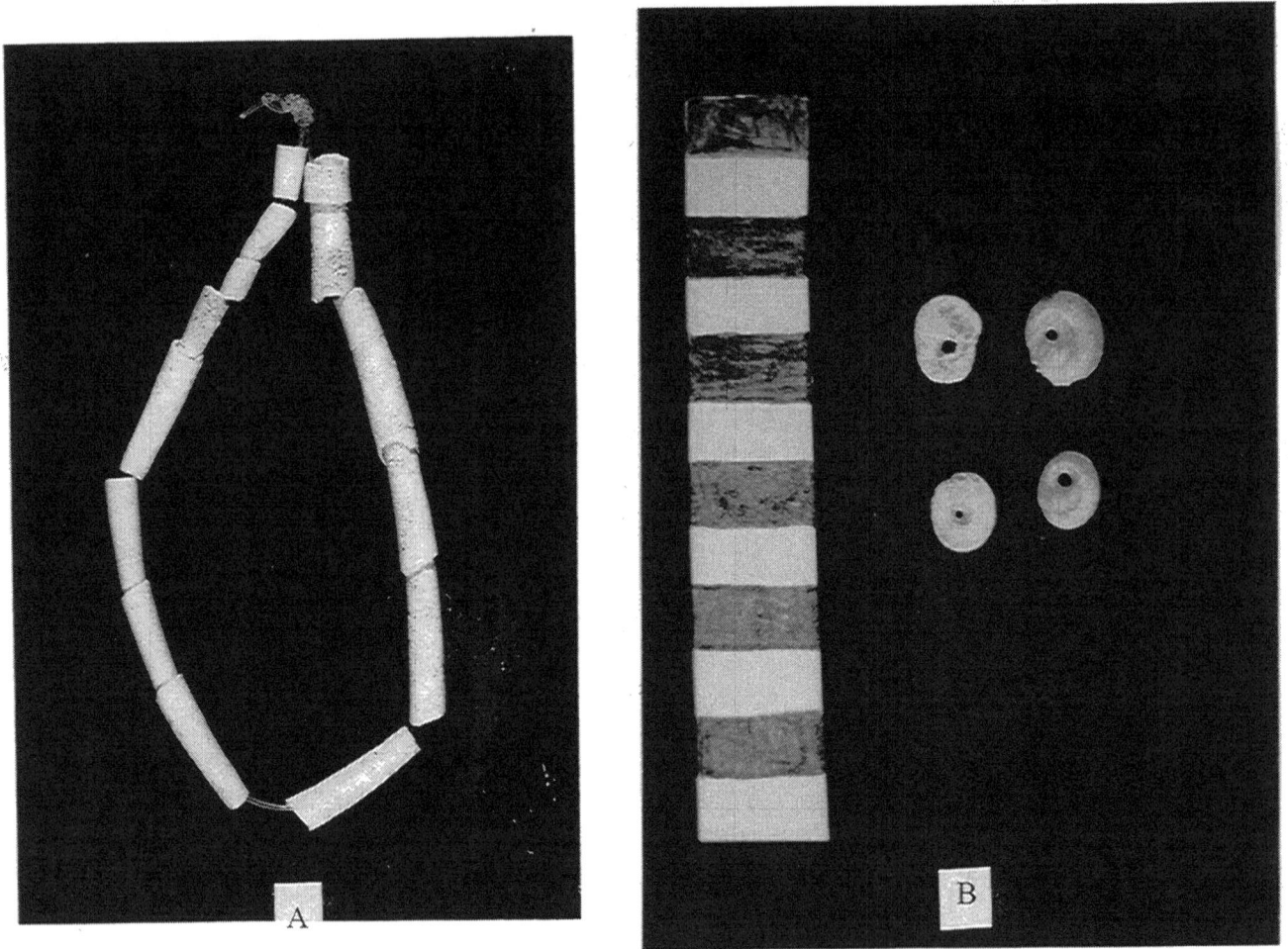

Fig. 30. A. Dentalium beads (Syros, site Kastro, EC, Grave 307, Nat.Arch. Mus. of Athens). B. *Operculum* with holes from Naxos (EC I-II, no 8827, Nat. Arch. Mus. of Athens, site Louros Athanassou)

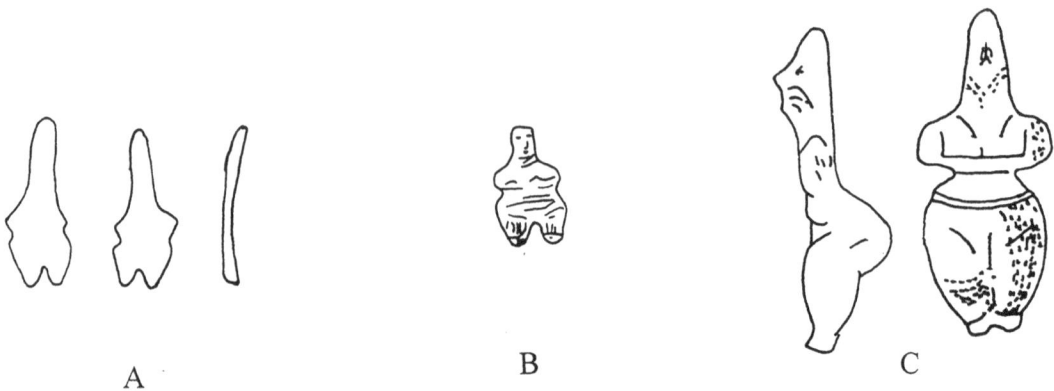

Fig. 31. Human-shaped figurines. A. Knossos; B. Central Crete (Ucko Pl. XXXIX, no. 10); C. Aigina (Welter 1938, Fig. 8).

Symbolic uses

Non-worked shells

Artistic representations

Seals

Vessels

Various objects

Fresco

Worked shells

Figurine

The conus shell game

Human shaped

Animal shaped

Polishing

Lead

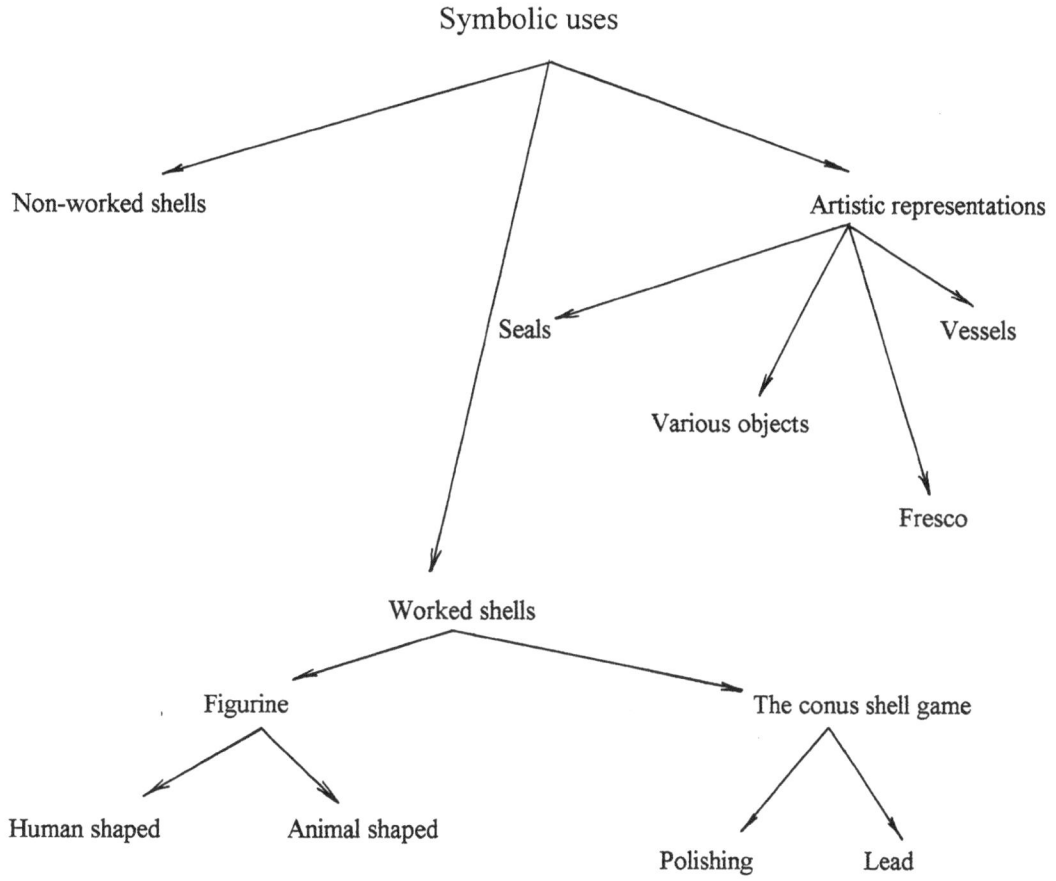

Fig. 32. Symbolic uses.

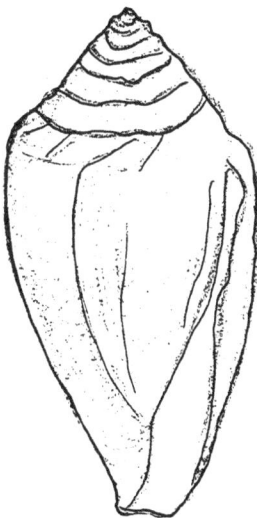

Fig. 33. Cone shells.

Other uses of molluscs

IV
Trade

surplus   value

buying demand

I

Building material

sediments   insulation

ingredients

III

Purple dye

-Murex trunculus L.
-Murex brandaris L.
-Thais (Purpura) haermastoma L.

II
Cardial Ceramic

incisions large and linear   incisions continuous and curvilinear

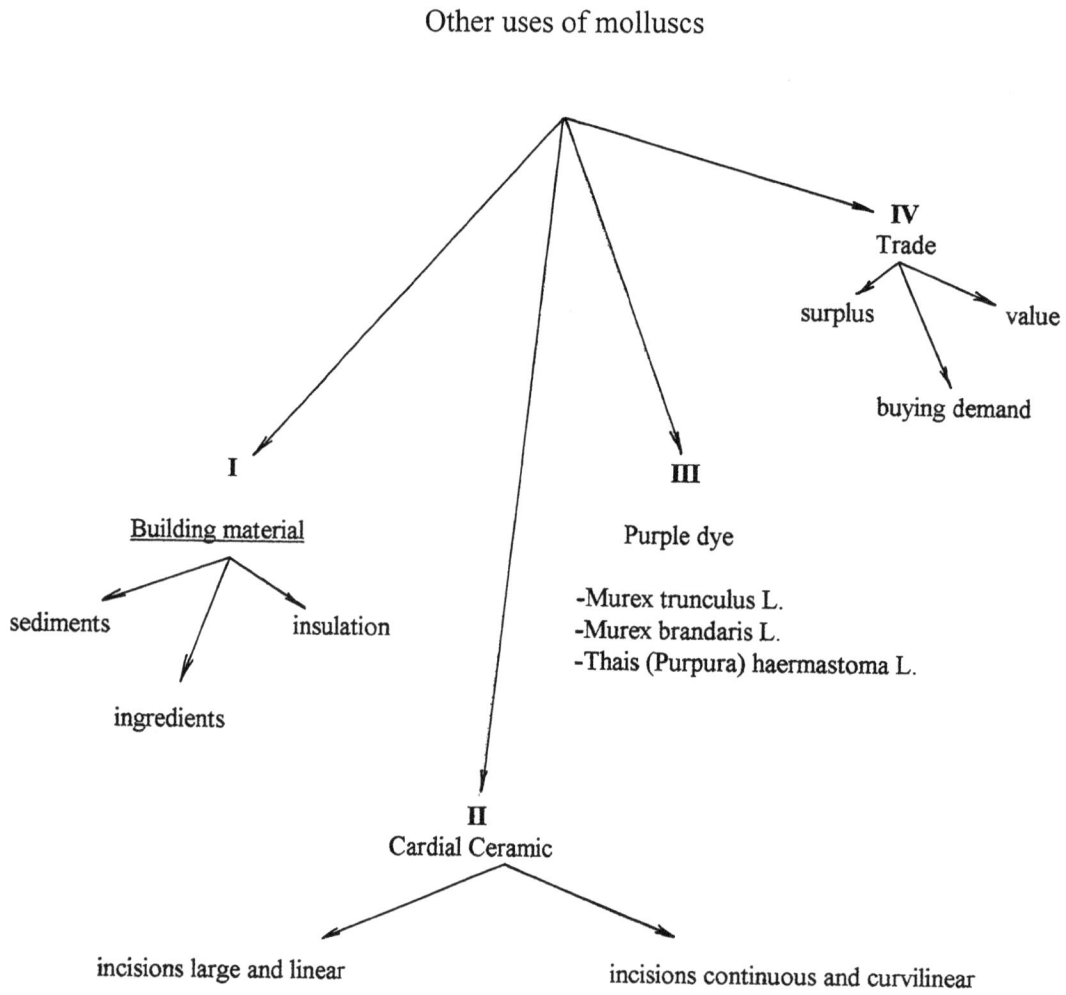

Fig. 34. Other uses of molluscs.

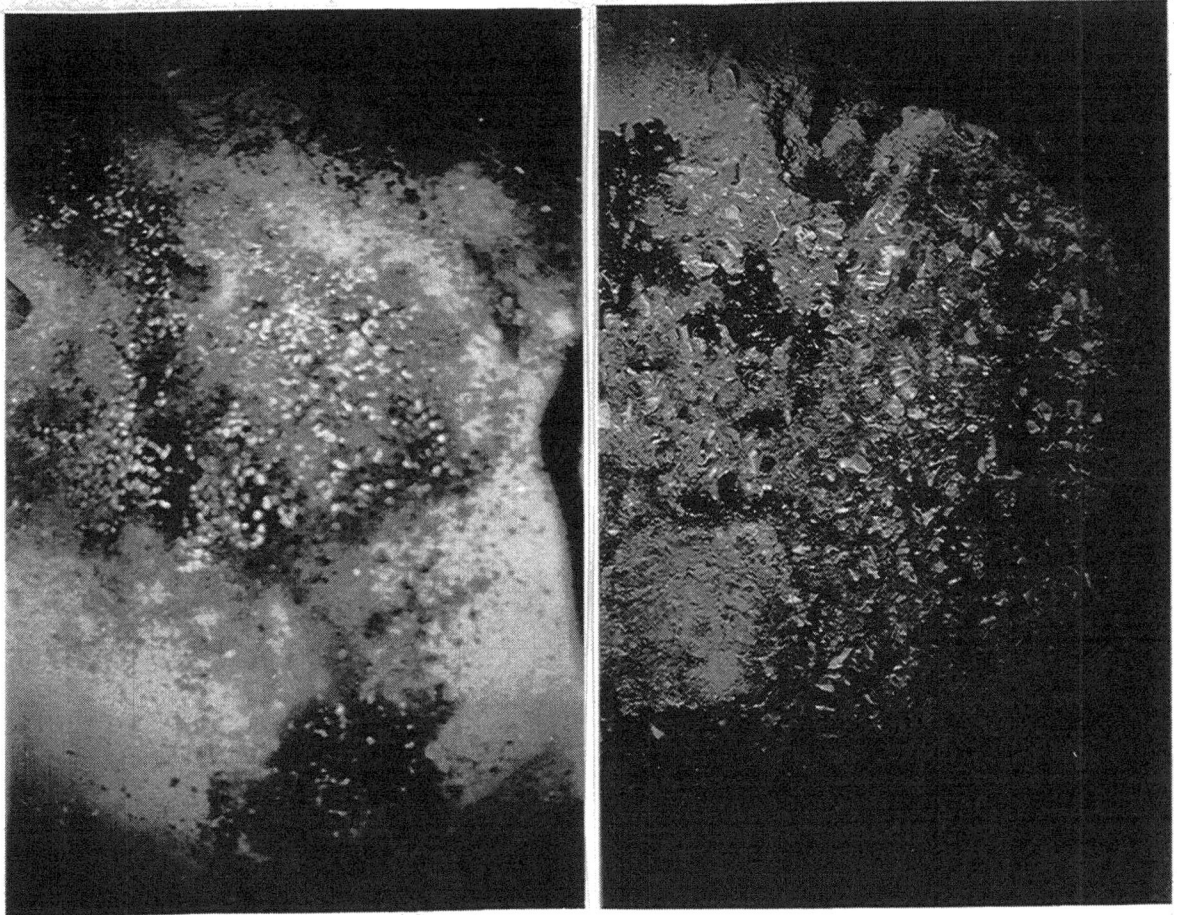

Fig. 35. Shell as building material (Rooms A2, B6, LC Akrotiri floors).

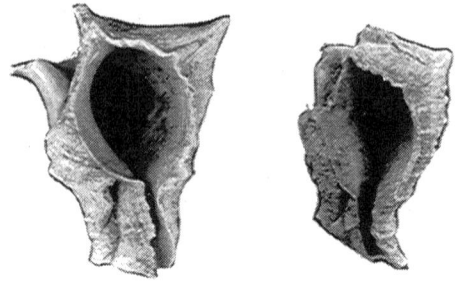

A

B

cm

C

Fig. 36. Purple-dye production: A-B. *Murex trunculus L.* C. Murex heaps from Akrotiri.

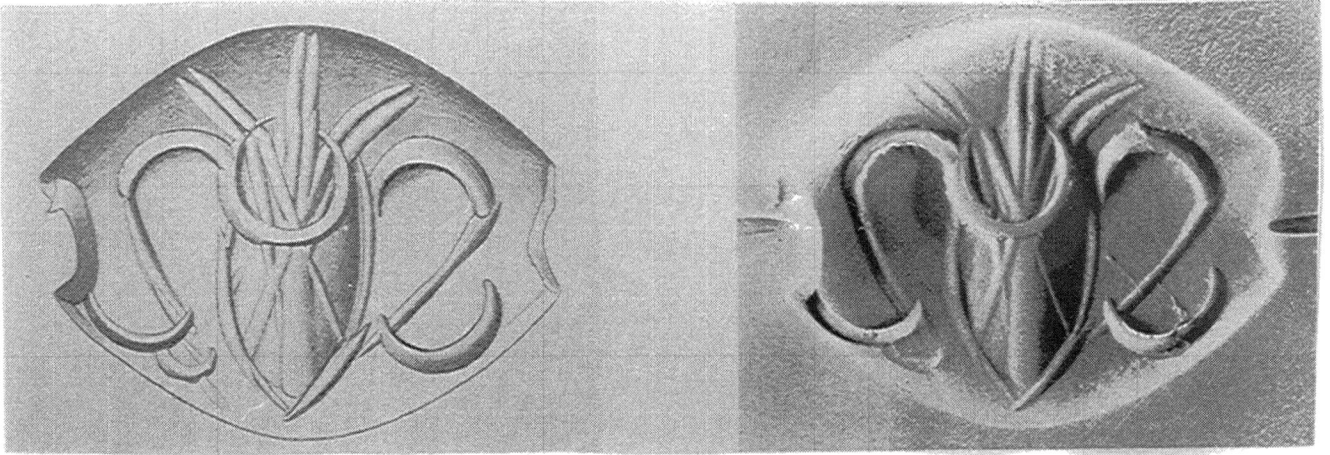

A

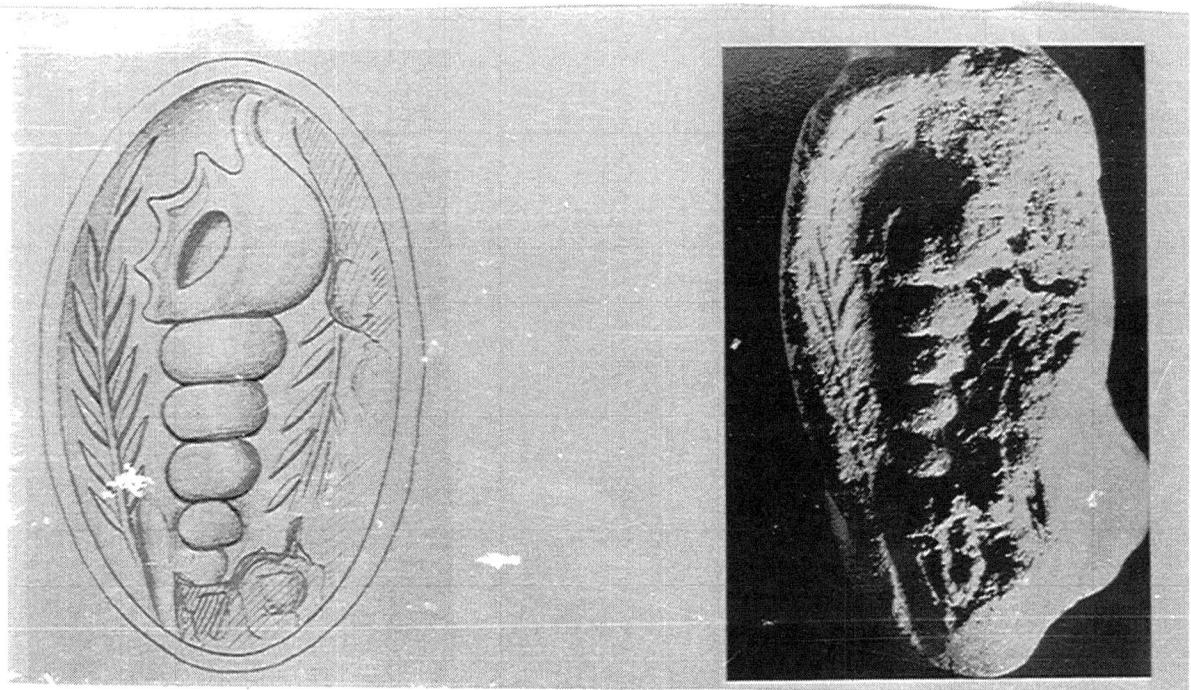

B

Fig. 37. Seals with sea species representations. A. Athens, SLG, Sigallas, Thera, no. 210);
B. Heraklion, Phaistos (C.M.S. II5) no. 305.

C.M.S. VII no. 219

C.M.S. VII no. 79

C.M.S. VII no. 80

C.M.S. IV no. 235

C.M.S. VII no. 177

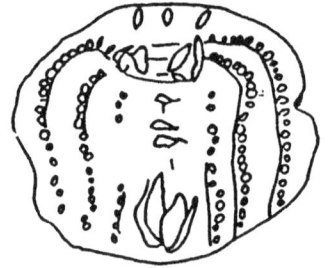

C.M.S. IX no. 184

C.M.S. IX no. 10D

C.M.S. VII no. 75

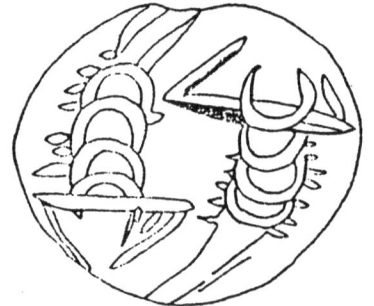

C.M.S. VII no. 76

C.M.S. VII no. 234

C.M.S. V₁ no. 205

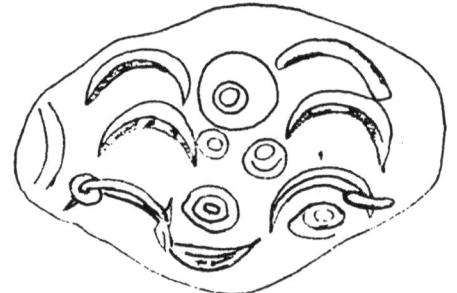

C.M.S. VII no. 78

C.M.S. VIII no. 51

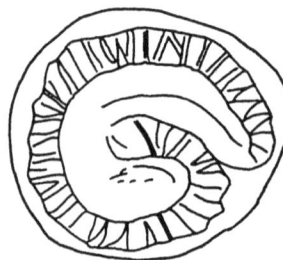

C.M.S. IX no 24

C.M.S. IIS, no. 304

Fig. 38. Sea species representations on seals.

Fig. 39. Vases of marine style A. Cretan rhyton with marine designs, c.1500 BC, Heraklion Museum; B. Cretan vase, floral and marine designs, c, 1600-1500BC, Heraklion Museum..

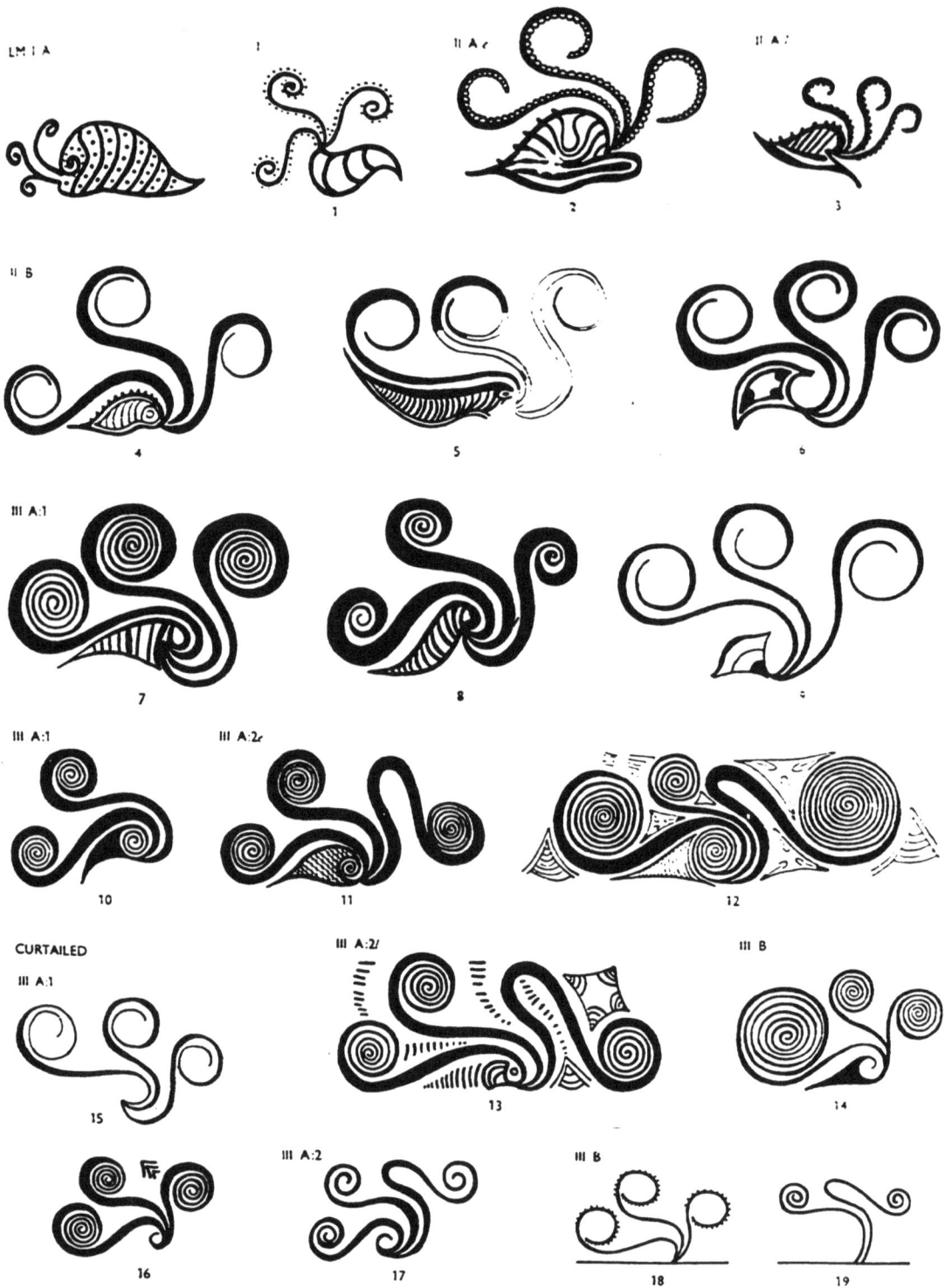

Fig. 40. The Argonaut motif (MP-motif number 22). Examples of shell motifs used in Minoan and Mycenenan art.

The Gastropod Shell

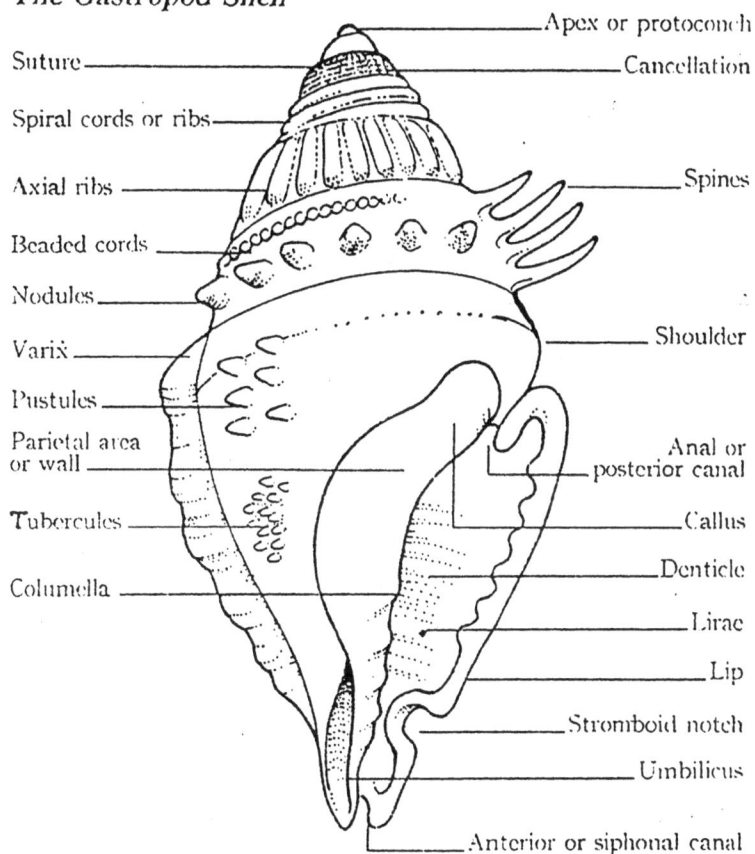

Suture

Spiral cords or ribs

Axial ribs

Beaded cords

Nodules

Varix

Pustules

Parietal area or wall

Tubercules

Columella

Apex or protoconch

Cancellation

Spines

Shoulder

Anal or posterior canal

Callus

Denticle

Lirae

Lip

Stromboid notch

Umbilicus

Anterior or siphonal canal

The Bivalve Shell

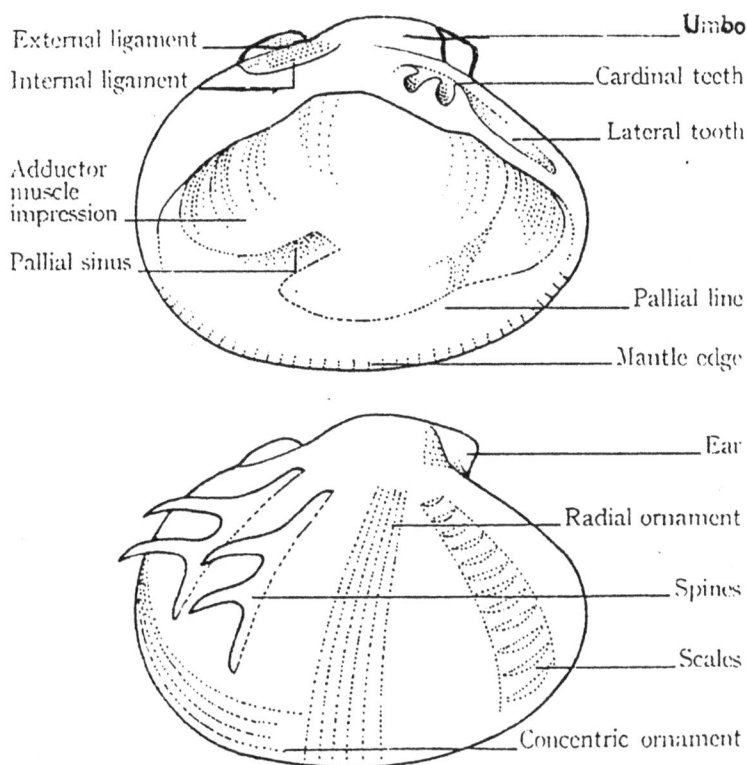

External ligament

Internal ligament

Adductor muscle impression

Pallial sinus

Umbo

Cardinal teeth

Lateral tooth

Pallial line

Mantle edge

Ear

Radial ornament

Spines

Scales

Concentric ornament

Fig. 41. Structural anatomy of Gastropod and Bivalve shell.

Atlas of sea shells found in Greece in archaeological contexts

A. Bivalvia

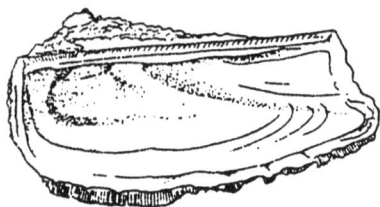

Arca noae L.

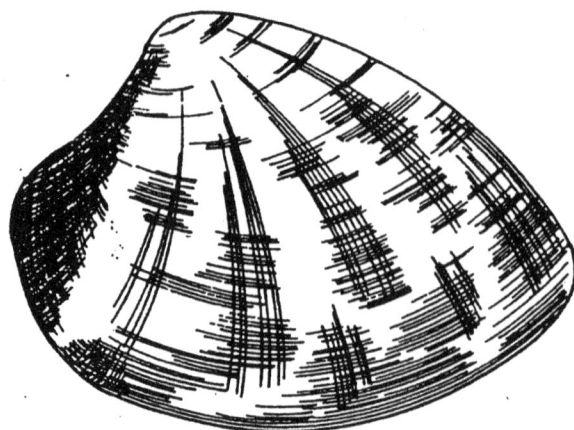

Callista chione L.

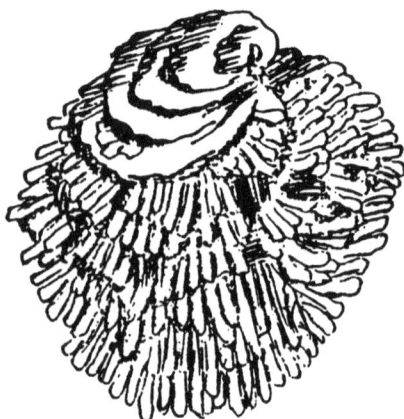

Chama gryphoides L.

Chlamys varia L.

Dentalium vulgare da Costa

Mesodesma cornea (Poli)

Ensis ensis L.

Glycimeris glycimeris L.

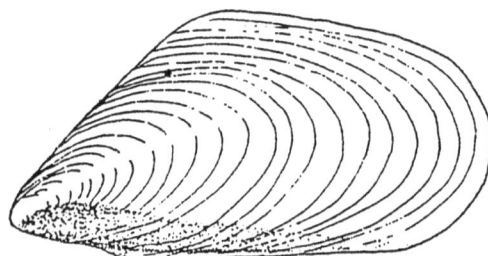

Mytilus galloprovincialis L.

Atlas of sea shells found in Greece in archaeological contexts

A. Bivalvia

Pecten jacobeus L.

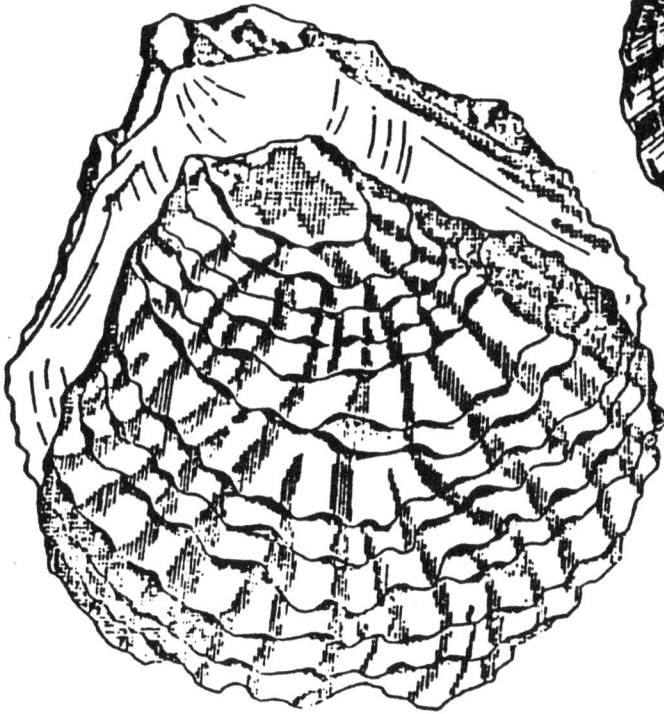

Ostrea edulis L.

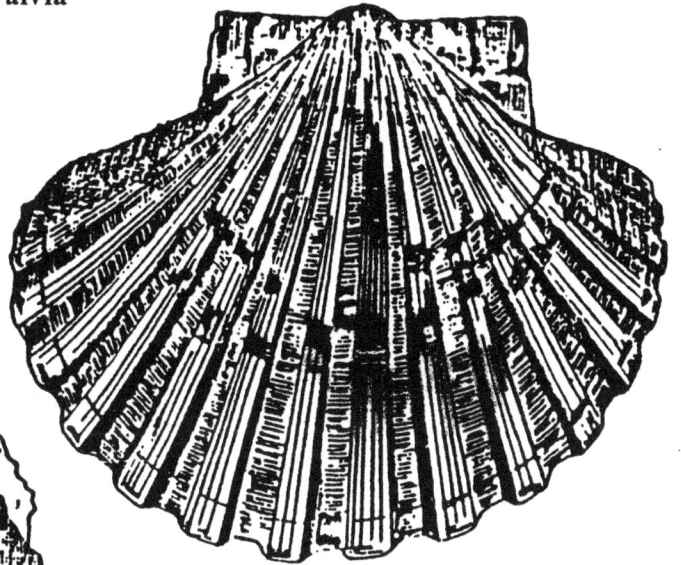

Cardium Sp.

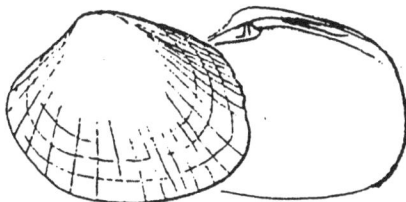

Tapes decussatus L.

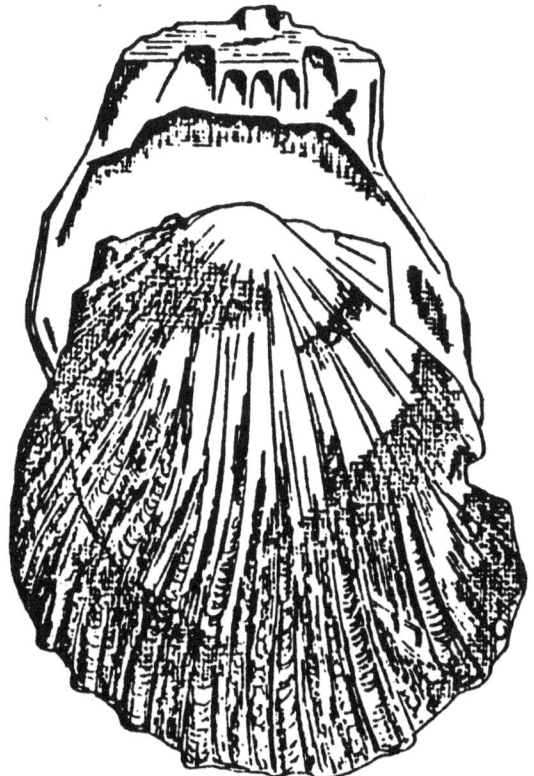

Spondylus gaederopus L.

Atlas of sea shells found in Greece in archaeological contexts

A. Bivalvia

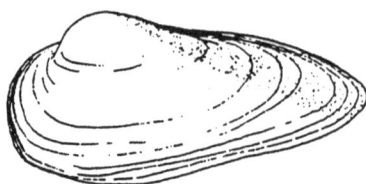

Unio Sp.

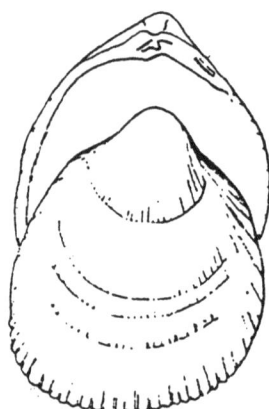

Venericardia antiquata Linne

Venerupis decussata L.

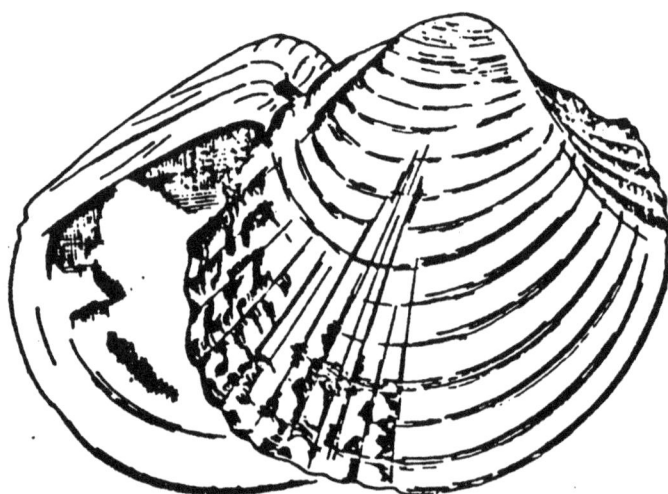

Venus verrucosa L.

Atlas of sea shells found in Greece in archaeological contexts

B. Gastropoda

Astralium rugosum Link

Cerithium ruprestre Risso

Bittium reticulatum da Costa

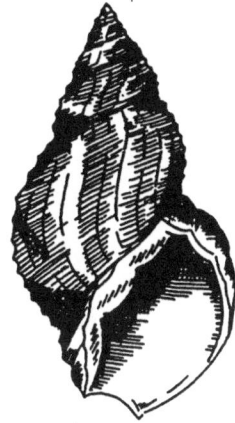

Buccinum undulatum L.

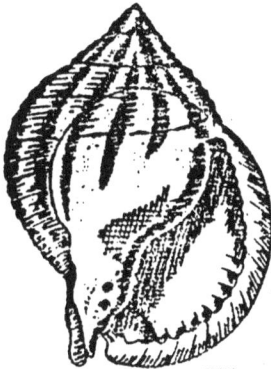

Columbella rustica L.

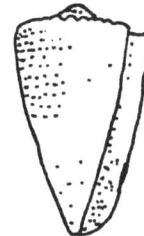

Cassis undulata (Gmelin)

Cerithium vulgare Br.

Conus Mediterraneus Brug.

Cassis Saburon Brug

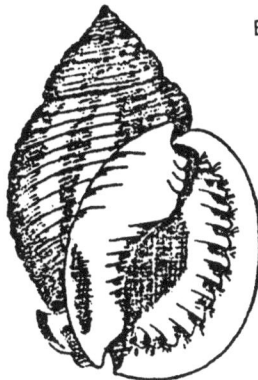

Cypraea Curida L.

Cypraea erosaria spurca L.

Cypraea Pyrum (Gmelin)

Atlas of sea shells found in Greece in archaeological contexts

B. Gastropoda

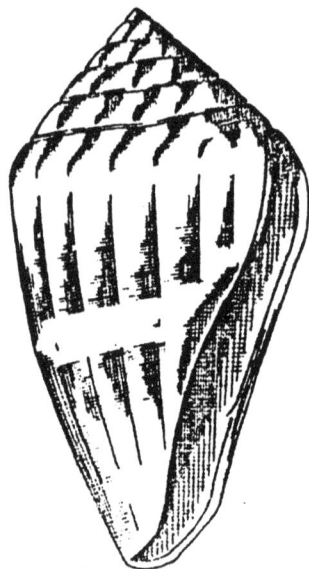

Conus venticosus Gmelin

Euthria Cornea L.

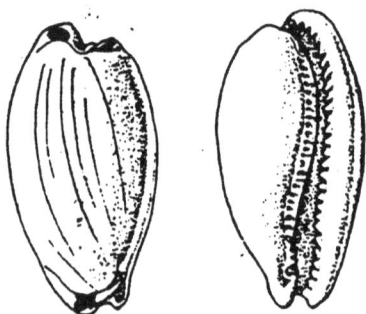

Cypraea Sp.

Luria lurida L.

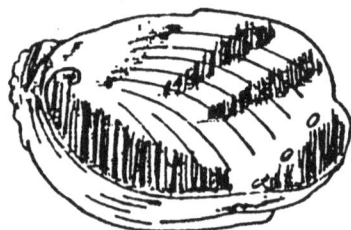

Haliotis tuberculata L.

Lementina arenaria L.

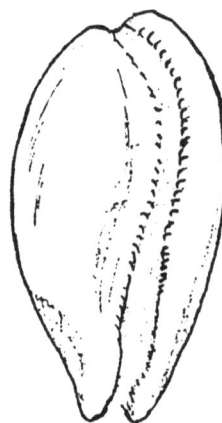

Gibbula adansoni P.

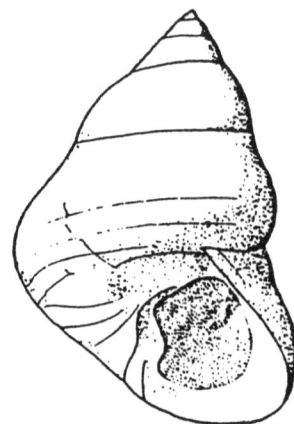

Monodonta articulata L.

Atlas of sea shells found in Greece in archaeological contexts

B. Gastropoda

Natica josephina Risso

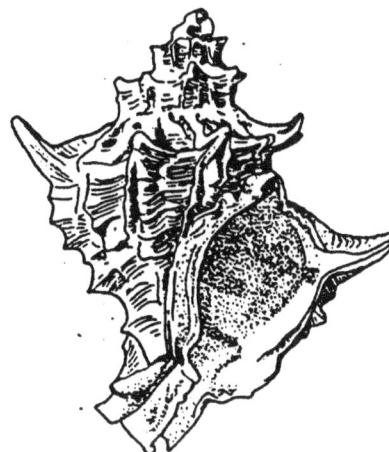

Murex trunculus L.

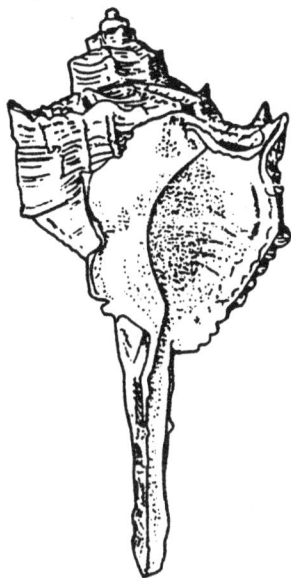

Murex Brandaris L.

Natica catena da Costa

Natica lebroea Martyn

Neritina flubiatilus L.

Nassa mutabilis L.

Nassa inerassata L.

Nassa reticulata L.

Patella coerulea L.

Patella aspera

Pisania Maculsa

Purpura Sp.

Atlas of sea shells found in Greece in archaeological contexts

B. Gastropoda

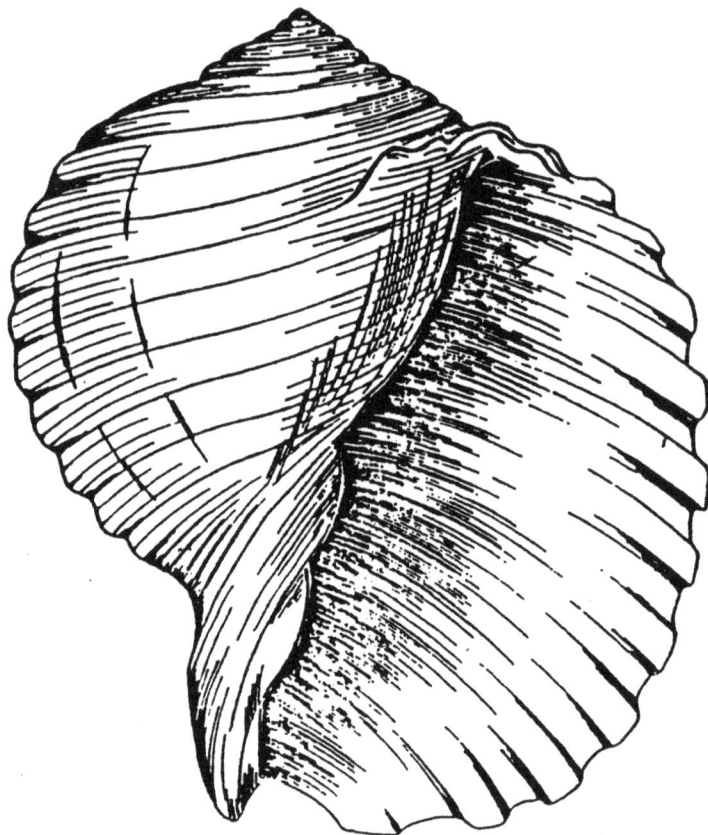

Tonna galea L.

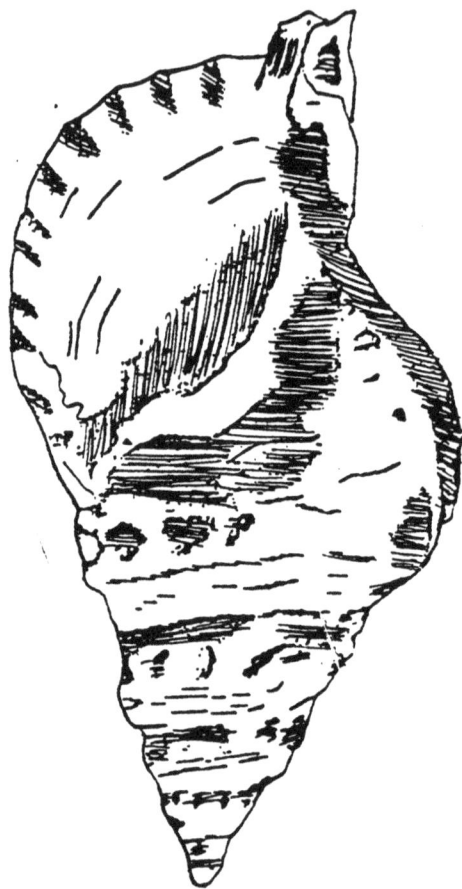

Tritonium nodiferum L.

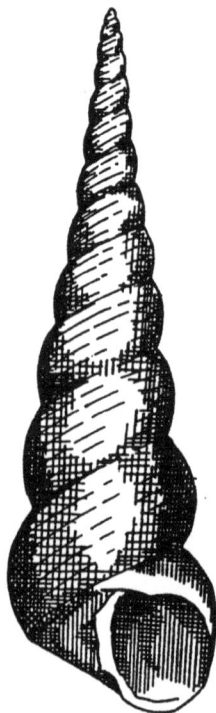

Tutritella communis R.

Atlas of sea shells found in Greece in archaeological contexts

C. Crustacea

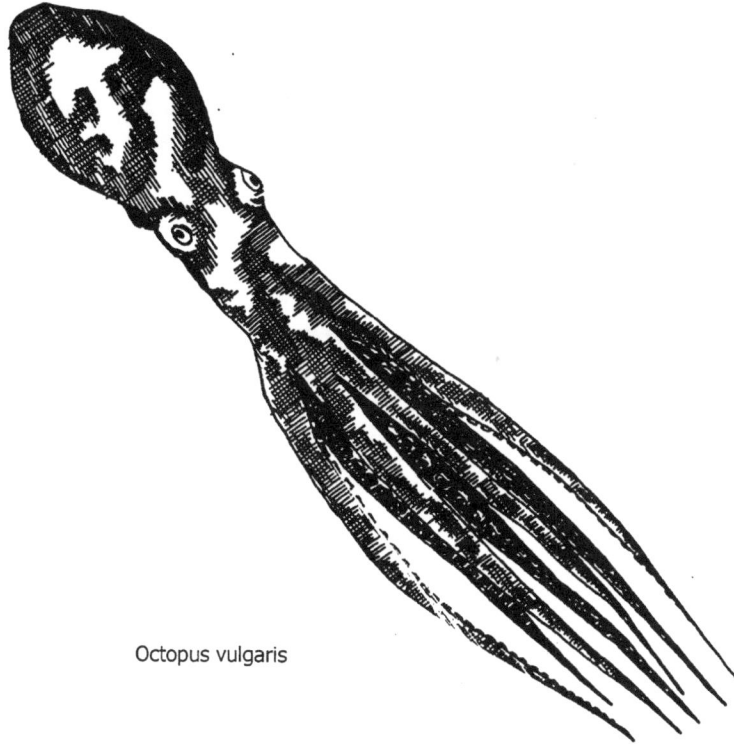

Octopus vulgaris

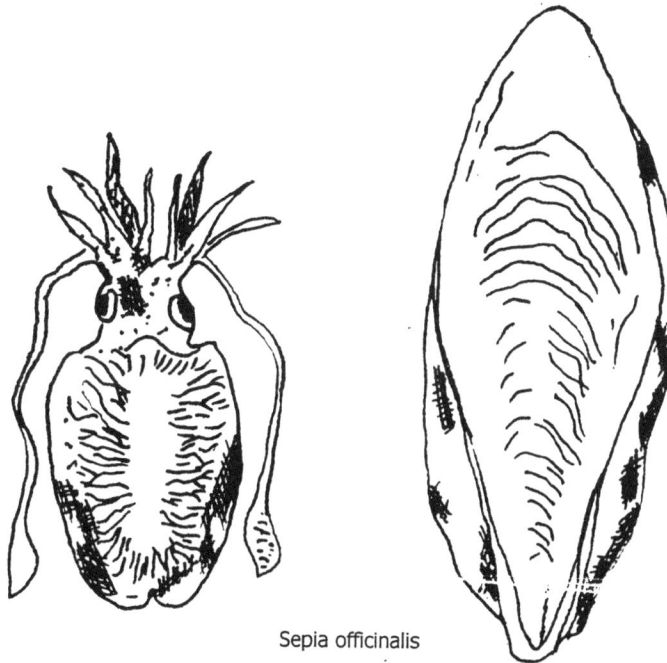

Sepia officinalis

GLOSSARY OF TERMS

The glossary includes not only those terms used in this publication, but also terms most commonly used in all standard conchological works.

A

Anterior. The front end of a shell. In gastropods, the end from which the head emerges; in bivalves, the end from which the foot emerges, furthest from the ligament. The opposite of *posterior*.

Aperture. The principal or anterior opening of a gastropod.

Apex. The tip of early whorls of the gastropod spire.

Apical. At the tip or apex.

Axial. Longitudinal, or in the direction of the axis of the shell.

Axis. The imaginary centre line of the shell, around which the whorls revolve.

B

Barnacle. A crustacean often found attached to shells.

Base. In spiral gastropods, the bottom of the shell; the extremity furthest from the apex. The anterior part, not including the aperture. Also, the flattened side of cowries.

Beak. The small rounded or pointed tip of a bivalve. Also called **umbo.**

Biconical. Shaped like two cones, base to base.

Bivalve. A shell with two principal valves or parts.

Body whrol. The final or largest anterior whorl of a spiral gastropod.

Byssus. A tuft of strong thread-like filaments that anchors some bivalves to other objects; secreted by the foot.

C

Calcareus. Consisting of calcium carbonate, usually white.

Callum. A thin calcareous covering of the gape between valves in some bivalves.

Callosity. The state of being calloused.

Callus (adj. calloused). A marked thickening of calcareous material, often enamel-like, usually around the aperture, often covering the umbilicus.

Canal. A semitubular extension of the aperture lip containing the siphon, in some spiral gastropods.

Cardinal teeth. The main hinge tooth or teeth of a bivalve directly beneath the beak.

Chitinous. Horny.

Columella. The central axial pillar of the spiral gastropod.

Concentric. Ridges or lines following the same direction as the growth lines on a bivalve. Also called **commarginal.**

Conic or conoid. Cone-shaped.

D

Decollate. Apex truncate or broken off.

Decussate. Latticed; having a crossing of sculptural lines, not necessarily at right angles. Cp. cancellate.

Dentate. Having tooth-like projections.

Denticle. Small tooth-like projection, especially around the margin.

Denticulate(d). Finely dentate.

Dextral. Right-handed. In gastropods, coiled in a spiral turning from left to right; opposite of **sinistral.** When the apex is pointed upward, the aperture is on the right side when facing the observer.

Discoidal. Disk-like; the whorls being coiled in nearly only one plane.

Divaricate. Having a surface composed of two different sets of parallel lines meeting at an angle.

Dorsal. In gastropods, the back, opposite or behind the aperture; in bivalves, toward the hinge area.

Dorsum. The back of the shell, opposite the aperture.

E

Ear. (auricle wing).

Endermic. Restricted to a particular locality or region.

Epidermis. (periostractum).

F

Fissure. A narrow slit or cut.

Flamed. Flame-like markings.

Fold. A spirally-wound ridge on the columella.

Foliaceous or **foliose.** Consisting of thin lamellae or leaves.

Foliated. Lead-like.

Foot. The muscular organ of the mollusc body used for moving.

Fossa. A groove or notch.

Fusiform or **fusoid.** Spindle-shaped; tapering toward each end.

G

Gaping. Having valves which only partially close.

Gastropod. A member of the class Gastropoda, such as a snail, slug or nudibranch, usually with a univalve shell.

Genus. A group of closely related species with common structural or phylllogenetic characteristics.

Girdle. The muscular material encircling the valves of a chiton.

Globose. Rounded or ball-shaped.

Granose or **granulate(d).** Covered with tiny grains or beads.

Growth lines. The impressed lines on the surface of a shell, parallel to the margin, caused by successive growth stages and rest periods.

H

Helical. Spirally coiled.

Hinge. The interlocking teeth and ligament of a bivalve.

Hinge line. The dorsal margin of the bivalve, where both valves are in permanent contact.

Holotype. The original specimen from which a new species is described.

Homonym. The later of two identical names given to two different species or other taxa.

I

Impressed. Indented.

Inequilateral. Not equilateral.

Inequivalve. Not equivalve; valves of unequal size and shape.

Inflated. Swollen; usually applied to very thin shells.

Inner lip. Part of the aperture which is next to the columella.

Interspaces or **interstices.** The spaces between teeth and other raised linear surfaces.

L

Lamella (pl. lamelllae). A thin, flat plate or scale.

Lamellate(d). Covered with thin plates or scales.

Lamina (pl. laminae). Lamella.

Lateral. Referring to the side.

Lateral teeth. The side teeth of a bivalve hinge, as opposed to the central **cardinal teeth.**

Left valve. The sinistral valve. On the left when the shell is placed with the posterior toward the observer and with the dorsal margin or hinge line upward.

Lenticular. Lens-shaped.

Ligament. The translucent elastic horny structure, usually internal, which joins the valves of a bivalve.

Lip. The edge of the aperture. (**inner lip** and **outer lip**).

Littoral. The tidal zone between high-and low-water marks.

M

Maculated. Spotted or splashed.

Mantle. The external fleshy membrane covering the soft parts of the shell. It secretes the shell and the periostracum.

Margin. The edge of the shell.

Mollusc. A member of the phyllum Mollusca; invertebrates with soft bodies, usually enclosed in or enclosing a calcareous shell.

Mouth. The aperture of a shell.

Muscle. The fleshy organ attaching the animal to the shell.

N

Nacre. The pearly or iridescent shell layer closest to the surface, consisting of extremely thin leaves of aragonite (calcium carbonate).

Nacreous. Pearly.

Nodose, nodulose or **nodular.** Having small knobs or tubercles.

Nucleus. The first-formed part of the gastropod, such as its apex, or of an operculum.

O

Oblique. Slanting.

Obtuse. Blunted or rounded.

Operculate. Having an operculum.

Operculum. The horny or calcareous plate attached to the foot of some gastropods, which seals the aperture of the shell when the animal is withdrawn.

Orbicular. Circular.

Orifice. An opening.

Ornament or **ornamentation.** The relief sculpture on a shell surface, not including the growth lines.

Outer lip. The margin of an aperture furthest from the columella.

Ovate. Egg-shaped.

P

Paratype. One of the original group from which a new species was described.

Parietal Lip. The posterior part of the inner lip in many gastropods.

Parietal shield. A shelf-like callus on the inner lip.

Pelagic. Relating to or living in open water-the oceans and seas.

Pelecypod. Former term for **bivalve.**

Periostracum. The outer hairy or fibrous covering of many shells. Also wrongly called the epidermis.

Periphery. The outermost edge of a whorl.

Peristome. The margin of the aperture of a gastropod.

Pillar. SEE **columella.**

Plate. In bivalves, a flattened calcareous structure.

Posterior. The apical end of a spiral gastropod; the back or siphonal end of a bivalve. The opposite of **anterior.**

Postnuclear. The whorls of a gastropod, other than the nuclear whorls.

Predatory. Preying on others for food.

Pyriform. Pear-shaped.

Q

Quadrate. Rectangular, or of roughly square shape.

R

Radial. Ray-like; in bivalves, referring to the surface decoration diverging from the beak.

Radula. The lingual ribbon of gastropods, to which rows of raspy chitinous teeth are attached.

Rib. A relatively broad elevation of the surface.

Right valve. SEE **left valve.** The right valve is usually lowermost in the Pectinidae and uppermost in the Ostreidae.

Rugose. Rough or finely wrinkled.

S

Scalloped. Having an undulated margin.

Scar. An impression on the interior of a bivalve left by the attachment of a muscle.

Sculpture. Ornament or ornamentation; a relief pattern on the surface of a shell.

Sedentary. Permanently attached.

Sinistral. Left-handed; turning from right to left. The aperture of the gastropod is on the left when facing the observer, if the apex is pointed upward.

Sinuate. Having a wavy margin.

Sinus. A deep notch, slit or indentation.

Siphon. A tubular organ of a shell through which water passes. In bivalves it is an extension of the mantle.

Siphonal canal or **groove.** A narrow tubular extension of the aperture margin through which passes the anterior siphon. Also called **anterior canal.**

Siphonal notch. A narrow slit at the end of the siphonal canal.

Socket. In bivalves, a depression in the hinge plate to receive the teeth of the opposite valve.

Spatulate. Having flattened spoon-like extensions.

Species. The subdivision of a genus, comprising a group of individuals with common specific characteristics and capable of interbreeding.

Spire. The visible whorls of a gastropod, from the apex to, but not including, the body whorl.

Stria (pl. striae). Fine lines or furrows on a shell, indicating growth stages.

Striate. Having sculpture in the form of extremely fine lines.

Substrate. The underlying living site of a mollusc, such as the sea floor, rocks and coral.

Suture. In gastropods, the spiral line or seam joining the whorls.

Synonym. One of two or more names for the same species or other taxa, customarily the latest of these.

T

Taxodont. In bivalves, having many uniform hinge teeth.

Taxon (pl. taxa). Any unit in classification, such as class, superfamily, family, genus, species, subspecies, etc.

Teeth. In gastropods, the tooth-like protuberances at the hinge.

Thread. A very fine raised line on the shell surface.

Transverse. The angle of bands or lines parallel to the axis of a gastropod, at a right angle to the growth lines of a bivalve.

Trochiform. Trochus-shaped, as in Trochidae.

Truncate. Having the end sharply cut off.

Tubercle. A protuberance or knob.

Turbinate. Top-shaped, as in Turbidae.

Type. SEE **holotype.**

U

Umbilicate. Having an umbilicus; navel-like.

Umbilicus. The hole or open axis within the whorls around which the gastropod coils.

Umbo (pl. umbones). SEE **beak.**

Undulated. Having a wavy margin.

Univalve. A mollusk with a single shell.

V

Valve. One of the halves of a bivalve, on either side of the hinge line.

Varicose. Having one or more varices.

Varix (pl. varices). Prominent raised ridges on the surface of the shell, formed originally at the aperture during rest periods in the shell growth.

Ventral. Referring to the margin area of a bivalve opposite to the hinge.

Ventricose. Inflated or swollen.

W

Whorl. A complete axial turn of a spiral gastropod.

Wing. An elongate, often triangular, projection of the bivalve shell extending from the hinge area, as on Pteridae. SEE **auricle.**

www.ingramcontent.com/pod-product-compliance
Lightning Source LLC
Chambersburg PA
CBHW060959030426
42334CB00033B/3297